DEBT

Debt *is volume six in the series*
21ST CENTURY STUDIES

Center for 21st Century Studies
University of Wisconsin–Milwaukee

Richard Grusin, *General Editor*

DEBT

Ethics, the Environment, and the Economy

Edited by Peter Y. Paik
and Merry Wiesner-Hanks

Indiana University Press

Bloomington and Indianapolis

This book is a publication of

Indiana University Press
Office of Scholarly Publishing
Herman B Wells Library 350
1320 East 10th Street
Bloomington, Indiana 47405 USA

iupress.indiana.edu

| Telephone orders | 800–842–6796 |
| Fax orders | 812–855–7931 |

© 2013 by the Board of Regents of the
University of Wisconsin System

All rights reserved

No part of this book may be reproduced or utilized in any form or
by any means, electronic or mechanical, including photocopying
and recording, or by any information storage and retrieval system,
without permission in writing from the publisher. The Association
of American University Presses' Resolution on Permissions constitutes the only exception to this prohibition.

⊖ The paper used in this publication meets the minimum require-
ments of the American National Standard for Information Sciences—Permanence of Paper for Printed Library Materials, ANSI
Z39.48–1992.

Manufactured in the United States of America

Cataloging-in-Publication Data is available
from the Library of Congress.

ISBN 978-0-253-00926-5 (cloth)
ISBN 978-0-253-00938-8 (pbk)
ISBN 978-0-253-00943-2 (eb)

1 2 3 4 5 18 17 16 15 14 13

Contents

Acknowledgments

THIS COLLECTION OF essays began life as a conference held at the Center for 21st Century Studies at the University of Wisconsin–Milwaukee. The idea for a major conference on the theme of debt came about from the effort to find a term that could tie together the various crises—economic, environmental, and ethical—affecting the nation and the world. The proposal for what became the conference was submitted at the end of September 2008, two weeks after the historic bankruptcy of Lehman Brothers shocked the global markets and sent them into a tailspin. The global financial crisis unfolded under the shadow of ongoing conflict in Iraq and Afghanistan and of alarms sounded by scientists about the devastating impact of greenhouse gases on the environment. Debt, both in the financial sense and in the sense of obligation and responsibility, seemed to be a thread running through the three crises, and so promised to open up productive standpoints from which to examine the present.

The conference provided two days of stimulating papers and engaging discussion. The presentations had a timeliness and a sense of energy which made possible striking points of convergence between scholars working in a wide variety of fields. The success of the event owed much to the resourcefulness and dedication of the staff at the Center for 21st Century Studies: Deputy Director Kate Kramer, Associate Director John Blum, and graduate student assistants Kris Knisely and Lea Gnat. John Blum also provided invaluable editorial assistance in putting together the manuscript. The editors also wish to thank Rebecca Tolen of Indiana University Press for her steadfast support of this essay collection. Finally, a deep and abiding debt is owed to Nan Kim, whose thoughtfulness and sagacity provided the inspiration for undertaking an intellectual exploration of the concept and experience of debt.

Introduction

Peter Y. Paik

This volume has its origins in a conference on the subject of debt that took place at the Center for 21st Century Studies at the University of Wisconsin–Milwaukee in late April 2010. The planning for the event began during the fall of 2008, under the shadow of the cataclysmic events that imperiled the entire global financial system. The sudden collapse in housing prices in the United States, triggered by a wave of foreclosures in the subprime mortgage market, wiped out the investment bank Lehman Brothers, which has proven to be the largest bankruptcy in history. The contagion threatened to spread to other financial institutions and was met by massive infusions of taxpayer money to prevent further meltdowns. The insurance company AIG, which had insured the risky securities that were backed up by subprime loans, turned to the Federal Reserve for emergency loans that amounted to the largest corporate bailout in history.[1] The US government nationalized the mortgage buyers Fannie Mae and Freddie Mac, while arranging the takeover of troubled firms like Merrill Lynch and Countrywide Mortgage by Bank of America. The situation was no less dire across the Atlantic. Iceland, one of the wealthiest countries in the world, became the first developed nation since 1976 to turn to the IMF for help after all of its banks collapsed and the value of its currency plummeted, freezing its foreign currency reserves.[2] In the United Kingdom, where the financial sector took up a greater share of the economy than in the United States, the cost of bailing out the failing banks was accordingly higher, but these rescue packages came with a stronger set of restrictions.

The tense and unnerving days of the crisis, when the contagion of defaults and bankruptcies brought the global economy to the edge of collapse, have given way in many places to a diffuse and inchoate sense of despair. Although official economic indicators state that the recession came to an end in mid-2009, rates of joblessness have remained stubbornly high, the already vast income disparities have continued to widen between the super-rich and the middle class, and declining tax revenues have forced governments to make painful cuts to social programs. The global financial system may have been saved by government intervention on a massive scale, but in the United States, efforts to help the poor and the middle class in the form of mortgage relief and job creation have proven paltry and inadequate. The global economy continues to lurch forward into this strange recovery, in which taxpayer funds have not only rescued the financial sector but enabled the banks to reap enormous profits, while increasing numbers of people in the United States fall out of the middle class into low-wage jobs that leave them exposed to the possibility of penury in the event of an accident or a health emergency.

These worsening inequalities and the disappearance for many of the chance to achieve or maintain a middle-class way of life have spawned protest movements across the globe. Mass demonstrations forced Iceland's promarket Independence Party from power, enabling a coalition of left-wing parties to take over. But in other countries, like Spain, Greece, and the United States, the protests were undertaken by groups expressing a fundamental discontent with the existing political system itself, a frustration over its apparent helplessness to provide a remedy for deepening economic disparities. The Occupy movement, which set up camps in the major cities across the United States, often near the city's financial center, arose in large part in response to the fateful decisions of the Obama administration neither to reform the financial industry nor to hold accountable any of the heads of the big banks whose exotic financial instruments brought about the catastrophic meltdown. Indeed, the bailouts of the major financial institutions were also a spark for the rage igniting the Tea Party, a right-wing populist movement with libertarian tendencies that champions drastic reductions in government spending.

The most heated and violent demonstrations in response to austerity measures aimed at reducing government deficits have taken place in Greece, where mass layoffs of state workers, deep cuts to salaries and pensions, and sizable tax hikes have threatened hundreds of thousands of Greeks with destitution. Although rioting in Greece has led to fatalities, the demonstrations there have had a clear political significance. The same cannot be said of the rioting and looting that swept the United Kingdom during the summer of 2011, in which looters attacked fellow residents and businesses in their own or nearby neighborhoods. The self-destructive and pointless violence of the rioters was divorced from any recognizable political demand, making their rage as excluded consumers more virulent than the responses of protesters issuing concrete demands, however difficult their realization.[3] The status quo is not only coming under the pressure of political movements calling for fundamental reforms but is also threatened by demands that no political or economic system can fulfill without jettisoning liberalism or democracy.

Although it is clear that the Anglo-American version of capitalism centered on privatization and deregulation has failed, the question of an alternative remains dauntingly elusive. As John Lanchester points out, a genuine recovery will not take place until we face up to the debts racked up by a series of bubbles caused by real estate prices, cheap credit, and years of deficit spending under the profligate administration of George W. Bush.[4] But this recovery can be made good only if there is a collective reckoning with the goals that have been taken to be self-evident in a capitalist economy: working hard for long hours toward an "always-receding vision of contentment."[5] Such a reckoning would ideally lead us to address the urgent issues that have been relegated to the margins in the midst of our economic emergency, such as the depletion of nonrenewable resources, which imposes insuperable limits on the spread of economic prosperity and is a primary cause for conflict among capitalist states. The cataclysmic jolts that nearly brought down the financial system ought to compel us to reflect not only on the debts recklessly accumulated by financial institutions in their relentless pursuit of ever higher profits but also on the other meanings of debt, which are bound up with our conceptions of justice, the good life, and our obligations to future generations. If questions such as how the economic system should change and what ought to replace it seem overwhelming, it is in part because they touch on concerns at the very basis of social and political order.

The elementary definition of debt is something one owes to another. Debt may take the form of capital that one has borrowed and must repay, a service that one is obliged to render or a duty that one must fulfill, or a transgression that must be expiated. In each of these instances, debt evokes limits and constraints on our range of action, as it calls to mind acts we might not perform and commitments we might not fulfill were we left wholly to our own devices. Loans must be repaid, obligations to society honored, and penitence for wrongful actions demonstrated. But if we typically regard economic debts as an undesirable state of dependency whose costs increase the longer they go unpaid, while the idea of collective atonement for historical injustices arouses controversy over how the past should affect the present, we often speak of debt in the sense of moral obligation as a vital social good. Debt in this sense is not something one should seek to terminate—it is not a burden to be escaped as soon as one has accumulated enough capital to pay it off. Rather, moral debt constitutes a commitment to be fulfilled over the course of one's lifetime, as the provision of one's membership in a community and as the obligation of citizenship. Debt as moral obligation strengthens the social fabric, makes individuals aware of needs and goods beyond their immediate interests, and sustains a network of reciprocity that stretches across generations and, ideally, transcends social, economic, and ethnic differences.

What renders debt in its nonfinancial meanings so elusive for us as an object of thought is the conception of freedom at the heart of modern liberalism. Although the fundamental ethical values of modern societies, such as respect for the dignity of others and concern to protect the environment, readily call to mind the condition of indebtedness, modern liberalism leaves the strength of any moral obligation for the individual to determine. Thus, while debt in the moral sense may possess a clear and straightforward meaning for most people, its symbolic force hangs very much in doubt. To speak of debt as a moral and social obligation, whether to the environment or even to one's own family, is necessarily to speak of it at a remove, since what in earlier periods was recognized as self-evidently authoritative has now become subject to individual preference. Indeed, it is difficult to argue that debts which are binding only to the extent that an individual is willing to acknowledge them as such can still be called debts at all. We come up against a paradox: we are free to fulfill those obligations we choose and accordingly free not to honor other commitments, but the very primacy of individual choice sabotages the capacity of individuals to join together to act on behalf of a common good. Debt, as moral obligation, ought to strengthen the social fabric, make individuals aware of needs and goods beyond their immediate interests, and sustain a network of reciprocity that stretches across generations and transcends social, economic, and ethnic differences. The fact that it does not, while nevertheless keeping us in a state of dependency and heteronomy, is perhaps the defining philosophical and political dilemma of liberal capitalist societies, for which the recognition of their long-term interests no longer amounts to a sufficient condition to pursue them.

The chapters in this collection take on the urgent and difficult task of thinking obligations and limits across a variety of disciplines. The chapters' themes meet and overlap in intriguing ways with other recent work on the subject of debt by writers who are not economists, such as Margaret Atwood's *Payback* and David Graeber's *Debt: The First 5,000 Years*. Atwood's book explores the concept in a series of digressive meditations that range from ancient notions of transgression and expiation to the dire environmental warnings of the Club of Rome, while Graeber's sprawling yet methodical study compares economic systems, marked by oscillations between virtual currencies and those backed by precious metals, across five millennia of human history. Yet what is common to both is an attempt to understand the problem of debt within a grand world-historical or cosmic scale. To analyze debt in this sense is to examine the very basis of human institutions. The essays collected in this volume work within a narrower and more specific frame of reference, yet also go to the heart of human beliefs and activities in imparting to us a stronger sense of what it means to inhabit a shared world.

The first group of contributors take on the subject of economic debt and its social consequences. Richard Wolff gives a lucid account of the present economic downturn that traces its sources to the patterns of increasing indebtedness among consumers, financial institutions, and the US government during the past three decades. Consumers have turned to credit cards and second mortgages in order to compensate for stagnant wages and to maintain their standard of living. Financial institutions rely on loans to leverage higher rates of profit on investments, while the budget of the government has gone into the red for the sake of providing services and maintaining a worldwide military presence without having to resort to the politically unpopular measure of raising taxes. Given the underlying fragility of such an economic system, in which meltdowns become increasingly destructive and recovery is rendered more difficult by huge debt burdens, Wolff calls for a restructuring of the economy to make economic decisions more accountable to producers and consumers alike. The inclusion of workers in boards of directors, for example, would constrain the pursuit of short-term profit that has resulted in the massive outsourcing of American jobs. The cooperative model of enterprise, which has already achieved great success in the technology sector, could be extended to other areas of the economy. Such a shift, though not a panacea for all economic ills, is likely to reduce the instability of the economy that has led to downturns of escalating magnitude since the 1980s.

If the meltdown of the mortgage market plays out as a familiar story of unrestrained greed and predatory practices, Elaine Lewinnek relates the often startling history behind the American dream of home ownership. The goal of home ownership in the modern United States was initially embraced most widely by an unexpected segment of the population—recent immigrants who were in most cases impoverished. Lewinnek cites the startling statistic that in 1939 the rate of home ownership among immigrants in Chicago, most of whom lived in slums, was 41.3 percent, compared to 21.7 percent for native-born whites. Immigrants bought houses because they felt a house could grant them some measure of security in straitened economic circumstances. But the realities of home ownership entailed bitter sacrifices for immigrants working in low-wage jobs. Mothers and children were compelled to enter the workforce to help make monthly mortgage payments, and it was common for families to forgo necessities such as indoor plumbing and even food. As Lewinnek points out, social workers were often shocked to find hungry and shivering children living in homes on which their parents had taken out mortgages. The image of the proletariat scraping by, leading precarious lives of underconsumption for the sake of maintaining home ownership, reveals striking resonances to the present-day crisis of the middle class, in which the collapse of housing prices and the rise of foreclosures have shattered for many the hope of maintaining their former way of life. It is instructive to note that while the middle class at the turn of the century did not consider home ownership to be vital for enjoying domestic stability, one of the heaviest burdens on the middle class is a house that one cannot sell, a problem that curtails the flexibility of the labor market.

In "Demonizing Debt, Naturalizing Finance," Mary Poovey examines what she considers to be the three "transvaluations" of economic debt in the modern period. The first transvaluation turned debt from an understanding of the human condition—to be a fallen creature in the sight of God and to exist in a network of interdependent and interlocking relationships—into a personal failing. Credit and trust were once considered indissoluble from belief in God, but the emergence of the capitalist economy and the rise of the secular conception of the autonomous self, in widening the bounds of human agency, increasingly turned debt into a matter of individual choice, and the outcome of a bad one at that. The belief that debt constituted a grave moral lapse led to the establishment of debtors' prisons and other punitive practices. But this Victorian transvaluation gave way to economic realities that left nations and people in chronic debt. The sheer difficulty of staying out of debt set in motion the second major transvaluation, in which certain forms of indebtedness were deemed necessary and virtuous. Moreover, the cost of financing wars led governments, like the United States during the Civil War, to sell bonds that blurred the distinctions between debt and investment. In this second valuation, the principle of thrift took hold as the standard by which to distinguish between debts that were economically productive and led to "full participation" in the economy, such as buying houses, purchasing insurance, and making investments, and debts that were wasteful and destructive. It is the limitation posed by the idea of thrift that is swept away by the third transvaluation, in which consumer spending becomes identified with the health of the economy. The practice of installment purchasing was a vital factor in this shift, in which the credit rating of the borrower overshadowed altogether the nature of his or her purchases. As Poovey points out, the linkage of national prosperity with personal consumer consumption essentially guarantees that personal indebtedness will increase. The unsustainable character of this predicament is triggering a fourth transvaluation whose shape and impact are still taking shape.

Michael Gillespie likewise addresses a fundamental shift in the conception of debt that has taken place in the modern world. The idea of debt in the ancient and medieval worlds is expansive and comprehensive, encompassing all the relations of human beings to each other as well as to nature and the cosmos itself. The dictum of the pre-Socratic thinker Anaximander that all things that come into being must pay a debt to time by passing away informs ancient conceptions of justice, and a no less encompassing view of debt is sustained by Christianity in the doctrines of forgiveness and original sin. But the modern reduction of debt to its economic sense proceeds from the emancipation of human powers and capacities to pursue scientific discovery and technological advancement. The modern world turns the natural world into an inert storehouse of resources to be used for economic development, but the capitalist economy makes possible a society in which growth and wealth become at last possible without war. A society's use of science and technology to overcome scarcities imposed by nature is a historical breakthrough that depends on emancipation from the stifling customs, constraints, and limitations of premodern societies. As Gillespie emphasizes, however, such emancipation proves to be a mixed blessing. A society based on economic growth, which increases vastly the freedom of the individual, is one that tends to lose sight of the vital obligations of the present generation both to its ancestors and to its descendants. For economic debt creates patterns of consumption and expansion that are self-perpetuating and difficult to alter, even if the ongoing economic crisis highlights the need for fundamental change.

The belief in limitless growth is the central idea of the capitalist economic system. As Joel Magnuson shows in "The Growth Imperative: Prosperity or Poverty," such a belief entails a debt that must be paid by future generations in the form of depleted natural resources and a degraded and polluted natural environment. The idea of perpetual growth represents the key myth of our time, and the need to maintain faith in this doctrine has discouraged both economists and the public from confronting the dire environmental repercussions of economic progress. Magnuson points out that such an economy tends to produce illusory growth in the form of asset bubbles because of the underlying imperative to generate profit. In such instances, wealth, in the absence of a real increase, ends up being redistributed upward. An economy centered on growth is also incapable of addressing the problem of greenhouse gas emissions—schemes involving energy credits cannot lead to substantial reductions, as corporations will find it more profitable to purchase credits that allow them to continue their environmentally destructive operations than to cut back on pollution. Magnuson also considers the overuse of resources that are otherwise renewable—water, topsoil, forests—and finds that so long as the economic system is shaped by the growth imperative there will be little chance of avoiding a calamitous loss of vital resources.

"Democracy's Debt: Capitalism and Cultural Revolution," by Stephen L. Gardner, takes a challenging and provocative approach to the troubled relationship between democracy and capitalism. What if the major problem of the era of global capitalism is not that bourgeois capitalism is too conservative but that it is in fact too radical? What if democracy, and the principle of equality of conditions, are not antithetical to the immense economic inequalities created by neoliberal capitalism but at the heart of them? According to Gardner, what we understand as democracy has become indissoluble from capitalism, throwing us into the "terrifying dilemma" whereby the act of abolishing the nihilistic individualism of contemporary society, its unconstrained pursuit of greed and relentless fixation with self-display, would also entail the demise of democracy. For Gardner, the cultural revolution carried out by the bourgeoisie is both more radical and thoroughgoing than the one imagined by its socialist rivals—witness the rapidity with which formerly socialist nations have embraced capitalist markets. But the bourgeois revolution opens up destructive forces that it may not be able to contain over the long run. While equality is a moral good, it nevertheless serves to exacerbate conflicts between individuals because democracy removes the traditional mechanisms for containing and quelling social conflict, such as religion, tradition, and social hierarchy. The principal method employed by democracy to keep social antagonism within acceptable limits, Gardner points out, is the expansion of debt, in the form of credit that makes possible the financing of a lifestyle based on consumption.

The pursuit of wealth, so long as a critical mass of people can maintain the belief that affluence is within their reach, prevents social antagonism from reaching explosive levels. The recent riots in London, in which most of the participants were young people who felt excluded from the consumerist utopia enjoyed by the rich, underscore the fragility of democracy in the absence of a growing economy. Gardner's bracing dictum that "markets are democracy in motion" underscores the reality that in a democracy what is left for equals to agree on as the criterion of value is money. Thus immense economic inequalities do not transgress or contravene what Gardner calls "democratic desire." Rather, such inequalities are born of the practices and institutions devised to fulfill the democratic desire for prosperity. Gardner's arguments defy the conventional categorizations of politics between Left and Right, underscoring the need for more heterogeneous and flexible approaches to political questions that can meet the challenge of theorizing the middle-class populism of the Tea Party in the United States as well as riots in which the looters are moved not by political passion but by the desire for participation in a fading consumer culture.

Morris Berman's chapter, "Is Debt the New Karma? Why America Finally Fell Apart," argues that the collapse of the real estate bubble represents the culmination of the greed and individualism that have become increasingly powerful forces in American society. Since the decade following its founding, American society has generally favored, at decisive forks in its development, individualist over community-based solutions. Thus the United States has become increasingly fragmented in recent decades, a fact driven home by its high rates of incarceration, use of antidepressants, and numbers of individuals living alone. The crisis into which American society has plunged might be intractable, since there is scant political will, even in the Democratic administration of Barack Obama, to remedy long-standing structural defects in the economy, especially the corrupt practices of the financial sector. Moreover, the faith in the American way of life, as Berman points out, can be maintained only so long as one represses the truth of living in a world where action engenders reaction. The possibility of recovery is thus undermined not only by political paralysis but by the inability of a society in decline to face the reality of its position in the world.

There is some debate among conservationists and others concerned about the destruction inflicted by industrial society on the environment as to the point when the human species went wrong in its relationship to the natural world. Some argue that the devastation of the natural world, the destruction of entire habitats, and the mass extinction of animal species were made inevitable with the coming of the modern age, when the advancement of technology and the spread of commercial activity enabled increasing numbers of human beings to make and possess a wide range of products as well as to accumulate vast wealth. Others locate the moment of the environmental fall at a far earlier moment, with the emergence of religions teaching the belief that human beings occupy a privileged and exceptional place in the cosmos and are to be elevated above animal life. Perhaps the turn to agriculture is where we should draw the more or less unbroken line that leads to a civilization endangered by rising sea levels and erratic weather patterns, or maybe the turning point was the discovery of tools. Although such debates seem fruitless and are in all likelihood impossible to resolve, they have the effect of making us conscious of the brevity of the duration in which human beings have inhabited the earth, and also of the vast yet inconspicuous patterns of natural life that typically escape the anthropocentric perspective.

As Julianne Lutz Warren points out in her chapter "Measures of Time: Exploring Debt, Imagination, and Real Nature," over the long run of evolutionary history, the number of species that have emerged through natural selection is greater than the number of those that have gone extinct. Nature is endowed with a capacity for self-renewal, and the more biodiversity there is in an ecosystem, the more resilient it tends to be. Industrial civilization impairs this self-renewing capacity, and the breakneck pace of economic growth sets in motion a wave of extinctions and the loss of biodiversity. As Warren emphasizes, the harm that unchecked growth inflicts on nature threatens economic development as well. For example, more than a third of the globe's arable land has been lost since the emergence of agriculture, but the bulk of this loss has taken place during the past forty years. The capacity of the planet to support life has been greatly reduced by an economy based on expansion. The absence of effective political measures to reverse the course of mass extinctions and the destruction of biodiversity have resulted in a situation in which it is left to literature to grapple with the harsh and calamitous future that unconstrained growth has set in motion. Bargains with the forces of darkness, the manifestation of justice as a punishing Fury, and the destruction of the natural world itself are the literary themes that Warren regards as the most meaningful and significant for our time.

Worsening levels of pollution, overfishing, and the destruction of entire ecosystems for the sake of gaining access to raw materials are setting in motion a mass extinction of animal life. Biologist and author E. O. Wilson notes that by 2022 as much as 20 percent of the world's animal species could be wiped out, with extinction levels rising to 50 percent shortly thereafter. "The Time of Living Dead Species: Extinction Debt and Futurity in Madagascar," by Genese Marie Sodikoff, explores conservation efforts on the island nation, which, because of its geographical location, the unique evolutionary trajectory of its native species, and its history of human settlement, offers unusual and unexpected insights into habitat recovery and the role of traditional belief systems in protecting various animal species. Sodikoff argues that the accelerated pace of mass extinction compels ways of thinking that exceed the more familiar time frames of the "near past" and the "near present" to engage the far more encompassing scale of geological time. The approaches to conservation that this vastly amplified temporal framework entails are those that make use of the metaphors of cosmology and resort to scientific intervention to restore various animal species by means of "resurrection" projects. Indeed, on Madagascar, mythical thinking and traditional folklore prove productive of a local knowledge that aids researchers and conservationists in locating "Lazarus species," that is, animals that are believed to have gone extinct but are revealed to be surviving in the depths of various habitats. Conservationists have relied on taboos against the killing of certain animals in order to preserve native and non-native species alike, but the force attached to these beliefs has waned in the face of modern techniques of resource extraction and habits of consumption. As Sodikoff's chapter and those by others demonstrate, modern science, in the search for limits to the destructive tendencies of economic development, has learned to be pragmatic with respect to traditional cosmological beliefs, seeking to extract from them warnings against human complacency and hubris.

The conventional wisdom, or even the governing ideology, of American democracy in the age of globalization combines the cautious skepticism of traditionalist conservative thinkers such as Edmund Burke toward radical social and political change with the belief that free market capitalism brings about the optimal social and economic outcomes for modern society. In "Unintended Consequences and the Epistemology of Fraud in Dickens and Hayek," Eleanor Courtemanche reveals that the system of beliefs that legitimates the pursuit of rational self-interest relies quite heavily on faith for its coherence. The defense of free market economics in the work of Friedrich Hayek brings together the warnings of Burke against reckless attempts to reshape existing institutions, the optimistic attitude of Adam Smith that individual selfishness has beneficial consequences for society as a whole, and the belief that a spontaneous order underlies the complexity of modern society. As Courtemanche points out, Hayek's system involves a certain selective skepticism—the category of unintended consequences applies to misguided government interventions in a free market that harm economic activity but not to economic activity undertaken in the spirit of fraud and deceit. The manner whereby the pursuit of self-interest works to the benefit of the greater society is left unexplained as well, as Hayek presents it as an effect of spontaneous order. As the global financial crisis makes clear, a theory of economics that, like Hayek's, does not address the possibility of fraud is limited indeed. Courtemanche looks to the novels of Dickens for a more comprehensive and truthful exploration of the mechanisms of economic fraud and the workings of unintended consequences, in which unexpectedly negative outcomes go beyond misguided benevolence and serve instead to underscore the condition of blindness and the possibility of hubris that attend all human endeavors.

While many of the contributors to this volume look to narrative as a way of drawing attention to the shortcomings and limitations of much contemporary economic thought, literary scholar Michael Tratner takes on what he considers to be the uncritical dependence of economists on stories to account for shifts in consumer demand. The near meltdown of the global economy has sparked a revival of interest in the theories of John Maynard Keynes, as governments of both the Left and the Right across the industrialized world have undertaken extraordinary measures to rescue their crippled financial systems. But as Tratner warns, the efforts to revive Keynesian economics in recent years have disregarded certain vital elements of Keynes's thought. Chief among these is Keynes's idea of "animal spirits," which refers to the irrational choices and decisions that are behind both market crashes and economic growth. For Keynes, the sources of irrationality in the markets have distinctly corporeal resonances—they relate to spontaneous urges to satisfy bodily needs. For the economists of the neo-Keynesian revival, irrationality issues not from the body but from false information, namely the misleading stories that people tell each other about the economy. The neo-Keynesian economists calling for stimulus measures to revive demand, Tratner argues, err in equating the present economic crisis with the one confronted by Keynes. In Keynes's time the problem was one of low levels of consumption, for which the cure was fulfilling the appetites of "strong, desire-filled working class bodies," while in our time the cause of the breakdown is a contraction in credit. The financialization of the economy corresponds to the rise of information as the dominant category of economics and reflects the troubling irrelevance of the body and labor in the postindustrial economy. Tratner closes his chapter with a remarkable reading of the science fiction blockbuster *Avatar,* which, while ostensibly calling for a return to nature, in fact portrays nature functioning as a kind of central bank that relays vital information to sentient life-forms.

The acknowledgment of indebtedness as an elementary condition of social existence is said to entail coming to terms with an essential state of interdependence. But a policy of deepening and heightening one's level of interdependence can expose all participants to unexpected crises and intractable conflicts, which may provoke them into undertaking courses of action that bring harm to them all. Relations of mutual dependence in trade can bring wealth and well-being to those who enter into them, yet they can also create dangerous imbalances, especially when the interests, needs, and habits of the parties cannot be reconciled. Donald Hester examines the points of vulnerability and friction that have arisen in the relationship between the world's two leading economies in "China and the United States: The Bonds of Debt." The meteoric rise of China from feudal poverty, war with Japan, and the catastrophic policies of Mao to become the globe's second-largest economy has been perhaps the most decisive historical development since the collapse of communism. The reforms initiated by Deng Xiaoping, such as the opening of the Shenzhen free enterprise zone in 1979, have enabled China to amass the world's largest foreign exchange reserves, while accumulating a trade surplus with the United States that rose to record levels in 2010 at $273.1 billion. As Hester points out, such a massive trade imbalance cannot form the basis of a new status quo. China may decide to cut back substantially on its purchase of asset-backed securities to finance consumption in the United States because of the fear of US default, leading to a fundamental transformation of the US consumer economy. Or the United States may choose to inflate its currency, resolving the problem of the trade deficit while inflicting severe harm on its economy. Less disruptive measures would entail a rise in consumer spending in China coupled with an increase in the savings rate in the United States. The situation is however complicated by the presence of conflicts that go beyond the commercial relationship between the two countries—the security of Taiwan, the crisis of entitlement spending in the United States, the need of the Chinese government to maintain high rates of growth as well as a deflated currency for the sake of avoiding social unrest, and the competitive nature of capitalism itself, in which countries must compete with each other for scarce resources.

In "Debt's Moral," Kennan Ferguson challenges the conventional framework for understanding debt. One influential conception regards debt as a wholly economic category, for which the question of moral evaluation is altogether an irrelevant concern. The rival view holds that debt entails moral responsibility and thus that lenders and borrowers must be held accountable for the consequences of their transactions. Both, for Ferguson, are inadequate because they rely on the presumption that debts will always balance out in the end. The economic perspective that views debt in wholly functional terms and the insistence that debt serve socially productive purposes succumb to a fantasy of equilibrium as the goal and purpose of social relations. In other words, both posit an imaginary point of balance toward which both financial and moral transactions ought to incline. The belief that debts, whether monetary or moral, economic or political, will balance out disregards the deeper reality of the human situation, in which to live is to be indebted. For Ferguson, even the theological condemnation of monetary debt found in Judaism, Christianity, and Islam relies on the implicit repudiation of interdependence as the inescapable condition of human life. Debt is by definition all-pervasive and excessive. Yet debt is not only a terrible and inexorable burden that extinguishes all that is free and joyful. Ferguson, by way of Shakespeare's *Merchant of Venice,* demonstrates that it is the experience of love that correlates most forcefully to the powers of debt as an unyielding commitment.

According to Gerry Canavan, the environmental crisis must be grasped as an example of the "unpaid costs" of capitalism, in which the immensity of the profits generated by the economic system do not reflect the true costs of commercial activity. The history of capitalism is one of disguising externalities, such as cheap labor provided by colonized peoples and the low cost of resources seized by means of military conquest and imperial domination. Global warming, the impact of which hits hardest the impoverished peoples of the global South, who bear the least responsibility for polluting the atmosphere, must be grasped alongside colonial exploitation as a direct consequence of capitalism's drive to unconstrained expansion and limitless growth. Canavan calls for the payment of ecological debt in the form of restitution to the peoples directly affected by rising sea levels, drought, and industrial pollution, as well as outlining a leftist environmentalism centered on self-renewing agricultural practices. Like several other contributors, Canavan looks to speculative fiction for clues to an emergent politics that might traverse the vast distance between what is necessary and what is possible, affirming the power of the literary imagination to awaken in readers a sense of what a sustainable and just future entails. A politics that does justice to ecological debt is one that must define ecological limits of economic operation within which a vision of a viable future can be fulfilled. For there is no humane alternative other than one that protects and sustains the environment.

The idea of debt is at the heart of the way we understand economics, ethics, and the environment. Debt awakens us to realities that we disregard at our peril, or to obligations that are vital to the well-being of society and to the possibility of human flourishing. We know that we need to live within our means, economically speaking, and to live in a manner that is environmentally sustainable, and that to do both is to lead an ethical life in a pluralistic and interdependent world. Yet the call to live modestly, to use resources responsibly, and to reform political and economic structures to enable the industrialized world to make the transition to a way of life not based on infinite growth or unlimited acquisition—all these objectives underscore the strange plight of advanced industrial societies. For it is our curious dilemma that we are obliged to go in search of limitations to impose on ourselves, to develop a different basis for social relations, and to turn ourselves toward unfamiliar horizons if we are to honor the most important debts of our time.

Notes

1. See John Lanchester, *I.O.U.: Why Everyone Owes Everyone and No One Can Pay* (New York: Simon and Schuster, 2010), 39–40.

2. Joseph Stiglitz, *Freefall: America, Free Markets, and the Sinking of the World Economy* (New York: Norton, 2010), 22.

3. See Zygmunt Bauman, "The London Riots: On Consumerism Coming Home to Roost," *Social Europe Journal*, September 8, 2011, www.social-europe.eu/2011/08/the-london-riots-on-consumerism-coming-home-to-roost/.

4. Lanchester, *I.O.U.*, 219.

5. Ibid., 218.

1 Debt

Richard D. Wolff

Debt as an Economic and Social Issue

Across the United States, unsustainable debt helps force millions out of their homes, undermines consumption, prevents the extension of new credit, and in these ways sustains massive unemployment. Record volumes of personal bankruptcies intertwine with debt-driven collapses of banks, hedge funds, insurance companies, and other financial as well as nonfinancial enterprises. Even government debt in rich industrial economies has reached problematic levels, provoking political confrontations in the streets of Europe and elsewhere, forcing far-reaching political and economic changes. Debt is everywhere central to capitalism's current, global crisis.

Debt is thus very much on today's social agendas and nowhere more so than in the United States. Yet sober assessments of the complexities of debt and its social effects are rare, and rarer still are analyses of the role of capitalism in generating unsustainable debt. Urgent and intense ideological, economic, and political stakes are involved in how debts—and especially unsustainable debts—get resolved. After all, history offers many examples of debt contributing to the collapse of civilizations from ancient Rome during the period of slavery to feudal Europe. Might it be contributing to the decline of ours? And if so, is someone or something to blame? Can the debt "problem" be corrected or fixed, and at whose expense? Given the role of the United States in world affairs, the effects of a US debt problem extend well beyond our borders. Moreover, the position and impact of debt in the United States parallel its positions and impacts in many other countries.

First, a few general points to clear away some of the overheated rhetoric that sometimes surrounds the topic.

Debt is an economic process that occurs when two economic entities, such as individuals, businesses, or governments, are brought by circumstances to engage in a particular kind of transaction. One, the borrower, obtains objects of value—a loan—from the other, the lender. The lender agrees to the transaction with these conditions: (1) the borrower must contract to return those objects or an agreed-upon value equivalent at an agreed-upon future date, and (2) the borrower must pay a fee—"interest"—to the lender for this temporary use of those objects. These days, debts are mostly about quanta of money.

Debt (borrowing/lending) is a ubiquitous economic process in many societies, past and present. Individuals, households, clans, villages, enterprises, governments, and other social groups and institutions have engaged in a maze of debt processes with one another. Like commodity production and exchange, saving, and investment, debt is one of the processes that together constitute the economic dimension of society. A vast array of different wants, needs, perceptions, and motivations propel lenders and borrowers to agree on and enter into debt processes. And debt processes react back upon those who enter into them in complex ways that also affect all the other economic processes and thereby the society as a whole. Debt is part of the dialectic of interdependence, interaction, and the resulting ceaseless change within and among all the processes that make up societies.

Depending on the conditions in which they occur, debt processes can satisfy both lenders and borrowers; they can enable economies to share the pains of economic setbacks and the gains of economic progress. However, debt can also enrich one part of a community at the expense of another; it can, as it does today, function to reduce the level of economic activity, incomes, and well-being of social majorities. Usually debt contributes to all these outcomes at the same time and unevenly across societies.

Debts are therefore not good or bad, or, to say the same thing, they are good and bad. They have many complex effects, just as they have many complex causes. Consider the many factors weighing on the minds of borrowers and lenders worried about the costs and benefits of agreeing to a loan versus refusing it. Debts are, at least formally, voluntary acts in modern societies, but the actors face pressures and conditions that are not of their own choosing. Decisions by lenders and borrowers depend on the totality of forces affecting them, both those they are conscious of and can calculate and those that elude their consciousness or calculations.

Much as the larger social conditions and contexts shape the nature and consequences of debt, the effects of debt also shape people's thoughts, feelings, and actions. Those who feel victimized or otherwise damaged by debt will often become critical, whereas those who find debt's effects positive will more likely celebrate or at least defend it. Differences over the causes and consequences of debt can become blame and vilifications of lenders or borrowers. History echoes with comments about lenders like those made today about Goldman Sachs and with comments about borrowers like those made today about the millions of Americans currently unable to sustain their mortgage payments.

When debt is seen as one of the causes or as the chief cause of economic and social distress, tensions over finance can become acute. Social and political movements square off in struggles about whether and how to change finance. Defenders of the status quo may blame irresponsible borrowers who could not afford their loans and dishonestly hid relevant facts from lenders. Defenders may also attack government policies for forcing wisely reluctant lenders into imprudent loans; the problem then is not debt but government intervention in debt processes. Critics of the status quo will more likely blame irresponsible lenders who misled borrowers, manipulated government regulators, and disregarded the proper limits and safeguards for their financial activities. The relative political strengths of defenders and critics usually determine whether financial regulations and reorganizations will occur, how far they will go, and how long they will last.

In contemporary society, where the capitalist system prevails, the intimate connections (not to mention the interlocking directorates) between private nonfinancial enterprises and their financial counterparts have produced mainstream economics textbooks that usually stress the positive aspects of debt. Thus, for example, banks allow some individuals and enterprises freely to save money by depositing it and then to lend those deposited savings to others who make productive use of it. Borrowers from banks, having used their loans productively, pay a portion of their gains as interest to the lender while keeping the rest for themselves. Banks, in turn, share the interest by subsidizing services and sometimes paying interest to depositors. In the more simplistic textbooks, modern capitalist debt yields repeated win-win outcomes.

The more nuanced textbooks sometimes acknowledge that debt can also be negative. Borrowers can make mistaken investments with borrowed funds and so be unable to pay interest or even repay principal. Then the borrower's investment error travels across financial market connections to become the lender's loss as well. Similarly, when loans are made for purposes of consumption, borrowers' short-term consumption gains from such loans are offset in the longer term because the obligation to repay the loans with interest will cut their future consumption possibilities. This dilemma has often provoked further loans into a downward spiral that can have long-term effects of mounting social inequality between creditors and debtors and the social tensions that rise with them.

Debt in the United States

During the last thirty years, all financial and governmental entities in the United States have accumulated massive, historic increases in debt, as table 1.1 shows. The debt increases involved households, enterprises, and the state. In addition to the other economic processes that these actors engaged in—buying and selling of resources and products, hiring, taxing, and producing goods and services—they *more rapidly* increased their borrowing and lending. The last column shows how debt rose faster than our most common measure of total economic activity, the gross domestic product (GDP).

This massively increased indebtedness brought wealth and prosperity to some. It served others as the means to postpone the impact of stagnant wages and salaries. It allowed millions to at least temporarily enjoy lifestyles associated with the "American dream." However, it also contributed crucially to plunging the world economy into the worst economic decline and crisis since the Great Depression of the 1930s. It worsened the gaps between haves and have-nots as it deprived tens of millions of workers of their jobs and home owners of their homes. Perhaps most importantly, the prevalent policy responses to the crisis in the United States and other countries make only minimal and marginal changes to the basic conditions of debt that generated the crisis. They refuse to engage the systemic question: What is the relation between capitalism and debt? As I shall suggest at the end of this paper, the failure to face and debate that relation may represent the gravest of threats to the global economy.

Some Basic Causes of Mounting US Debts

Central to the debt story in the United States has been the relationship between wages earned by workers and the goods and services that workers produce for their employers to sell. Real wages (money wages adjusted for the prices of goods and services purchased with those wages) have stagnated in the United States since the 1970s. In contrast, productivity (output per worker) has continued to rise steadily across the same three decades. In short, employers have obtained ever more goods and services to sell per hour of their employees' effort while not having to pay those workers any more. The result has been a growing gap between the value added per worker and the value paid to workers. In Marx's terms and language, this has represented a stunning, long-term rise in the surplus appropriated per worker, and thus in what Marx called the "exploitation of labor."

The 150 years before the 1970s were different in a crucial way. During those years, while productivity rose faster than real wages, the latter rose every decade in the United States. Few if any other capitalist countries delivered so long-sustained a period of rising real wages to their working classes. This American "exceptionalism" was sustained by enduring labor shortages in the United States, which successive waves of immigration mitigated but never overcame. One result was the sense of US workers that they were somehow guaranteed a rising standard of living in exchange for the ever-harder work they performed to generate the rising productivity. Those workers embraced the American dream: for themselves, as a promise to their children, and as a measure of their own individual self-worth. They came to believe—with much encouragement from conservative ideologues—that the United States guaranteed the freedom and an equal opportunity for all to prosper sooner or later.

Imagine, then, the trauma inflicted at the end of this idyll as real wages stopped rising while productivity increases continued. That circumstance delivered ever greater

Table 1.1 Outstanding US Debt by Sector (Current $ Billions)

Year	Total	Household Total	Business Total	State & Local Governments	Federal Government	Total Debt % of GDP
1980	4531.6	1396.0	2056.2	344.4	735.0	162.5
1990	13448.5	3580.9	6382.1	987.4	2498.1	231.9
2000	26323.9	6987.3	14753.6	1197.9	3385.1	264.5
2009	40353.5	13536.0	26650.0	2362.2	7805.4	283.4

Sources: Federal Reserve, "Flow of Funds Accounts of the United States," *Federal Reserve Statistical Release*, September 20, 2012, Debt Growth, Borrowing, and Debt Outstanding Tables, www.federalreserve .gov/releases/z1/current/z1r-2.pdf; Bureau of Economic Analysis, "National Economic Accounts," www .bea.gov/national/index.htm#gdp.

wealth to employers and those who could participate directly in that growing wealth, such as stockholders, financiers, and top managers. Inequality of wealth and income grew, and the American dream became ever harder to obtain or sustain.

The end of rising real wages resulted from four major developments that became important in the 1970s. First, the computerization of almost all worksites hit its stride, an automation that sharply reduced the demands for all sorts of labor. Second, the profit-driven movement of jobs to offshore sites, where wages and taxes were lower and environmental standards weak, reduced the number of jobs available for US citizens. Third, US women began moving massively into paid employment in addition to their labors as homemakers and mothers. Fourth, new waves of immigrants, especially from Latin America, arrived. Rising supplies of labor power met reduced demands, with the predictable consequences for real wages. Employers no longer needed to raise wages to get or keep workers, as they had had to do for the previous 150 years. It was not the case that US workers became suddenly less disciplined, educated, or motivated, absolutely or relative to other nations' workforces, as has been suggested so often by popular as well as academic pundits. On Main Street and Wall Street, employers large and small, financial and otherwise, stopped raising real wages because "good business practice" as well as typical capitalist competition warranted doing what labor market conditions made possible.

In reaction, the US working class did *not* abandon the American dream and all it had come to symbolize. Instead they devised ways to secure rising levels of consumption despite stagnant real wages. First, more family members were sent out of households to perform more hours of paid work. The extra hours of work would compensate for the end of rising real wages per hour. Adult men took second or even third jobs, teenagers and retired persons took jobs, but most socially significant were the millions of US women who added paid work outside the household to all they already did inside.[1] Partly those women were responding to or participating in the women's liberation movement since the 1970s by seeking equal access with men to paid jobs and careers. They did that also to raise their families' standards of consumption when their husbands' real wages stagnated. In joining the paid labor force, women both reacted and contributed to stagnant real wages.

One of the social consequences of all this extra work was the deep crisis in US capitalism today. As of today, US workers do more hours of paid labor per year than the workers in any other advanced industrial country. Our working classes are exhausted. More importantly, the work of women outside the home proved to be a costly "double shift" given their continuing roles as primary house-worker and parent. Women could no longer perform the emotional work supporting the integrity of US families as they had so long done—at least not with the time and energy they had previously devoted to such work. So the last thirty years have seen vast shifts to the point that the "dysfunctional family" has become a cultural icon, a staple of the entertainment industry. Nor did all the extra work solve the problem of rising consumption in the face of stagnant real wages. The extra paid work by household members, especially women, required new sets of clothes, additional cars, the substitution of prepared for home-cooked meals, and added psychological self-care, such as costly drugs and/or psychotherapies. The extra work, in short, yielded little in the way of net extra consumption beyond that necessitated by the extra work itself.

So the US working classes turned, in some desperation, to the only remaining individual act available to raise consumption given stagnant wages. They went on a borrowing binge of epic proportions, mortgaging their homes (the only collateral most workers have) and making increasing use of that new product of 1970s economic changes, the credit card. Driven by advertising, especially "easy credit," by the absence of any other remaining way to boost consumption, and most of all by a dogged determination not to give up on the American dream they had promised to themselves and their families, American workers borrowed more, eventually, than many could afford. The entire history of the country had brought them to that point. By 2007, they were physically exhausted, emotionally stressed by dissolving family ties, and increasingly anxious about unsupportable levels of personal debt. US economic history culminated in a major crisis with deep historic roots and causes. The severity of this crisis means it will not be a shallow, quick "cycle" or be curable by standard doses of Keynesian monetary and fiscal policy prescriptions.

Meanwhile, at the other end of the social distribution of wealth, US employers were raking in fast-rising surpluses as productivity kept climbing while real wages did not. Parts of these surpluses were paid out to shareholders as dividends and to top managers as ballooning salaries and bonuses. The latter promoted an altogether different explanation for their rising net revenues from that provided above: their companies' good fortune was the result of their own stunning entrepreneurship. A cult of the innovating entrepreneur—or, more accurately, CEO—arose around businessmen like Lee Iacocca and Jack Welch. This worked out nicely, since it could reasonably be argued that if entrepreneurship or top management caused the great new wealth, then such entrepreneurs and managers deserved corresponding rewards in the way of luxurious packages of salary, bonus, and stock options. The rich in the United States became stunningly richer, creating a new market for financial management: the provision of investment strategies for "high–net worth individuals" by "hedge funds" and other new "financial instruments."

Another part of employers' mounting surpluses was deposited in banks, which thereupon began searching for and eventually creating new outlets for the profitable disposition of those deposited surpluses. One such profitable disposition that began in the 1970s was the mass marketing of credit cards. The banks also invented new types of mortgages to entice ever greater numbers of ever less wealthy Americans to borrow against their homes. They also invented new types of securities backed by packages of variously selected and grouped mortgage, credit card, auto, and student loans as well as by packages of industrial and commercial loans. Under conceptual euphemisms like "diversification of risk" and "financialization," many aspects of the economy were invaded by floods of loanable funds proffered by those who had gathered the rising surpluses yielded by increasingly exploited and vulnerable workers.

Those who had gotten their hands on those surpluses looked for ways to turn a profit by loaning them out to others willing to borrow. Workers desperate to maintain rising living standards were one key group of such borrowers. Corporations seeking to solve their problems also turned increasingly to loans. The multiplying loans and securities backed by loans spawned immense increases in related "financial services," including the rating of the risks of each loan and each loan-backed security, the insurance of such loans and securities (via the invention of "credit default swaps"), and the peddling of "investment advice" to the growing collection of individuals not rich enough to warrant hedge fund fees but with enough to buy such services. Since the 1970s, the financial industries have grown much faster than other industries. Not surprisingly, consumer debt and corporate debt zoomed.

Finally, government debt also soared. Except for a few years in the 1990s when the stock market bubble produced capital gains that brought in new tax payments, the federal, state, and local governments borrowed ever more alongside consumers and corporations. Government debt in the United States, as in many other countries, emerges from a kind of political stalemate. On the one hand, a distressed working class resents and fights further taxes even as it demands more and better government-provided services. These citizens have the power of numbers in an electoral system. On the other side, corporations and the wealthy evade and avoid taxes even as they demand that government undertake the costly activities they prefer, such as lavish defense spending and subsidies for technical research, transportation facilities, and public education of future employees. These citizens have the power of wealth to fund parties and campaigns, to lobby, and to finance think tanks shaping public opinion.[2] Opposing political parties almost always navigate these two groups' contradictory demands without imagining, let alone advocating, social changes to overcome such contradictions by transforming the two groups. During periods of economic crisis such as the one today, the government is typically called upon to undertake even more spending to maintain effective demand while not increasing taxes (for the same reason). The result then is an upsurge of extra national debt.

Notwithstanding their rhetorics, especially during electoral campaigns, the major parties differ only marginally in how they utilize the national debt to manage capitalism's contradictions in and out of crisis. That is, they all borrow against "the full faith and credit of the state" to provide many government services and activities that both sides want without having to tax both sides additionally to pay for such services. Leading party politicians hope this makes them popular, and they know that the problem of eventually repaying their borrowings will fall on their successor parties and politicians. So long as governments can find lenders, the rising national debt works as the politicians hope. It provides a kind of coping mechanism for the contradictions of the capitalist economy (but one burdened with other contradictions of its own).

In the United States, government activities include maintaining a vast global military presence, including multiple active wars. These commitments are always expensive. Especially when the wars also are unpopular, it becomes politically impossible to impose either mass taxes to pay for them or taxes on the rich and the corporations. Hence the US government borrows to pay for its global reach on top of borrowing to manage, or, better said, paper over the internal contradictions between employers and employees over what the state should do and who should pay for it.

The highly profitable, innovative, and fast-growing financial industry in the United States globalized over the last thirty years alongside many other industries. Multinational corporations, immense US trade deficits, and the continuing global role of the United States as capitalism's champion (and safest haven) drew capital into the United States in ever growing quantities. Much of the world's savings flowed into financial investments in US consumer, corporate, and national debt. The US position as the world's greatest debtor nation expanded. The United States needed these foreign cash inflows to feed the borrowing frenzy that grew out of the post-1970s widening disparity between real wages and productivity.

Some Basic Consequences of Mounting US Debt

The historically sudden growth of the surplus accruing to employers and via their distributions to shareholders and top managers led to a kind of euphoria that capitalism has seen before. It expresses itself in what former Federal Reserve chairman Alan Greenspan once called "irrational exuberance" and what others have called "bubble and bust sequences." The combination of fast-rising profits, the need to find investments for them, and competition among those seeking to manage them combine to produce speculative bubbles that eventually burst. In the United States, the first such bubble since the 1970s arose around the stock market and especially the Internet-related companies vying for investors. Individuals and corporations suddenly enriched by the stagnation of real wages sought stock market gains by bidding up shares, especially in the 1990s, until that bubble burst early in 2000. Then the money shifted instead into real estate investments of all kinds, producing a bubble there that burst in 2007. The bursting of the real estate bubble produced a collapse of the entire financial industry that turned out to have built an unsustainable mountain of debt and debt-backed securities.

In part, debt helped to cause the current crisis. Large numbers of US workers could no longer service the debts they had accumulated on a base of stagnant wages. They defaulted especially on their mortgages. First, this deflated the values of mortgage-backed securities. That in turn plunged the companies that had insured those securities into financial disaster. Banks and other creditors could no longer trust existing or potential borrowers because suddenly no one knew who had how many and how badly deflated debt-backed assets on their books. No one's solvency could be verified. The credit markets seized up. The debt expansion that had fueled capitalist globalization now froze it into a spiraling global recession, the worst since the Great Depression of the 1930s.

However, the explosion of debt itself demands explanation if we are to comprehend the deeper causes of the current crisis. A nation that had a long history of celebrating frugality and savings changed into one with stunningly low savings rates among its people and exploding, unsustainable debt levels for its consumers, enterprises, and governments. The United States had suffered a massive capitalist breakdown seventy-five years earlier and had attributed it in part to unsustainable debts and financial speculation. In its wake, the US government instituted all sorts of regulations and controls to prevent its recurrence. Yet over recent decades it had enabled its financial industry to evade, weaken, or eliminate those regulations and controls and thereby to repeat economic disaster. And now Americans watch as first a Republican and then a Democratic government increase the national debt on an enormous scale to relieve the private corporate debt while proposing many of the same financial regulations that proved inadequate and nondurable before, *as if nothing else could be done*. To complete the tableau, the very financial enterprises saved from collapse by the government's infusion of funds to them in 2008 and 2009 have spent huge sums to lobby against new federal regulations that might prevent them from repeating the activities that led to the crisis. That spectacle, together with a "jobless recovery," continues to sharpen domestic political tensions.

Behind the Debt Issue Lies the Organization of Production

The economy of the United States had no sudden, mysterious conversion to debt accumulation in the 1970s. What happened was a particular interaction between changed labor market conditions and typical capitalist corporate decision making. As the supply and demand for jobs inside the United States changed—for many complex and international reasons—capitalist employers in the United States grasped an opportunity. Because the long-standing labor shortages in the US economy were gone, employers realized that they no longer needed to keep raising wages to attract or retain employees. So they froze pay rates and thereby kept for themselves the fruits of rising productivity over the last thirty years. That was the logical, institutionally validated profit-maximizing strategy that made sense to employers from Main Street to Wall Street.

Employers did not consider the economic and social consequences that might follow from their decisions to end the long US history of rising real wages. They did not imagine that those consequences might come back to haunt or destroy them. They did what capitalism programs them to do. The ceaseless conflict located at the heart of capitalist enterprises between employers and employees motivated the technical changes and the relocation of production to lower-wage regions that reduced the relative demand for jobs in the United States. It likewise motivated the cessation of rising wages when that became possible for employers. That other interests can unite employers and employees in shared goals and purposes should not obscure the reality and consequences of their clashing interests. Yet exactly that obscurity infuses the mainstreams of thought and action among business, political, media, and academic leaders. Beyond and because of them, it has congealed into a one-sided common sense.

Even a moment's distance from such mainstreams nevertheless opens the way to alternative solutions that might finally break the repeated cycles of more and less government interventions into a capitalism recurringly punctuated by crises. Suppose we reorganized the major, economically dominant enterprises—capitalist corporations. Suppose we ended the system in which small groups of individuals situated at the peak of corporations—boards of directors selected and accountable to the small groups of major shareholders—made all the key economic decisions: what to produce, how and where, and what to do with the profits.

Such reorganized boards of directors would respond differently—in noncapitalist ways—to changing social conditions. To take the 1970s in the United States, had enterprises been so reorganized, their boards would *not* likely have ended the long history of rising real wages in the United States. Nor would they likely have moved jobs out of the United States. Such fundamental causes of the debt explosion, bubble, and crisis discussed in this paper would thereby have been removed.

Enterprises that are run democratically by those who work in them and that share powers with similarly democratic residential communities are also practices that have long histories in the United States and elsewhere. They have been realized as well in many experiments from cooperatives to communes to collective firms from California's Silicon Valley to Spain's Mondragon. What many of these experiments have in common is the desire of workers to share in the economic decisions that affect their lives.[3] Thus in one case workers want decision-making power over the division of surpluses/profits between (1) dividend-like payouts to the owners of the enterprise (these same workers or possibly others) and (2) allocations to research and development of new products or new technologies. In another case, workers want decision-making power over choices between more or less environmentally destructive techniques, especially when they and their families and neighbors have to live with pollution that a distant capitalist board of directors would view and decide about differently. In still another case, workers want the right to decide the division of output between wages and surplus for distributions elsewhere so that, for example, when their productivity keeps rising, they can raise their wages rather than enlarging the surplus.

Of course, enterprises reorganized in such noncapitalist ways will generate their own problems. The point is that they will be different from the recurring problems of a cyclically unstable capitalism imposing vast social costs very unevenly on the populations of the world. And any serious, honest debate about how to react to and correct the latter would have to include assessments of the costs and benefits of reorganizing enterprises. Those who have concluded that modern economies can do better than capitalism would then have their opportunities to make and defend their arguments. The inadequacies of previous experiments with noncapitalist economic systems might then become sources from which useful lessons for the future could be drawn, rather than functioning, Cold War style, as excuses for never questioning capitalism per se.[4]

Debt works its effects on the rest of society depending on how it interacts with other social processes. The set of economic processes that make up capitalist enterprises can interact with debt so as to provoke and then sustain systemic global economic crises. That's where we are now as successive "recoveries" prove temporary and very limited in scope and threaten to become punctuations in long-term economic decline processes in many countries.

Since the crisis hit in 2007, governments in most industrialized capitalist economies have nationalized the debts that became unsustainable for the individuals and enterprises that undertook them in the private sector. Now those governments are imposing austerities on their increasingly resistant citizens to service and pay off those nationalized debts. The austerity crises—whether at the national level as in Europe or more at state and local levels as in California and so many other states—are just displacements of the unresolved problem of capitalism and debt. If we can open discourse to ask formerly taboo questions about capitalism and debt, we will have greater opportunities to prevent still more capitalist crises than if discourse remains closed. That is a central issue of our time.

Notes

1. See the pathbreaking work of Arlie Hochschild, including *The Second Shift: Working Parents and the Revolution at Home* (New York: Viking Penguin, 1989) and *The Time Bind: When Work Becomes Home and Home Becomes Work* (New York: Metropolitan/Holt, 1997).

2. Since the 1970s, employers used their rising surpluses to pay for enhanced political interventions. They began pouring larger sums than before into (1) the campaigns of candidates they favored; (2) armadas of well-budgeted lobbyists inundating federal, state, and local legislatures and

executives; and (3) think tanks publicizing employer-friendly interpretations of economics, politics, culture, and nature. Business saturated the political spaces of US society just as stagnant wages, overwork, stress, and debt anxiety drove millions of workers to withdraw their participation and then even their interest in politics and civic affairs; see Robert D. Putnam, *Bowling Alone: The Collapse and Revival of American Community* (New York: Simon and Schuster, 2000). In such conditions politics shifted sharply rightward in the United States: not because many folks changed their minds but rather because those who withdrew had different values and priorities than those who rushed in equipped with massive new money to spend on politics.

3. For recent discussions of such reorganized enterprises, see the following: "Beyond the Capitalist Economy: Another World Is Possible," special issue of *Working USA: The Journal of Labor and Society* 13, no. 1 (March 2010); Richard D. Wolff, "Taking Over the Enterprise: A New Strategy for Labor and the Left," *New Labor Forum* 19, no. 1 (Winter 2010): 8–12; and Richard D. Wolff, *Capitalism Hits the Fan: The Global Economic Meltdown and What to Do About It* (Northampton, Mass.: Olive Branch Press, 2010).

4. The most sustained recent experiment with one kind of socialism as an alternative to capitalism occurred in Russia/Soviet Union between 1917 and 1989. How much of an alternative was it? What lessons does its history teach in terms of movement beyond capitalism? Is the definition of socialism exhausted by positing social instead of private property and planning instead of markets? Or are such macrolevel definitions insufficient without accompanying microlevel transformations inside enterprises of the sort sketched in the text? These questions are treated systematically in Stephen Resnick and Richard Wolff, *Class Theory and History: Capitalism and Communism in the USSR* (New York: Routledge, 2002).

2 "I Consider It Un-American Not to Have a Mortgage"

Immigrant Home Ownership in Chicago

Elaine Lewinnek

I̶N A 1953 *New Yorker* article, E. B. White fantasizes about accompanying Senator Joseph McCarthy on a trip to Walden Pond to investigate whether Henry David Thoreau was a communist. The trip gets off to a poor start because White's fictional McCarthy doesn't enjoy fresh air or walking, and then McCarthy is told that Thoreau had no mortgage. "I consider it un-American not to have a mortgage," declares the senator in E. B. White's humor piece. "Besides, it's probably a lie."¹ It's a fascinating sentiment, succinctly combining ideas about debt, citizenship, and the unreliability of historical financial evidence.

When White puts this comment attacking a classic American individualist into the mouth of an imagined McCarthy, he does so to make a joke and to mock McCarthy's witch hunts. But it wasn't a joke when Thoreau's own friend Ralph Waldo Emerson lamented, at Thoreau's funeral in 1862, that Thoreau "had no ambition." Instead of becoming a business leader—which probably would have involved going into debt—Thoreau had been content to be merely "captain of a huckleberry-party."² That is a remarkable thing to say at a man's funeral. But just how un-American or unambitious was it to live a life without debt?

In his fascinating study *Financing the American Dream*, Lendol Calder observes that Americans have a "myth of lost economic virtue." Since the mid-nineteenth century, Americans have been declaring that we have fallen from the thrift of our grandparents, from a golden age of relatively little debt that is always imagined to be about seventy years before each speaker. But such thrift never existed, as Calder explains:

"A river of red ink runs through American history."[3] The Pilgrims, many pioneers, and most founding fathers were all in debt, even though some of them also moralized against debt. In the wonderful phrasing of historian Daniel Boorstin, "The American dream was bought on the installment plan."[4] To Calder, this is actually an inherent part of capitalism: although moralists may be reluctant to admit it, debt disciplines workers, externally forcing Americans to budget their money in order to pay monthly bills. "What Americans did on the installment plan was to transform consumer culture into a suitable province for more work. . . . A bumper sticker sums it up accurately: 'I owe, I owe, it's off to work I go!'"[5] Instead of reflecting hedonism, debt actually pressures consumers to go to work to pay their debts. Perhaps this is what E. B. White meant by joking that eschewing a mortgage might be anticapitalistic, almost communist.

Such debt is sometimes portrayed as imposed on Americans by a manipulative capitalist system. My research into Chicago's working-class housing between 1870 and 1930 suggests, however, that many workers used mortgages as a way to engage in small-scale business ventures that they hoped would let them find a haven from the pressures of industrial corporate capitalism. Ironically, individuals went into debt in an effort to gain some economic control, although this control frequently eluded them. My analysis begins with a brief overview of the history of debt in America, then focuses more closely on the specific case of turn-of-the-century housing debt.

At first, most American debts were personal and private debts to friends, neighbors, and merchants. Few Americans borrowed formally from banks, but in the early republic paper money itself was a kind of debt, a promise that each issuing bank made to redeem paper currency for gold, although this promise was not always kept. Before government greenbacks first appeared in 1863, more than 1,500 US banks all printed their own currency, each valued slightly differently by other banks in other places. This dizzying economy, expanding into remote markets, relied on a tenuous trust but also encouraged speculation and gave us the term *confidence man* or *con man*. In her excellent narrative of America's first banking collapse, which happened in 1809, Jane Kamensky explains that the "alchemy" of speculative paper currency "made all Americans gamblers."[6]

Similarly, historian Scott Sandage explains that "nineteenth-century Americans understood that solvency and selfhood were speculative ventures."[7] Economic historians agree that in the middle of the nineteenth century one in five American households went bankrupt. In the 1850s, between half and two-thirds of San Francisco merchants failed. In more settled Poughkeepsie, New York, 30 to 60 percent of small businesses defaulted on their debts within three years.[8] Many others probably teetered on the brink, tenuously avoiding formal bankruptcy at a time when declaring legal bankruptcy was considered unmanly. As older ideas of honor mixed with the burgeoning market economy and the newer surveillance systems of credit-rating agencies, the "self-made man" faced the terror of becoming his own opposite: the "failure," the bankrupt, the loser. Such individualistic explanations ignored, of course, the structural forces that meant nineteenth-century Americans faced a severe recession once every twenty years, caused not by visible sources such as drought or war, as in the past, but by the far less tangible forces of maturing capitalism.[9]

In 1888, Edward Bellamy famously imagined all of society as "a prodigious coach," pulled by masses of desperately hungry people who were straining in agony against their harnesses, while a few lucky people sat on top of the coach, enjoying the breeze without having to do any work. These fortunate ones, pulled along by the laboring masses on the ground, lived off the interest income of their investments. They were moreover terrified by the fact that their comfortable seats "were very insecure, and at every sudden jolt of the coach persons were slipping out of them and falling to the ground, where they were instantly compelled to take hold of the rope and help to drag the coach on which they had before ridden so pleasantly." Bellamy imagines that at particularly steep patches of the road the rich sitting on top would commiserate with the poor harnessed down below by promising possible compensation in another world and occasionally chipping in "to buy salves and liniments for the crippled and injured." But the rich would take care never to do more than that, "for there was always some danger at these bad places of a general overturn in which all would lose their seats."[10] Bellamy's capitalist bus remains one of the most vivid imageries of bankruptcy in American culture. Everyone feared it, and many suffered from it, continually falling out of their seats of credit.

After 1880, pawnbrokers, housing developers, mass retailers, and immigrant-organized microlending societies all expanded access to consumer credit in America. Levels of debt ballooned in the 1920s with the advent of automobile-company financing. As Mary Poovey explains in her contribution to this collection, during the Progressive Era most Americans began to view debt more as an opportunity than as a burden. Americans' debt expanded again after 1957 with the introduction of credit cards. It swelled again in the 1980s and continues to do so, as Richard Wolff discusses at greater length in this volume. Our personal rates of indebtedness are now far higher than they ever were—we are almost thirty times more in debt than we were in the 1950s—but the condition of personal indebtedness is not new, nor are the questions that debt raises about ethics, identity, and the market economy.[11]

Before the twentieth century, debt was often divided between good "productive debt" and bad "consumptive debt." Many of us still recognize this division: we tend to believe that it is acceptable to borrow money to pay for a college education because that is a productive debt that will eventually allow the borrower to earn more money, while it is less morally permissible to borrow money to pay for a designer purse. Yet the line between productive and consumptive debts can be slippery. Is a car productive or consumptive? An automobile is a consumer good, of course, which loses value as soon as a purchaser drives it off the lot, but it can also enable that purchaser to drive to a job.

The definition of productive and consumptive debt is subjective. In their classic study *Middletown,* sociologists Robert and Helen Lynd were shocked to discover in the 1920s that twenty-one families in Muncie, Indiana, purchased a car before they purchased indoor plumbing. Middletown's residents had different ideas than did the researchers about what constituted a necessity.[12] This may have resulted in part from the fact that it was easier to obtain financing for an automobile than for home improvements, but it also seems to have been a personal choice. As a rural informant told a shocked US Department of Agriculture researcher in the 1920s, "Why, you can't go to town in a bathtub."[13] This statement captures the ways in which Americans have, literally and metaphorically, used debt to go to town. What it does not reveal, but what contributed to the perplexity of the Lynds and the USDA researcher, is that the people whose finances were so fragile that they had to choose between a car and a bathtub were all home owners. There was no landlord to pay for the bathtub.

Home ownership was important to working-class Americans at the turn of the twentieth century. It offered them housing, of course—a better alternative to the tenements and boardinghouses that were so crowded that they had dire rates of infant mortality. It also offered workers a way to invest their tenuous savings that was safer than banks, which were unreliable before the advent of federal banking insurance in the 1930s. In Chicago, homes were actually advertised as "better than a bank for a poor man."[14] Homes were seen as potentially productive spaces, offering the possibility of gardens, tenants, or small, home-based businesses such as laundries. Homes were also a tangible investment that workers hoped they could control through the sweat equity of their own home improvements. Home ownership, workers hoped, was a way to assert individual control in the face of corporate capitalism. Yet homes were also giant debts that entangled individuals in the uncertainties of the capitalist economy through lending institutions and property value markets that were ultimately beyond their control.

In every North American city where researchers have investigated turn-of-the-century rates of home ownership—Boston, Chicago, Detroit, Toledo, Toronto, Johnstown (Pennsylvania), New Haven (Connecticut), and Newburyport (Rhode Island)—the immigrant working class owned homes at far higher rates than the wealthy, who preferred to rent.[15] In Chicago, in 1939, only 21.7 percent of native-born white residents were home owners, while 41.3 percent of immigrants were. In 1913, in the stockyards district of Back of the Yards—the notoriously poverty-stricken, immigrant-filled setting of Upton Sinclair's *The Jungle*—even 30 percent of female-headed households owned homes, 47 percent of male-headed households earning less than two dollars a day owned homes, and, of the rest of male-headed households, a remarkable 95 percent owned homes. As David Roediger declares: "Immigrant[s] did not so much 'buy into' the American dream of home ownership as help create it."[16] I am not sure whether E. B. White knew this when he had McCarthy declare, "I consider it un-American not to have a mortgage," but White may have noticed that when Thoreau built his cabin at Walden Pond in 1845 he used wood that had originally been part of an Irish laborer's "shanty," covered in dirt, "dank, clammy, and aguish," yet with salvageable boards for which Thoreau paid $8.03, his single largest housing expense.[17] Thoreau and his readers took it for granted that working-class immigrants would own humble homes before native-born Americans owned middle-class homes.

This raises two questions: How did America's turn-of-the-century immigrants pay for their widespread home ownership, and why did they buy houses? Some working-class people, like Thoreau, used their own sweat equity to pay the cost of houses by building them for themselves. Richard Harris has examined the practice of owner-building in Toronto's working-class suburbs before 1920, while Becky Nicolaides has studied similar owner-building practices in working-class suburbs of Los Angeles as late as 1940.[18] Chicago also had owner-builders, but by the 1880s Chicago's active reformers promulgated strict building codes that limited the possibilities for owner-building. Chicago's working-class suburbs were the result not of owner-building but of creative home financing. As Chicago's Progressive housing laws became national, and as standards of living rose to include heating and plumbing that were not easily built by amateurs, the situation of turn-of-the-century Chicagoans became the situation of most Americans: people bought their houses by going into debt.

The average annual wage for Chicago's factory workers in 1890 was $590.23, while the average cost of a small house was $1,500, or about three years' wages.[19] To buy a house, most workers had to borrow money. Chicago's banks offered real estate loans to larger customers after 1869, although, until the amortized mortgage became widespread in the 1920s, these mortgages generally followed the risky balloon plan: borrowers paid off the interest at regular intervals, while paying off the principal only in a lump sum at the end of five or six years.[20] In the early twentieth century, Chicago's banks offered modified balloon plans, in which the final payment was about two-thirds of the initial loan, but these were still a viable financing plan only for people planning to sell off their initial investment as soon as the loan came due in order to meet the balloon payment.[21] One Chicago social worker reports meeting an elderly couple who were planning to die before their balloon mortgage came due.[22] Most of Chicago's working-class immigrants rarely qualified for such bank loans, often distrusted banks in the first place, and usually could find better deals outside formal banks, so, as that same social worker explained in 1924, "The bank is practically never resorted to."[23]

Chicago's workers preferred to borrow from friends or relatives, from realtors and real estate developers, or from a building and loan society. In the late nineteenth century, many of Chicago's subdivision developers offered installment payments, at first due annually in four equal payments over four years at 8 to 10 percent interest, then evolving to a now familiar pattern of 10 percent down, then monthly payments at 6 percent interest, in an arrangement that dealers promoted as "just like rent." The main difference from present-day arrangements of housing financing was that in turn-of-the-century Chicago dealers usually kept the title in their own name until the purchaser made the final payment, so that one missed mortgage payment could mean forfeiting the entire house.[24]

That is the story that underlies Upton Sinclair's famous novel *The Jungle*. This muckraking novel about grinding poverty and nauseating industrial meatpacking is also, oddly, a novel about home ownership. Dissatisfied with sleeping in shifts in a boardinghouse cleaned only intermittently by hungry chickens, Jurgis Rudkus and his family purchase a flimsy house two miles south of Chicago's stockyards, where the twelve members of the extended Rudkus family crowd into four rooms. They are surprised by hidden costs, including interest on the mortgage, home owner's insurance, water fees, and property taxes. To pay for the home, they skimp on heat and food, then send the women and the children of the family out to work. After three years of struggle, they miss one month's payment when Jurgis is jailed for beating up the boss who raped his wife, and because of that one missed payment they lose their entire investment.[25] That mortgage foreclosure is the turning point in Sinclair's novel. Without the house, the family falls apart and scatters.

The Jungle may have exaggerated conditions of labor but not those of home buying. Book reviewers in 1906 hardly even remarked on the home ownership plot: it seemed ordinary and unremarkable to them. Chicago's social workers confirmed this: "It is not unusual when a case has been referred to the United Charities because children are underfed or underclothed that a visit will disclose that the family is making regular monthly payments on a house."[26] In the early 1920s, social worker Mary Bruton visited eighty-four of these home owners seeking charity. She found that, like the fictional Rudkus family, 51 percent of these home owners had financed their homes by contracting with developers, 13 percent by borrowing from friends, and 6 percent by using their own savings. Another 16 percent refused to answer her questions, suspecting that she had come to raise their taxes or condemn their houses or otherwise threaten their investments.[27] Such suspicions indicate how precarious these poor home owners felt.

The most secure of these charity-receiving home owners, Bruton concluded, were the 6 percent who had financed through building and loan associations. Unlike banks, building and loan associations offered a plan allowing monthly payments on both interest and principal. And unlike developers' contracts, building and loan associations allowed their members to hold title to the property that they were paying for. They were what we would now call an immigrant microlending society. Every member bought "shares," paying as little as 50 cents a month, in the expectation that at "maturity" (usually a period of about ten years) they would receive back their entire investment of $60, plus $40 in interest. The promised payouts were high because each month members bid for the right to borrow from the groups' collective savings, paying back with a structured monthly plan of fees and 8 percent interest. Building and loan associations boasted that they offered "the only plan by which the working man can become his own capitalist, and create a source of wealth from which he can supply all reasonable demands." Using the language of Americanness as well as the language of small-scale capitalism, they declared that this was a mutual plan "of the people, by the people, and for the people."[28] This system of "mutual help for self-help" began in Scotland in 1815, spread to Philadelphia in the 1850s, and reached Illinois by 1872, carried by immigrants familiar with building and loan associations in Europe.[29]

When the *Chicago Tribune* reported on these societies in 1883, the newspaper felt the need to explain to its native-born readers how Czech, German, Irish, and Polish immigrants pooled their savings to purchase a house.[30] In 1931, an official history explained, "The Building and Loan Associations, the poor man's device for financing home-buying, is in Chicago essentially an immigrant institution. It is said by Czechs that a girl of that nationality will scarcely consider a marriage proposal of a suitor who has not a 'book,' a membership in such an institution."[31] This is a fascinating idea: I won't marry you unless you're in debt. It was not only Czechs who boasted of their own home financing. More than one social worker noted, "Each of the foreign building and loan representatives visited described his own particular nationality as having the largest proportion of homeowners."[32] Immigrant groups used home ownership to strive for American domesticity and middle-class respectability. In Chicago, Italians appeared to prefer private "debts of honor" without paperwork or firm deadlines, and African Americans borrowed directly from realtors until the rise of black-owned Chicago banks in the 1910s, but all other racial and ethnic groups among Chicago's workers relied on building and loan associations.[33]

These associations were more limited and stable than turn-of-the-century banking, but they were still risky. In 1894, in America's worst depression before 1930, fourteen of Illinois's building and loans went bankrupt, while secretaries of two others attempted to embezzle $47,442.25. The attorney general of Illinois closed down twelve other building and loans, eleven of which were in Chicago, generally for irresponsibly making "loans on worthless real estate" that cost their shareholders $928,050.[34] These are huge sums to lose, representing many people's 50 cents per month. In 1898, Illinois's building and loan associations owned $6,141,723.06 worth of real estate, almost all of which they had gained through foreclosed mortgages.[35] Using the associations' own estimate of $1,500 per house, these statistics suggest at least 4,094 lost homes in the late 1890s alone. The developers, neighbors, and family members who also loaned money did not leave auditor's accounts revealing how many other mortgages were foreclosed, but knowing that building and loans financed 6 percent of homes can allow us to calculate that if 6 percent lost 4,094 homes, then 100 percent lost at least 68,233 homes—or more, since building and loan debt was generally recognized as the most stable of all debt options. In 1900, Chicago's total population was 1.7 million people, or approximately 340,000 households, so that a conservative estimate amounts to a foreclosure rate of approximately 20 percent.[36] A turn-of-the-century realtor believed that a majority of Chicago's "working people" who bought land in the middle of the nineteenth century eventually lost it to foreclosures.[37] One book review of *The Jungle* casually mentions that "of course" they lost their home; this was a well-known hazard of what the review called buying a house on "the installment plan."[38] With a foreclosure rate between 20 and 50 percent, the turn-of-the-century housing market makes our current housing crisis pale by comparison.

Chicago's immigrants faced sometimes-swindling realtors, a racist property market (a special challenge to African American home owners, who recognized that their property values would rarely ever rise), and a turbulent economy whose seasonal layoffs made it difficult for workers to repay their monthly debts.[39] Still, they bought homes. They bought for reasons of business: the equivalent of two to four years' rent would buy a house, permanently, and many Chicagoans from rural backgrounds knew how to use their yards for truck gardening or small commercial laundries.[40] They would also often take in boarders. They hoped their homes could become small businesses, a small-scale capitalism to help them weather the vicissitudes of industrial capitalism. They also bought for reasons of comfort: they wanted to move out of cramped and polluted tenement neighborhoods to raise their families in larger and more open conditions.

For his sociology dissertation at the University of Chicago, Julius John Ozog interviewed Chicago's Polish home owners in the 1930s and concluded that, overall, "economic ambition" was their prime motive for home ownership, intertwined with "a vague desire" for "social benefits and prestige." Ozog explained that land ownership meant economic, social, and political capital to the Poles he interviewed because in the peasant societies from which they had immigrated land had been a crucial tool of production and also, often, a prerequisite for political power.[41] Many of Chicago's social workers dismissed this attitude as naive peasant nostalgia, without noticing that American urban land could also be a tool of production for people who ran small shops from their homes.[42] American property ownership also brought political power in a government based on property taxes, while homes owned in ethnic neighborhoods could bring political power through Chicago's ward system.[43] The "peasant attachment to land" that middle-class Chicagoans criticized actually had a material basis in modern Chicago.

Chicago's immigrant workers told interviewers that owning a home gave them a sense of citizenship. They foreshadow McCarthy's imagined comment: "I consider it un-American not to have a mortgage." Yet in the Progressive Era, Chicago's middle-class observers had great difficulty recognizing the foreigner's domesticity. Chicago's settlement-house workers observed, "The ambition of the immigrant to own property in America is one of his most striking characteristics. For it he will make almost unbelievable sacrifices both of his own comfort and of that of his wife and children, since the heavily mortgaged house too often calls for the united wage-earning power of the entire family."[44] This could not be middle-class "American" domesticity, they argued, because it involved women's waged work, child labor, and extreme underconsumption in order to afford a home.

Chicago's reformers asserted that the "land-hunger of the European peasant" in Chicago caused problems of "not simple poverty, but undue frugality."[45] Reformers worried that immigrants' desire to own homes "means in some cases the sacrifice of the children's education, the crowding of the home with lodgers, or the mother's going out to work," or all three, transgressing middle-class domesticity in order to achieve it.[46] "The foreign worker wants to own his own home as soon as possible and often before he ought to," settlement-house leader Mary Eliza McDowell complained. "This thrift is not a blessing but too often a curse to the family and not good for the community."[47]

To pay for homes, Chicago's workers did engage in severe underconsumption. They skimped on clothing, food, and heat, sometimes crowding all sleepers into a single heated room, in what reformers called an "un-American standard of living."[48] They skimped on maintenance, making life even harder for their many boarders and tenants. They skimped on municipal services, so that Chicago's working-class suburbs often featured poor schools or few utilities. They skimped on home improvements: West Hammond's homeowners lacked "amenities" like private toilets and bathtubs as late as 1939.[49] Building homes without bathrooms in cities without sewers led to especially high costs later on, when new housing standards forced cities and home owners to add services. This raises the question whether, instead of being a dream of upward mobility, such home ownership might have been a nightmare of misplaced resources.

Chicago's social workers believed that too many children lost opportunities for class mobility because "at all times the need of keeping up the payments on a house outweighs the need of keeping a child in school."[50] Historian Olivier Zunz concurs, in his study of Detroit: "Considering the large number of day laborers owning a home, it may well have been a brake to mobility."[51] In his classic statistical study of Newburyport, Rhode Island, Stephan Thernstrom agrees, concluding that the limited mobility that allowed parents to own property had no effect on the mobility of those parents' children. "Ruthless underconsumption" allowed immigrant workers to own homes, but at the cost of "immense sacrifices—sacrifices so great as almost to blur the dichotomy between 'property' and 'poverty.'"[52]

The policy of Chicago's charities at the time was to insist that clients sell their homes because renting appeared cheaper to the charity directors and seemed to call for less extreme sacrifices.[53] The poor knew of this policy and apparently resisted it. Social workers complained that poor home owners pretended their mortgage payments were rent, in a ruse to get charities to help them with home ownership.[54]

What alternatives did these immigrant home owners have? Few immigrants had access to quality education for their children, but many immigrants encountered Chicago's numerous subdividers, building and loan associations, and others in the business of encouraging home ownership. Few immigrants could find a more secure venue for their meager surplus earnings or other routes to claiming middle-class American status. A home was better than a bank for a poor man. It was, nevertheless, a great risk.

Even Thoreau wrote that, in the spring of 1845, he "borrowed an axe and went down to the woods by Walden Pond, nearest to where I intended to build my house, and began to cut down some tall arrowy white pines" on land loaned to him by Emerson. "It is difficult to begin without borrowing, but perhaps it is the most generous course thus to permit your fellow-men to have an interest in your enterprise."[55] Thoreau borrowed both the ax to build his house and the land on which he built it. Although he spurned most of the economy of his time, he recognized debt as part of a web of interdependence.

Chicago's immigrants had the ambition that Emerson accused Thoreau of lacking, though Emerson would probably not have approved of the sacrifices they made for home ownership. Their American dream may seem more like an American ordeal, but their story reveals that the current foreclosure crisis is part of an all-American, immigrant-designed pattern. Chicago's immigrants went into debt not from capitalist coercion or misunderstandings born of ignorance but from a calculated choice, although it was a choice made from limited options.

It is a familiar story: "My grandparents came over from the old country, skimped and saved and bought their own home, pulling themselves up by their bootstraps." Few mention that these were heavily leveraged bootstraps and that, for between 20 and 50 percent of home owners, those bootstraps broke. Few recognize that these immigrants' American dream led to a sprawling built environment that was moreover segregated, separating skilled workers from unskilled workers and separating earlier arrivals from later waves of migrants.[56]

Immigrant home ownership left a cultural legacy that may be even larger than its environmental and social legacy. The independent and creative efforts of immigrants at home financing made it seem as if success or failure were due solely to individual merit.[57] This notion has lost little of its influence, as seen in today's public discussion of who "deserves" a bailout: debt is perceived to be a problem of individual morals and individual strategies instead of a structural issue dependent to some degree on the contingencies shaping when people entered the housing market. As in the past, we still see the vulnerability of poor people struggling to access middle-class status through home ownership and debt. As in the past, the poor, who have the most to lose from volatile housing prices, turn out to be most at risk.

Notes

1. E. B. White, "Visitors to the Pond," *New Yorker*, May 23, 1953, quoted in Rebecca M. Dale, ed., *E. B. White: Writings from the New Yorker, 1927–1976* (New York: HarperCollins, 1990), 44. At Walden Pond, of course, Thoreau built his tiny cabin himself in 1845, using a borrowed ax and borrowed land, while spending just over $28 on supplies.

2. Ralph Waldo Emerson, "Thoreau (Eulogy, 1862)," quoted in Scott Sandage, *Born Losers: A History of Failure in America* (Cambridge, Mass.: Harvard University Press, 2005), 1–2.

3. Lendol Calder, *Financing the American Dream: A Cultural History of Consumer Credit* (Princeton, N.J.: Princeton University Press, 1999), 26.

4. Daniel Boorstin, *The Americans: The Democratic Experience* (New York: Random House, 1973), 426, quoted in Calder, *Financing the American Dream*, 11.

5. Calder, *Financing the American Dream*, 303.

6. Jane Kamensky, *The Exchange Artist: A Tale of High-Flying Speculation and America's First Banking Collapse* (New York: Penguin Books, 2008), 11.

7. Sandage, *Born Losers*, 27.

8. Kamensky, *Exchange Artist,* 11; and Sandage, *Born Losers,* 3–4, 29.

9. Sandage, *Born Losers,* 3–4, 29.

10. Edward Bellamy, *Looking Backward* (1888; repr., New York: Signet Classics, 1960), 29–30.

11. Calder, *Financing the American Dream,* 10, 25.

12. Ibid., 201.

13. Joseph Interrante, "You Can't Go to Town in a Bathtub: Automobile Movement and the Reorganization of American Rural Space, 1900–1930," *Radical History Review* 21 (1979): 151–68.

14. See Elaine Lewinnek, "'Better Than a Bank for a Poor Man? Home Financing in Chicago, 1870–1930" *Journal of Urban History* 32 (December 2006): 274–301.

15. For Detroit, see Olivier Zunz, *The Changing Face of Inequality: Urbanization, Industrial Development, and Immigrants in Detroit, 1820–1920* (Chicago: University of Chicago Press, 1982), 152–53. Margaret Marsh confirms this observation for Boston in *Suburban Lives* (New Brunswick, N.J.: Rutgers University Press, 1990). Douglas Rae notes this in New Haven in *City: Urbanism and Its End* (New Haven, Conn.: Yale University Press, 2003), 95–96, while Stephan Thernstrom confirms it for Newburyport in *Poverty and Progress: Social Mobility in a Nineteenth-Century City* (Cambridge, Mass.: Harvard University Press, 1964). Richard Harris offers the best explanation of this phenomenon in *Unplanned Suburbs: Toronto's American Tragedy, 1900 to 1950* (Baltimore, Md.: Johns Hopkins University Press, 1996). For further comparison between cities, see David Roediger, *Working toward Whiteness: How America's Immigrants Became White. The Strange Journey from Ellis Island to the Suburbs* (New York: Basic Books, 2005), 158–59.

16. Roediger, *Working toward Whiteness,* 159.

17. Henry David Thoreau, *Walden; or, Life in the Woods* [1854], reprinted in *Walden and Other Writings,* ed. Joseph Wood Krutch (New York: Bantam Books, 1989), 137, 141.

18. Harris, *Unplanned Suburbs,* and Becky Nicolaides, *My Blue Heaven: Life and Politics in the Working-Class Suburbs of Los Angeles, 1920–1965* (Chicago: University of Chicago Press, 2002).

19. Richard Sennett, *Families against the City: Middle Class Homes in Industrial Chicago, 1872–1890* (Cambridge, Mass.: Harvard University Press, 1970), 85. There was little wage inflation in these years. Chicago's Immigrant Commission Study of 1904–14 found that one-third of immigrant families earned less that $500 annually, while another third earned less than $750. See Sophonisba Breckenridge, *New Homes for Old* (New York: Harper and Brothers, 1921), 36–37.

20. F. Cyril James, *The Growth of Chicago Banks,* vol. 1, *The Formative Years* (New York: Harper and Brothers, 1938), 396; and Calder, *Financing the American Dream,* 66, 281.

21. Fred Feasel, "The Financing of Urban Residential Construction" (MA thesis, University of Chicago, 1920), 23, 34.

22. Mary Frances Bruton, "A Study of Tenement Ownership by Immigrant Workingmen in Chicago" (MA thesis, University of Chicago, 1924). Bruton reports that the elderly Italian immigrants Mr. and Mrs. B used all their savings for a down payment on a small house, taking out a loan on the rest that they were aware they could never pay back. Their son moved into the attic while they settled in the basement, renting out their home's main floor for $30 a month in order to pay the loan interest and property taxes, and, they hoped, fund a modest retirement for themselves. The damp basement exacerbated their rheumatism, so that Mr. B was confined to his bed for twelve years, trapped, and spending all spare income on medicine (48–49).

23. Ibid., 32.

24. Ibid., 30.

25. Upton Sinclair, *The Jungle* (1906; repr., New York: Penguin Classics, 1986), 81–86, 122, 212–14.

26. Bruton, "Tenement Ownership," 50. The same sentence appears in Abbott, *Tenements,* 387.

27. Bruton, "Tenement Ownership," 36, 7–8.

28. Edmund Wrigley, *The Working Man's Way to Wealth; a Practical Treatise on Building Associations: What They Are and How to Use Them* (Philadelphia: James K. Simon, 1869), 43, 5. This popular book went through at least six printings in the 1860s and '70s.

29. See H. Morton Bodfish, *History of Building and Loan Associations in the United States* (Chicago: U.S. Building and Loan League, 1931), 4, 11.

30. "Chicago Building Societies Which Represent an Investment of $5,000,000," *Chicago Tribune*, March 25, 1883, 23.

31. Everett Charington Hughes, *The Growth of an Institution: The Chicago Real Estate Board* (Chicago: University of Chicago Society for Social Research, 1931), 49.

32. Edith Abbott, *The Tenements of Chicago, 1908–1935* (Chicago: University of Chicago Press, 1936), 391 n. 12. See also Bruton, "Tenement Ownership," 30.

33. Bruton, "Tenement Ownership," 33, 16. See also Work, *Negro Real Estate Holders*, 15, 19.

34. David Gore, *Third Annual Report of the Auditor of Public Accounts of Building and Loan Associations of the State of Illinois: 1894* (Springfield, Ill.: Ed F. Hartman, State Printer, 1895), 5.

35. J. S. McCullough, *Seventh Annual Report of the Auditor of Public Accounts of Building, Loan and Homestead Associations of the State of Illinois: 1898* (Springfield, Ill.: Phillips Brothers, State Printers, 1899), vi–vii.

36. Of course, the fact that 6 percent of charity-seeking home owners used building and loans does not necessarily mean that 6 percent of all home owners did; 4,094 building-and-loan-owned houses in 1898 does not necessarily mean that all 4,094 foreclosures happened in one year; and the population of 1900 did not necessarily live equally divided, five people to a household. My calculation is unreliable, but it is an attempt to put into perspective the turn-of-the-century housing market.

37. Homer Hoyt, *One Hundred Years of Land Values in Chicago* (Chicago: University of Chicago Press, 1933), 42, 76.

38. "Jurgis Rudkus and 'The Jungle,'" *New York Times Book Review*, March 3, 1906, 128.

39. Monroe Nathan Work, "Negro Real Estate Holders of Chicago" (unpublished MA thesis, University of Chicago, 1903), 37.

40. Citizen's Association Committee on Tenement Houses, *Report* (1884), quoted in Bessie Louise Pierce, *A History of Chicago*, vol. 3, *The Rise of a Modern City, 1871–1893* (New York: Alfred A Knopf, 1957), 270.

41. Julius John Ozog, "A Study of Polish Home Ownership in Chicago" (MA thesis, University of Chicago, 1942), 52, 57, 63, 103. See also Bruton, "Tenement Ownership," 9–10, 21, 38.

42. In Ozog's sample group, 6 percent had shops in their homes, and 12 percent took in boarders, a practice that had subsided by the time of Ozog's study. Earlier, before home ownership, 56 percent of Ozog's sample had taken in boarders.

43. For Chicago's reliance on property taxes, see Robin Einhorn, *Property Rules: Political Economy in Chicago, 1833–1872* (1991; repr., Chicago: University of Chicago Press, 2001), as well as Pierce, *History*, 333. For the power of ethnic wards, see Karen Sawislak, *Smoldering City: Chicagoans and the Great Fire, 1871–1874* (Chicago: University of Chicago Press, 1995), 259.

44. Louise Montgomery, *The American Girl in the Stockyards District* (Chicago: University of Chicago Press, 1913), 4. See also Edith Abbott, *The Tenements of Chicago, 1908–1935* (Chicago: University of Chicago Press, 1936), 377–78.

45. Sophonisba Breckenridge and Edith Abbott, *The Delinquent Child and the Home* (New York: Russell Sage Foundation, 1912), 81.

46. Sophonisba Breckenridge, *New Homes for Old* (New York: Harper and Brothers, 1921), 107.

47. Mary Eliza McDowell, "Housing" (1921), 3, in Mary Eliza McDowell Papers, folder 14, "University of Chicago Settlement-Housing," Chicago Historical Society. See also Bruton, "Tenement Ownership," 37.

48. Edith Abbott and Sophonisba Breckenridge, eds., "Housing Conditions in Chicago, Part III: The Twenty-Ninth Ward Back of the Yards," *American Journal of Sociology* 11, no. 4 (January 1911): 450.

49. Joseph C. Bigott, *From Cottage to Bungalow: Houses and the Working Class in Metropolitan Chicago, 1869–1929* (Chicago: University of Chicago Press, 2001), 142.

50. Montgomery, *American Girl*, 21. See also Breckenridge and Abbott, *Delinquent Child*, 15: castigating "the cupidity of parents who preferred the purchase of a house to the education of their children."

51. Olivier Zunz, *The Changing Face of Inequality* (Chicago: University of Chicago Press, 1982), 161, 152. Zunz was one of the first to observe that "homeownership at the turn of the century was neither particularly middle class nor American."

52. Stephan Thernstrom, *Poverty and Progress: Social Mobility in a Nineteenth-Century City* (Cambridge, Mass.: Harvard University Press, 1964), 136–37, see also 152–55.

53. See Bruton, "Tenement Ownership," 60.

54. Ibid., 54.

55. Thoreau, *Walden*, 135.

56. Margaret Garb, *City of American Dreams: A History of Home Ownership and Housing Reform in Chicago, 1871–1919* (Chicago: University of Chicago Press, 2005).

57. This American belief in individual meritocracy is pervasive, as Kathryn Dudley shows in her marvelous ethnography of the 1980s farm crisis, *Debt and Dispossession: Farm Loss in America's Heartland* (Chicago: University of Chicago Press, 2002).

3 Demonizing Debt, Naturalizing Finance

Mary Poovey

This essay seeks to illuminate several chapters in the history of debt. I am not primarily concerned with tracking the fluctuating totals of monetary debt, whether for nations or individuals. Nor am I primarily interested in the spiritual dimensions of debt. While I will argue that both calculative and theological frameworks figure in the history of debt, their prominence (in absolute terms and relative to each other) properly belongs to the history of the connotations of debt—the historical matrix of interpretive frameworks and meanings by which debt has been understood over time. To recover even a schematic overview of this matrix—as I seek to do in the first section of this essay—is to resist any claim that debt is a natural or inevitable part of the human condition.[1] It is also to claim that as the frames by which debt is understood change, so too can debt be transvalued—changed, for example, from an ordinary part of everyday experience to a moral failing to be avoided at all cost, or changed again, from an ethical lapse into a financial opportunity.

I begin this schematic history (somewhat arbitrarily, I admit) in the early modern period in western Europe, with an emphasis on Great Britain. While the history of debt could certainly be pursued in earlier periods and different geographical locations, my own expertise makes sixteenth-century England a logical place to start. There are two major transvaluations in my historical narrative. The first, which began to unfold in the late eighteenth century and then reached a point of consolidation in the nineteenth century in Britain and the United States, transformed debt from the ubiquitous feature of everyday life that it was in the period from the sixteenth century through the middle of the eighteenth into a personal failing, which could—at least in theory—be avoided. The second—whose origins can be traced to the late seventeenth-century creation of the English national debt but rather suddenly took effect in the United States in the 1920s—transformed debt from an ethical failure, which allowed the past to hold sway over the present, into a positive opportunity, which allowed the present to benefit from anticipated (future) gains. The overlapping trajectories of these two transvaluations, as well as the long period during which each unfolded, call for a more sustained examination of the precise dynamics by which each transformation occurred than I am able to provide here. As a down payment on such detail, I turn in the second part of the paper to two events that helped convert debt from a personal ethical failure into a financial opportunity: the US government marketing of Liberty Bonds in the 1920s and the acceleration of installment buying in that same decade. In my brief conclusion I argue that, as political connotations of debt, which have been animated by the financial crisis of 2008, begin to focus attention on the role that modern governments have played in mediating debt for individuals, a third transvaluation might now be under way.

The theoretical framework that undergirds this schematic history assumes that, at any given time, any social behavior (like borrowing) occurs within a matrix of overlapping interpretive frames that establishes the parameters by which such behaviors are typically (or normatively) understood.[2] Crucially, such frames are always multiple, and the relationships among them are always subject to change. Indeed, it is the changing nature of the relationships among these overlapping interpretive frames that accounts for both the extended period typically required for significant change to occur in the normative meaning of debt and the tensions among various interpretations that obtain at any given time. Even though this archaeological metaphor might be misleading (because the interpretive frames are not exactly superimposed upon each other), I think of these frames as *layers of mediation* whose relative (and changing) prominence shapes the social meaning(s) normatively attributed to the behavior in question. Thus, even though debt is always a social relationship (because it always entails both a borrower and a lender), the meaning of its sociality is not always the same: when the social frame overlaps with a theological frame, as it did in the early modern period, the social connotations of debt carry strong resonances of spiritual obligation and redemption. When the social frame begins to be informed by a legal framework buttressed by natural law theory, as it did in the eighteenth century, then the social connotations of debt take on the coloration of a secular obligation enforced by coercion rather than encouraged by the promise of redemption.

Understanding Debt: A Schematic History

The history of debt is actually a history of the changes within the interpretive matrix by which debt is understood normatively. It is a history, in other words, of the mediation of debt through an internally dynamic, hierarchically arranged matrix of systems of meaning, frames, or codes. The best account of the meanings associated with debt in early modern Europe (especially Britain) is Craig Muldrew's *The Economy of Obligation*. Muldrew argues that in the sixteenth and seventeenth centuries credit and debt were deeply embedded in *social* networks (which were also informational, because they were the conduits through which news and information were transmitted). In this context, credit *was* sociality—an essential part of the network of bonds that held families and communities together.[3] To be alive was thus to be in debt—not simply because of some philosophical or biological reason but because the nation's chronic shortage of money and the interdependence of relational systems required individuals to devise modes of communal support that made debt ubiquitous. Because they still inhabited a Christian world, moreover, early modern Britons also tended to view debt in *theological* terms. In this vocabulary debt was linked to redemption, just as credit (along with trust) was linked to belief in God.[4] While the balance between the theological and social connotations of debt shifted over the course of the two centuries, with the latter coming to rival, if not displace, the former, the two interpretive frames continued to dominate the way debt was understood, even as the more abstract relations associated with market society emerged. "Personal social relations were seen in terms of trust," Muldrew explains, "but as market competition and disputes became common, 'society' came to be defined, not just as the positive expression of social unity through Christian love and ritual as had been the case in medieval England, but increasingly as the cumulative unity of the millions of interpersonal obligations which were continually being exchanged and renegotiated."[5]

Social networks—and with them, monetary obligations—became more geographically extended during the eighteenth century, and, as this happened, creditors increasingly turned to the courts to settle claims.[6] This turn to law went hand in hand with the elaboration of natural law theory, which emphasized the relationships between individual contracting agents over the general, primarily spiritual obligations that "humankind" owed to a universal God. Even though theological discourse and a rhetoric of sociability continued to inform understandings of debt in the eighteenth century, the ideas that society and government were based on contract and that competition and uncertainty made this contractual government necessary increasingly supported rivals to theological explanatory frameworks. These rivals included *legal* rubrics, which were promulgated through an emergent secular juridical apparatus and bolstered by the criminalization of debt and the founding of prisons specifically devoted to debtors' incarceration; *ethical* explanations, which either vilified or naturalized self-interest over altruism and spiritual abjection; and *calculative* languages (like those associated with bookkeeping, banking, and insurance), which dispassionately and apparently objectively tallied up debts and obligations in quantitative, monetary terms. In tandem with the increasing adoption of paper substitutes for the still insufficient supply of gold and silver coin, the emergence of these interpretive frames, alongside but sometimes in competition with social and theological frames, laid the groundwork for what I have described as the first critical transvaluation of debt: the slow process by which debt was denaturalized—deprived of its apparently natural, because ubiquitous status—and personalized as a condition one could (apparently) fall into or avoid. Gradually, debt came to seem less like an aspect of the human condition and more like the outcome of a series of choices either voluntarily or inadvertently made.

The personalization of debt was one sign of changes that were also gradually altering the normative model of the self. As the networks of credit, debt, legalized responsibility, and calculative practices began to assume a recognizably modern form during the eighteenth century, a more robust model of an autonomous self began to displace the socially embedded form of subjectivity that characterized the early modern period. Muldrew points out that the autonomous self did not become practical until institutions like banks, nondomestic workplaces, and all kinds of insurance schemes could provide economic support for an individual potentially marooned from family and kin networks; once these institutions were in place, it was no longer necessary to market one's self constantly in order to secure status and economic security.[7] By the beginning of the nineteenth century, as this autonomous self gradually shrugged off the theological terms in which subjectivity was once conceptualized, debt began to be understood in the quasi-psychological, quasi-theological, quasi-ethical terms associated most notably with Protestant evangelicalism. Even though debt continued to be a legal category (with imprisonment for debt not abolished in England until 1869 and a national bankruptcy law not passed in the United States until 1898), the compound of *psychological, theological, ethical,* and *social* understandings of indebtedness dominated the Victorian period on both sides of the Atlantic.

Two additional nineteenth-century developments in the cultural connotations of debt are important to note. First, at the beginning of this century, the debtor-creditor pairing underwent a decisive geographical split. With the financial centers in France and the Netherlands disrupted by war, London emerged as the financial capital of the West, and Britain became the most important creditor nation in the world. Among its many sovereign borrowers were the United States and India, and the financial interdependence of these nations played an important role in their relative wealth and autonomy for the entire century. Like the French before them, Americans had financed their revolution with a combination of borrowed and fiat money, and the young republic continued to amass debt, even as it freed itself from the tyranny of British taxation and rule, then succumbed to the financially disruptive Civil War. Across another ocean, the subcontinent of India also racked up debt to the British government—first indirectly, through the intermediary of the East India Company, and then, after 1857, directly, through the annual "tribute" exacted by the British government. The geographical reworking of the debtor-creditor dyad enhanced the *political* connotations of debt; and the rough alignments of democracy with chronic debt (in the United States) and "barbarism" with another form of chronic debt (in India) simply complicated the political meanings that could be read into perpetual indebtedness.

The second point to make about Victorian connotations of debt is that the middle decades of this century marked the rise in importance of the *financial* dimension of debt. This heralds the second of the two major transvaluations of debt I chronicle here. Strictly speaking, it had been possible for Britons to conceptualize debt in financial terms since the late seventeenth century, when William III had instituted a public (national) debt to pay for England's ongoing wars. Practically speaking, however, the purely financial connotations of such a debt—the idea that investing in the nation could be a source of personal gain—did not attract widespread attention in England until the early years of the nineteenth century, when the prolonged war with France made the idea of retiring the national debt through some sort of sinking fund seem both impossible and unnecessary—if for no other reason than that the Consols (shares in the consolidated national debt) had become the "gilt" securities that underwrote the well-being of every Briton who could afford them. In the United States at midcentury, Abraham Lincoln's government experimented with its own version of financialized investment opportunities when it issued short-term, high-interest bonds to help pay for the campaign against the Confederate States. These bonds were attractive to investors because they were rumored to be redeemable in gold, not greenbacks, the inflationary government-issued currency. After the Civil War, in 1869, the US government made the gold payback official, and, in 1870, with the Funding Act, it solidified its own relationship to investors' bonds by replacing the floating bonds with longer-term, lower-interest bonds.[8]

At this point (and with the help of Lendol Calder's *Financing the American Dream*), I want to focus in more detail on the United States. In the last decades of the nineteenth century, as the United States pulled out of the recession of the 1870s, debt was conceptualized in terms of what Calder calls "the Victorian money ethic."[9] The Victorian money ethic made explicit the implications of denaturalizing debt: this ethic cast debt as a personal failure that violated God-given natural law, not a universal condition that proved God's willingness to forgive. According to Calder, however, even though late nineteenth-century Americans conceptualized debt primarily in the ethical terms associated with evangelicalism, they also made allowances for the potential benefits of some kinds of indebtedness. They did so, in part at least, because the difficult monetary and economic conditions of the still-struggling nation made staying free of debt (both for individuals and for state and local governments) virtually impossible. By distinguishing between what they called "productive credit"—indebtedness that allowed an individual to invest in his business, for example—and "consumptive debt"—borrowing money to indulge in unnecessary luxuries or vices—Americans were able both to preserve the evangelical virtue of thrift and to lay the groundwork for the development that realized this second transvaluation: the new century's consumer revolution.[10] This revolution was enabled by the democratization of credit (through the 1917 Uniform

Small Loan Law, which reformed lending practices and helped push loan sharks out of the lending business), the incidental suturing of patriotism to certain kinds of debt (through Liberty Bonds), and the widespread adoption of installment buying.[11] One effect of the consumer revolution was to push the *theological* and *ethical* rubrics lower in the hierarchy of interpretive frames through which debt was understood. While *social* connotations certainly persisted, moreover, they no longer typically stressed the social embeddedness or the commonality of individuals and instead emphasized the distinctions that separated a few, advantageously indebted individuals from the undistinguished (but also indebted) masses. (Think here of the black American Express Card or the million-mile, elite-flyer status that George Clooney's character "earns" in the Hollywood film *Up in the Air.*) Similarly, the *legal* connotations of debt were still enshrined in various bankruptcy laws, but over the last half of the twentieth century the stigma (as well as the penalty) attached to bankruptcy decreased. Throughout the twentieth century and up to the present, debt has continued to be subject to *political* connotations (as when the Tea Partiers protest their own and the nation's escalating indebtedness), but the dominant frame through which debt was until very recently understood has been *financial*. As part of the elevation of the financial connotation of debt, the original meaning of the word *finance* (the settlement of a debt) morphed into something approaching its opposite (the science of funds management—that is, the science of making money from debt).

Debt and National Well-Being: Making Debt Patriotic

> A second consecutive month of increases in auto loans and the slowing of the decline in credit-card borrowing could be an indication that consumers are beginning to feel more confident about increasing their spending and taking on more debt. That development is seen as critical to providing support for the overall economy, which is still struggling to recover from the worst recession since the 1930s.
>
> —*New York Times*, March 6, 2010

Contemporary economists remain divided about the role that Americans' willingness to incur individual debt plays in the prosperity of the nation as a whole. For this topic even to emerge as a question in the academic literature, chronic indebtedness *for the sake of consumption* had to reach a level sufficiently high for consumption to be driven by borrowing—that is, for consumption to exceed what individuals could earn or save. The unprecedented levels of consumption—and indebtedness—reached (and, until the last few years, sustained) in the 1980s constitute one outcome of the consumer revolution that began in the early years of the twentieth century, accelerated in the 1920s, and, after a momentary pause during the Great Depression, continued to transform American life for the rest of the twentieth century. As we will see in the next section, this revolution was facilitated by innovations in modes of lending and changes in the way that saving, spending, and debt were conceptualized in the period. In this section, I discuss two related innovations of the twentieth century's early years: the promotion of national thrift and the government's campaign to market patriotism through the sale of wartime Liberty Bonds. While not as central to the consumer revolution as innovations in saving, lending, and buying, these two campaigns helped naturalize "saving to spend"—in part, by removing debt from the Victorian interpretive frame that emphasized self-control and the ethics of restraint and giving it another valence that was no less ethical for stressing patriotism and "wise spending."

At first glimpse, thrift might seem to be the opposite of debt, since saving is theoretically both a way to avoid debt and a means of getting out from under the monetary obligations an individual has incurred. The campaign that tried to make thrift a central component of American values did so, however, not primarily by castigating indebtedness but by promoting certain kinds of spending—even, in some circumstances, borrowing in order to spend—as an expression of patriotism. Historians disagree about the precise nature of the relationship between the thrift movement and the overtly patriotic, government-sponsored promotion of Liberty Bonds, but in retrospect both can be seen to have contributed to the early twentieth-century transvaluation that reframed debt, so that it came to be seen less as personal failure than as financial opportunity.[12]

The first Thrift Week was held in 1916, as an offshoot of the activities of the Committee on Thrift Education, which was founded in 1915. Thrift Week began on January 17, the birthday of Benjamin Franklin, America's great apostle of thrift, and it was celebrated annually until 1966, when a lack of sponsors led to its unheralded demise. In the early years of Thrift Week, the meetings of the Committee on Thrift Education were also held annually, in conjunction with the meetings of the National Education Association. These conferences were sponsored by a variety of unlikely organizational bedfellows, ranging from the YMCA to the American Bankers' Association, the National Retail Dry Goods Association, the Association of Life Insurance Presidents, and the Associated Advertising Clubs of the World. If the Boy Scouts, the National Kindergarten Association, and the US Chambers of Commerce were also willing to lend their support to this quasi-governmental, quasi–private enterprise event, it was because a certain version of thrift could be promoted as a cornerstone of democracy and a bulwark against the modes of imperialism and nationalism then fueling the war in Europe.

The version of thrift promoted by organizers of the 1924 National Conference on Thrift Education helps reveal the vision that brought these organizations together. Echoing President Harding, a spokesperson for the New York State League of Savings and Loan Societies explained that keeping democracy safe required increasing the numbers of American home owners—something that could be facilitated through the kind of "wise spending" that savings and loan societies encouraged.[13] Thrift also encompassed the elimination of "waste"—through various kinds of standardization that a Commerce Department spokesperson consolidated into the slogan "simplification of practice."[14] Most important, thrift was an educational agenda, which was designed to counteract, from childhood up, the "reckless expenditure" that organizers of the conference feared would undermine the virtues of wartime restraint.[15] As an educational project, thrift aimed squarely at improving physical well-being through lessons on health and fitness, improving the percentage of taxpayers and savers by fighting illiteracy, and inculcating providence as a life ethic. The virtuous behaviors amalgamated under the rubric of thrift are best captured by John Goodell, executive secretary of the National Thrift Committee of the International Committee of the YMCA: "The financial creed [of the YMCA] runs as follows: work and earn; make a budget; record expenditures; have a bank account; carry life insurance; own your own home; make a will; invest in safe securities; pay your bills promptly and share with others. You will notice it completes the circle of personal and family economic education, including earning, spending, saving, investing, and giving."[16]

As the items in this "circle" make clear, "thrift" encompassed not only saving but also investing and spending. Had thrift not been so understood, chambers of commerce would not have been eager to endorse it; had thrift not also entailed purchasing life insurance and a home, insurers, banks, savings and loan societies, and realtors might well have viewed it as a threat. Because thrift meant "wise spending," however, and because financial intermediaries like banks and savings and loan societies helped transform saving into investing, thrift could seem compatible (at least momentarily) with American capitalism, as well as democracy. In his *History of the Thrift Movement* (1920), S. W. Straus repeatedly emphasized these connotations of thrift. Thrift, Straus proclaimed, consists of "prudent spending as well as of wise saving"; "ask any rich man," he continued, "and you will find out, and you will learn that the accumulation of money begets the fixed habit of demanding a full return on outlay—that is thrift."[17]

Straus, who was the first president of the American Society for Thrift, was also an innovative (and successful) salesman: in 1909, he originated and, for the next two decades, sold real estate mortgage bonds. Straus marketed these bonds as supersafe (because "senior," or first-mortgage) bonds, and he guaranteed purchasers an annual return of 6 percent. According to an article published in the *New York Evening Post* in 1924, contemporaries equated purchasing these bonds with "safe investing"—that is, the embodiment of thrift—and, along with Liberty Bonds, real estate bonds helped make saving to invest seem like the obvious thing to do with one's money:

> Real estate bonds have been sold perhaps more widely than any other type of bond; they have been placed with the small investor so well in cases that many have come to regard them as the personification of safe investing. Real estate mortgage bonds have probably done more to increase the investor class in this country than any other influences since the Government war bonds selling campaigns; they have demonstrated that new buyers of bonds, in large numbers, can be created by intensive merchandising methods (not necessarily undignified methods). In doing this the real estate banker deserves no little appreciation from the bond business in general and from general business and the public at large.[18]

At the beginning of the 1920s, Straus's claim that purchasing his real estate bonds was a proper expression of thrift held true; but as the decade progressed and standards of lending were relaxed, Straus began passing off "junior" liens (second and third mortgages) as "senior" liens. In 1926, the failure of one of Straus's competitors sparked an inquiry into the real estate mortgage bond industry, and with the revelation that many of these ventures were essentially Ponzi schemes Straus's bonds lost the popularity they had briefly enjoyed.[19] Nonetheless, Straus's personal association with the thrift movement, as well as the equation of thrift with both saving and investing, helped suture connotations of prudence and virtue even to a mode of investing that had its shady side.

When the 1924 *Evening Post* writer associated Straus's real estate mortgage bonds with government war bonds, he highlighted the other campaign that helped purge debt of its pejorative ethical connotations and blur the boundary between saving and investing. Liberty bonds were initially marketed in 1917–18 as a way for individuals to express their patriotism and, when the United States entered the European conflict, as the vehicle through which noncombatants could contribute to America's overall war effort. Between 1917 and 1919, the US government sold $27 billion in Liberty Bonds and Victory Bonds to finance the war against Germany. Over twenty-two million Americans, from nearly all income groups and occupations, bought war bonds. As Michael E. Parrish notes, this was for many a first taste of the "mysteries of the securities market," and the popularity of this campaign encouraged more individuals to buy stocks and more corporations to issue them: "The spectacular success of the government's wartime bond program encouraged more and more corporations to seek public financing in the next decade. . . . By 1919, excluding people who owned multiple shares, there were probably 1.5 to 2 million stockholders in American corporations."[20]

Although initially rather expensive (in 1917 the smallest Liberty Bond was $50), war bonds were issued rapidly in denominations suited to nearly every American citizen. Saving stamp books were given out to schoolchildren, and a $5 certificate was contemplated for laborers, women, and children.[21] Most important, from my point of view, is the way that the Liberty Bond campaign brought together individual savers, government officials, and private banks in a network that seamlessly transformed individual savings into interest-bearing investments, which were intended to benefit the individual saver/investor, the government, and the private banks that borrowed from the government in order to lend to the small investor. As James Grant notes, this transaction often constituted an early opportunity for individuals to buy on margin. Early in 1917, Grant explains,

> It was clear to the Treasury Department that the people's savings would fall short of the needs of the government. To augment the stock of real capital, the government directed the banking system to loan would-be investors the price of their bonds. The Federal Reserve, in turn, would lend to the banks. In effect, the worker-investors would buy on margin—an experience that some of them would repeat in the

stock-market boom of the 1920s. [George F.] Baker's bank [the First National Bank of New York] became the very model of the patriotic financial institution. It purchased Liberty bonds for its own account, lent them to facilitate their purchase by others, and took the extra, and at the time novel, step of borrowing from the Federal Reserve Bank of New York to extend its reach.[22]

Even though not every purchaser of a Liberty Bond understood that he or she was now an investor, much less that the investment had been made on margin, the Liberty Bond campaign helped Americans conflate saving and investing, just as it cast incurring at least some kinds of debt as a patriotic action.[23]

Installment Buying: Spreading Debt over Time

The government campaign to sell Liberty Bonds in the name of patriotism and thrift did not completely alter the spending habits (or habits of mind) of all Americans, but it did reinforce the impression many already had that buying products in installments carried a virtue all its own. Installment buying has a long history in the United States, but promoting patriotic savings books and the stamps to fill them surely extended this purchasing model in ways and to a segment of the population that the mid-nineteenth-century marketing of part-payment schemes for farm equipment or sewing machines had not done.[24] To understand the role that installment buying played in the twentieth-century transvaluation of debt, it is helpful briefly to rehearse the history of this purchasing model, before turning to the way that installment buying helped neutralize any lingering Victorian (pejorative) connotations of debt.

Edwin R. A. Seligman was the first economist to write extensively about installment purchasing. In 1927, when installment plans were already common in the United States, Seligman explained that this mode of payment typically involved some kind of down payment, then regular payments through the duration of the loan, interest charges on the unpaid balance, and a legal provision that allowed the seller to repossess the purchased commodity if the purchaser defaulted. Even though installment buying is "as old as credit itself," Seligman continues, modern versions of this practice first appeared in the nineteenth century.[25] From government arrangements to collect taxes on a partial-payment system to part-payment insurance and real estate sales, the system of periodic payments was applied to the purchase of commodities like furniture (beginning in 1807); sewing machines, pianos, and books (from the mid-nineteenth century); and automobiles (beginning in 1910). Some nineteenth-century merchants extended credit themselves, according to Seligman, but the popularity of installment plans for large-ticket items whose sales were also seasonal eventually gave rise to the twentieth-century finance company—organizations dedicated to financing installment purchases for customers and, not incidentally, to assuming the risk and supporting manufacturers and merchants during the periods in which sales lagged. One of the longest-lived finance companies, the General Motors Acceptance Corporation (GMAC), was founded in 1919. By 1925, the number of finance companies devoted to automobile sales alone had reached sixteen or seventeen hundred, and somewhere in the vicinity of 70 to 75 percent of all automobile sales were financed through these companies.[26] The popularity of installment buying was so great that the system began to be applied to less expensive purchases, including phonographs, radios, vacuum cleaners, washing machines, refrigerators, and ready-made clothing.[27] As Calder points out, installment plans were so common by 1910 that the phrase already functioned as a metaphor for any kind of any expenditure (of money or energy) spread over time.[28] Another sign of the effect that installment selling had on the transvaluation of debt was the gradual replacement of "consumptive credit," the old pejorative term for borrowing to buy (luxury items in particular), with "consumer credit," a phrase that emphasizes the creditworthiness of the borrower rather than the diseased nature of the purchase.[29]

Installment buying ushered in what historians call the consumer revolution of the early twentieth century. This revolution is connected intimately to the increasingly urban nature of the US population, as well as to the industrialization that accompanied the large-scale shift of the population from farms to cities. With incomes for industrial workers spread evenly over the year in the form of weekly wages instead of being correlated to seasonal harvests, single-payment loans made less sense than loans whose repayment could also be spread evenly over time. As wage income rose, moreover, at a rate of about 1.3 percent a year between 1860 and 1920, individuals further down the social scale found themselves short of the cash necessary for large purchases (like furniture or sewing machines) but with sufficient disposable income to make regular credit payments.[30] Even though doubts continued to be expressed about the ethics of borrowing, even when payments were made regularly and on time, installment buying was gradually accepted as a means by which workers and middle-class families alike could emulate their betters, acquire the heretofore unaffordable items necessary to improve their standard of living, and, in general, enjoy luxuries their parents had not dreamed of. When an article extolling the benefits of installment buying, written by the public relations counsel for the National Thrift Committee, appeared in *Forbes Magazine* in 1926, any remaining doubts about installment buying seemed to fade.[31] What William H. Whyte Jr. later called "budgetism" could seem beneficial for working- and middle-class families because it signaled the ability to spread out (and satisfy) obligations over time.[32] Even after the stock market crashed in 1929, the consumer revolution underwritten by installment buying did not end. Not only did the government response to the economic downturn and the resulting high unemployment encourage borrowing for large purchases like houses, but the Great Depression itself made "spending to save" seem a more reasonable response to economic hard times than saving to spend could possibly be. As "the debt way of life" became the American way of life, consumer credit—which extended the logic of installment buying beyond the purchase of an individual item to purchasing in the abstract, as an activity always and everywhere possible—came to seem as natural as condemning debt had once seemed.

As this link between installment buying and installment credit suggests, it is possible to evaluate installment buying in two, nearly antithetical ways. On the one hand, some historians of consumer society have viewed installment buying as inculcating virtue because it provided an external version of the discipline once (theoretically) imposed by the individual upon him- or herself.[33] On the other hand, installment buying can seem like a gateway to the kind of installment credit that proliferated in the 1980s, when banks mailed credit cards to minors, pets, and even the deceased.[34] Both views can find plenty of support. On the one side, the relatively low rate of default on credit card debt (before the economic downturn of 2008) suggests that the discipline of buying on time has generally worked in the United States, even if the high interest rates charged by card-issuing banks have meant that borrowers pay handsomely for the privilege of enjoying apparently limitless credit. On the other side, the steady increase in household and personal debt since 1970 suggests that Americans can't get enough of a privilege that has come to seem increasingly necessary.[35] The relatively anemic rate at which Americans pay down their debt, moreover, might be said to portend more problems to come, especially if unemployment remains high, mortgage refinancing continues to be difficult, and banks begin to restrict the lines of credit that some previously used to consolidate existing debt.[36] As part of the history of the interpretive matrix by which debt has been understood, however, the important point is not whether such borrowing to spend is inherently beneficial or harmful but that this financial use of debt has become so taken for granted that moral categories now have to be superimposed upon it.

Reframing Personal Indebtedness: The Political Returns

The demotion of the ethical frame in which debt was normatively understood in the Victorian period to a lower position in the relevant hierarchy of interpretive frames registers in the difficulty that some historians, journalists, preachers, and politicians have encountered in recent decades in their intermittent attempts to encourage people to think about indebtedness as something other than a financial opportunity. Until very recently, in fact, there were more commercials for consolidating debt (with an eye to increasing consumption again) than sustained discussions about the benefits of paying off credit card balances (not to mention destroying the cards themselves). Most discussions of personal debt, moreover, whether they celebrate or warn against it, have tended to omit any sustained consideration of the role that the US government has played (and continues to play) in the twentieth century's transvaluation of debt—in making it seem like a financial, rather than an ethical, matter. One side effect of the global financial crisis of 2008, however, has been to highlight the government's role in encouraging individual borrowers to spend. Ultimately, this emphasis—by pundits on the political Left and Right—upon elected officials' endorsement of federal and state policies that actively encourage individual indebtedness may alter once more the hierarchy of interpretive frames in which debt is understood, so that indebtedness comes to be understood not primarily in *financial* terms but in *political* ones. As a contribution to this (emergent) transvaluation, I offer this brief account of the US government's role in what James Grant calls the "socialization of risk."[37]

As Grant has argued, the "democratization of credit" that began in the 1920s was made possible by this socialization of risk—the US government's decision to guarantee bank deposits, promote home ownership through various federal initiatives and tax incentives, and back home mortgages through government-sponsored agencies like Freddie Mac and Fannie Mae. According to Grant, the socialization of risk has had the unintended effect of linking national prosperity to personal consumer consumption—a situation almost guaranteed to increase personal indebtedness, especially in periods in which the Federal Reserve keeps interest rates artificially low (as it has done since 2001) and in which installment purchasing technologies (like credit cards and PayPal) are readily available. Grant's summary of the federal initiatives implemented to cushion individuals from personal risk and encourage borrowing to spend makes it clear that the very decisions that helped the United States pull out of the Great Depression laid the groundwork for the run-up of leveraged buying that culminated in the crash of 2008. These initiatives include the National Credit Corporation of 1931; the Federal Home Loan Bank Board, created in 1932; and the 1933 and 1935 Banking Acts, the first of which created the Federal Deposit Insurance Corporation and the second of which increased the amount of insured deposits to $40,000. (The dollar value of insured deposits was increased to $100,000 in 1980 and to $250,000 in 2009.) Beginning in the 1960s, a new series of legislative measures encouraged yet more borrowing: in 1963, the comptroller of the currency ruled that banks could borrow new capital instead of earning it; in 1968, the Federal Housing Act lifted restrictions on real estate lending; and in the late 1960s, banks began capitalizing on consumers' desire for easy credit by issuing credit cards and extensive lines of credit.[38] In the 1970s, the US government vastly increased its commitment to mortgage lending. According to Grant, Fannie Mae and Freddie Mac "collected mortgages by the hundreds of billions of dollars' worth. They packaged them for sale as mortgage-backed securities, and they guaranteed the securities against default." In the decade from 1970 to 1980, the federal government's support for residential mortgages grew from $26 billion to $206.5 billion; by 1989, this total had topped $1 trillion.[39]

A decade and a half after the publication of Grant's book, the global financial crisis has spurred more analysts to see debt in the terms Grant presciently deployed in 1992. It has also led them to reevaluate facets of twentieth-century US history that previous historians tended to celebrate. In the aftermath of the bursting of the US housing bubble and the near collapse of the global financial system, for example, legislative measures that freed the US banking system from many of the regulations imposed in the 1930s have begun to seem dangerously lax—and politically charged. Thus passage of the 1994 Riegle Neal Interstate Banking and Branching Efficiency Act (which lifted rules that had limited interstate banking), the enactment, in 1999, of the Financial

Modernization Act (which repealed the Glass-Steagall restrictions on mixing investment banking with deposit banking), and the passage of the 2000 Commodity Futures Modernization Act (which facilitated over-the-counter derivatives trading) now appear to many Democrats, Republicans, and Tea Partiers alike to be questionable pieces of legislation—possibly driven by political interests, and almost certainly (depending on one's politics) underwritten by financial interests whose relation to American well-being is either obvious or questionable. The vicious congressional debate that began in 2008 over passage of the Troubled Asset Relief Package (TARP), which split along party lines, made it clear that, however else one interprets it, debt now indisputably lies at the heart of the American political debate.

The relationships among the interpretive frames by which debt is understood do seem to me to be shifting—with the political frame vying with, if not displacing, financial understandings of debt, even as ethical connotations come roaring back. Meanwhile, with additional revelations yet to be made public—about the cost of those "toxic" assets the United States underwrote for financial institutions deemed "too big to fail" in 2008 and the total amount that will eventually be necessary to save Fannie Mae and Freddie Mac (and, with them, the housing market)—it is impossible to predict how the relationships among political, financial, and ethical frameworks for conceptualizing debt will eventually sort out.[40] The financialization of debt in the context of the socialization of risk has certainly destabilized what had become a commonplace—that a financial understanding of debt could help individuals (and nations) surmount the gloomy Victorian money ethic so as to achieve ever greater levels of prosperity.[41] Whether the new political connotations of debt will spur reforms of public policies and private behaviors that will occasion yet another transvaluation of debt remains an unanswerable question, for this story belongs to the future we are only just beginning to live.

Notes

1. To say that human beings are always or always already in debt seems to me, at most, a biological claim about the fact that human infants are born without the physical resources to maintain life. While this is undeniably true, it tells us very little about the semantic connotations of indebtedness—the meanings that human beings attribute to debt and dependency. Only when debt is invested with such meanings—only when debt means something—does it become part of the human condition in any sense beyond a mere biological one.

2. By introducing the word *normatively,* I want to indicate that it is always possible for people to apply interpretive frames that depart from the norm. In doing so, however, they introduce interpretations that are either *idiosyncratic* or *interested* in some way that calls attention to their departure from social norms. Thus it is possible for a twentieth-century American to interpret incurring debt as an affliction visited by the devil or as an act without the legal or social obligation to repay, but neither interpretation would correspond to what most Americans understand debt to mean or entail. The historical transvaluations of behaviors like incurring debt are typically marked by such contests over the frames in which the behaviors are understood.

3. Craig Muldrew, *The Economy of Obligation: The Culture of Credit and Social Relations in Early Modern England* (New York: Macmillan, 1998), 97 and ch. 4.

4. Ibid., 130.

5. Ibid., 123.

6. Ibid., 195.

7. Ibid., 156.

8. Walter T. K. Nugent, *Money and American Society, 1865–1880* (New York: Free Press, 1968), 9–11 and ch. 4.

9. Lendol Calder, *Financing the American Dream: A Cultural History of Consumer Credit* (Princeton, N.J.: Princeton University Press, 1999), ch. 2.

10. Ibid., 93, 100–103, and ch. 2.

11. Ibid., 124–34 and Part III.

12. Calder treats the thrift movement as part of a campaign by bankers to counteract the government's efforts to encourage investing in Liberty Bonds, since the purchase of Liberty Bonds decreased the money available for deposit (*Financing the American Dream*, 223–24). James Grant, in *Money of the Mind: Borrowing and Lending in America from the Civil War to Michael Milken* (New York: Farrar, Straus, Giroux, 1992), presents the two campaigns as contributing, more or less equally, to the naturalization of investment (146, 150, 152, 173, 174). David M. Tucker, in *The Decline of Thrift in America: Our Cultural Shift from Saving to Spending* (New York: Praeger, 1991), judges both campaigns to have been failures in their stated aim of increasing Americans' thrift. He does not consider either campaign from the perspective of naturalizing debt or consumption (ch. 7).

13. "We are promoting thrift by promoting home ownership," the speaker declared. President Harding, along with his commerce secretary Herbert Hoover, repeatedly sounded this line: "No greater contribution can be made towards perpetuating the democracy of our country than to make our Nation a nation of home owners." See Committee on Thrift Education, *Thrift Education: Being the Report of the National Conference on Thrift Education; Held in Washington, D.C., June 27 and 28, 1924, under the Auspices of the Committee on Thrift Education of the National Education Association and the National Council of Education* (Washington, D.C.: National Education Association, 1924), 9, http://lcweb2.loc.gov/gc/amrlg/htmlguid/lg26.html.

14. "Simplification of practice means the reduction of variety in sizes, dimensions, and immaterial differences in everyday commodities as a means of eliminating wastes, decreasing costs, and increasing values, in production, distribution and consumption. . . . 'Too many varieties' is recognized as the mother of excessive investment, slow turnover, rapid obsolescence, decreased profits, and economic waste" (Ibid., 67–68, 70–71).

15. Ibid., 4.

16. Ibid., 14.

17. Simon William Straus, *A History of the Thrift Movement in America* (New York: Lippincott, 1920), 23, 111.

18. Quoted in Grant, *Money of the Mind*, 163.

19. Grant, *Money of the Mind*, 165–69. Straus escaped with only a reprimand from the New York State attorney general, but his bonds did eventually suffer a catastrophic fall in value during the panic of 1931–32 (200).

20. Michael E. Parrish, *Anxious Decades: America in Prosperity and Depression, 1920–1941* (New York: W. W. Norton, 1992), 228. Cedric Cowing estimates that the number of Americans who held securities rose to seventeen million because of Liberty Bonds. See *Populists, Plungers, and Progressives: A Social History of Stock and Commodity Speculation, 1890–1936* (Princeton, N.J.: Princeton University Press, 1965), 95. While he agrees that the number of people investing in stocks increased after 1915, David Hochfelder attributes this rise as much to the effective campaign against illegal bucket shops as to the Liberty Bond campaign. See "'Where the Common People Could Speculate': The Ticker, Bucket Shops, and the Origins of Popular Participation in Financial Markets, 1880–1920," *Journal of American History* 93, no. 2 (September 2006): 335–58.

21. Tucker, *Decline of Thrift*, 84. It is not clear to me whether these certificates were ever sold.

22. Grant, *Money of the Mind*, 150.

23. Grant invokes an article published in the magazine *Factory* in 1918 that describes workmen thinking they had simply made a gift to the government when they purchased their bonds. Others thought that they owed the government money, and many forgot to collect their principal when the bond matured. See *Money of the Mind*, 151.

24. Edwin R. A. Seligman, the first economist to theorize installment purchasing, explicitly cites the purchase of Liberty Bonds as an instance of installment buying. See *The Economics of Installment Selling: A Study in Consumers' Credit* (New York: Harper and Brothers, 1927), 1:7.

25. Ibid., 1:6.

26. Ibid., 1:48–49.

27. Ibid., 1:51.

28. Calder quotes an article published in the *Saturday Evening Post* in 1910, which refers to "beaver dams . . . built on the instalment plan" (*Financing the American Dream*, 167). He also cites references in fiction: in Charles M. Flandrau's *Harvard Episodes* (1897), reference is made to buying a piano or books on such a plan; and in Charles Fort's *The Outcast Manufacturers* (1909), two characters claim that "you can get anything on the installment plan nowadays" (*Financing the American Dream*, 167).

29. Ibid., 280.

30. Ibid., 168.

31. Ibid., 235.

32. Ibid., 297.

33. This is Calder's judgment. See ibid., 207, 300–303.

34. James Grant expresses this skepticism about the "democratization of credit" (the phrase is Arthur J. Morris's). See *Money of the Mind*, especially chs. 9–11 and "Afterword."

35. Grant reports that "in 1970, only 22.9 percent of households in the $4,000 to $6,000 income bracket had installment debt outstanding. In 1977, 30.7 percent did" (*Money of the Mind*, 313).

36. US household debt is now nine times what it was in 1981, and it has risen twice as fast as disposable income during this period. Nelson D. Swartz reports that the portion of disposable income spent on paying down debt has increased only slightly—from 10.7 percent in 1981 to 12.6 percent in 2010 ("Americans Face Tighter Credit," *New York Times*, April 11, 2010, A-1). It should also be noted that both the increasing rate of household debt and the slowing pace with which Americans repay debt are occurring within the context of a dramatic decline in the wage rate. James Livingston points out that beginning in the 1980s, business investment stagnated along with incomes; these two factors led to a fall in the rate of saving as well as the increase in the use of credit documented by all historians of consumption. James Livingston, "The Incommensurability of Crisis," paper presented at "The Culture of the Market" conference, Said Business School, Oxford, March 10, 2010.

37. Grant, *Money of the Mind*, 181.

38. American Express issued the first plastic cards in 1959; but MasterCard (from 1969) and Visa (from 1977) made these cards popular (ibid., 309, 311).

39. Ibid., 352.

40. For an analysis of the risk Freddie Mac and Fannie Mae pose to the economic recovery of the United States, see Gretchen Morgenson, "Ignoring the Elephant in the Bailout," *New York Times*, May 9, 2010, Sunday Business section, 1.

41. It is the combination of the financialization of debt and the socialization of risk that seems to me to be so dangerous. Were risk merely to be socialized—as it is in mandated insurance plans and state health care systems—there would be less inequality in rewards and losses. Were debt merely to be financialized—as it can be in opportunities to invest in government debt or even private

corporations—it would not necessarily lead to the kind of unsustainable leverage that investment banks like Goldman Sachs and JP Morgan used in the first decade of this century. In 2007, at the peak of the housing bubble, investment banks like Goldman and Morgan had a debt-to-capital ratio of 32 to 1 (up from the nineteenth-century level of 6 to 1). See Andrew Ross Sorkin, *Too Big to Fail: The Inside Story of How Wall Street and Washington Fought to Save the Financial System—and Themselves* (New York: Viking, 2009), 4.

4 On Debt

Michael Allen Gillespie

THE NOTION OF debt is rooted deeply in our understanding of ourselves and our world. This becomes apparent if we reflect for a moment on the old philosophical saw, *Ex nihilo nihil fit,* "Nothing comes from nothing." Or to put it another way, everything comes to be from something else. Nothing is self-made or sui generis, and every individual thing is thus *indebted* to something else for its being.

The first to examine this idea philosophically was Anaximander of Miletus, who lived from 610 to 546 BC. Anaximander was the student of Thales, also a Milesian, who is generally regarded as the founder of Western philosophy and science. Thales is best known for his declaration that everything arises out of water. To most people today this notion seems ludicrous, and it is consequently difficult for us to take him seriously. What could he possibly have meant by such a bizarre claim? To make sense of Thales' assertion, it is important to recognize the cultural limitations of the Greek world in which he lived. The reigning cosmological notion, articulated in Hesiod's *Theogony,* that the cosmos originated out of the coupling of Mother Earth (Gaia) and Father Sky (Uranos) was fundamentally anthropomorphic. Thales' assertion, by contrast, is decidedly materialistic. Moreover, as Friedrich Nietzsche pointed out, Thales' assertion has to be understood within the linguistic possibilities of his time.[1] What he was actually trying to say was something profound and important—that every individual thing arises from and consists of undifferentiated matter or being—but every time he opened his mouth to express this glittering insight, all that came out was "water." Twenty-five hundred years later we have learned to say "matter" or "energy," but in a fundamental sense we have not gone very far beyond Thales' brilliant beginning.

Anaximander accepted his teacher's revolutionary notion but went a step further, declaring that everything came to be out of what he called the *apeiron,* which is variously translated as the "infinite," the "unlimited," or the "unbounded." In the earliest extant philosophical fragment in the Western world, he describes this origin as follows: "The beginning of all beings is the unbounded and from there is the coming to be of all things and into there is also their passing away according to necessity and they pay each other their justified debt and penance for their injustice according to the law of time."[2]

The first philosophic assertion is thus also the first philosophic consideration of debt. Anaximander ties debt to the very being of things. Indeed, it would not be too much of an exaggeration to say that for Anaximander, to be is to be indebted. Moreover, this debt in his view requires payment, atonement, or penance that is paid by passing away, by ceasing to be. But what does this claim mean? Anaximander is asserting that all beings are *as they are* only because they have a particular form or limit, because they are bounded. There is no abstract matter apart from concrete things, but there are also no finite or bounded things that do not occupy matter. Furthermore, the total amount of matter is limited. All things thus come to be only by displacing other things and occupying or embodying the matter that hitherto constituted something else. They thus exist only because they displace, consume, or destroy another being. This is the injustice Anaximander refers to, and the injustice that everything must atone for by paying its debt, that is, by passing away, being displaced, destroyed, or consumed by other things.

This pre-Socratic insight into the ontological or phenomenological nature of debt offers us a clue to its deeper significance and continuing importance. We see this notion prominently reflected in the greatest philosophical and theological works of the ancient world, from the initial definition of justice in Plato's *Republic* as "paying one's debts to men and the gods" to Christ's injunction that his followers pray that God will "forgive us our debts as we forgive our debtors." But what can this mean for us? All of these claims seem much more abstract than the notion of debt we typically employ. What then does this excursus into the distant reaches of the history of philosophy and religion have to do with our notion of debt?

We today almost invariably think of debt first and foremost in monetary terms. This is no accident. The development of a monetized economy that continually produces and employs capital has been integral to the development of the modern world. While this development has had enormous advantages for economic and social development, dealing with debt in this narrow manner conceals a more comprehensive notion of debt that is rooted in a debt to our ancestors and the natural world. The failure to recognize or take account of this deeper debt poses great dangers for our civilization. Anaximander's ancient claim remains crucially important for us today.

In an obvious sense Anaximander is clearly right that everything that exists is indebted to something that came before it and that thus caused it to be or brought it into being. A rose, for example, can exist only because it draws upon and embodies the minerals in the soil, the water that it absorbs through its roots, the energy of the sun that makes photosynthesis possible, and the previous genetic developments that culminated in the rose as an organism. It is indebted to everything that it comes from as well as what it consumes and destroys in order to sustain itself, and it pays these debts by producing more of its kind and by becoming "food" for something else. All things are displaced by other beings that come to occupy the substance in which they subsist. Debt is thus closely bound up with the justice or injustice by which all things come to be and pass away according, as Anaximander puts it, "to the law of time."

We moderns operate with a much less expansive notion of debt. In the first place, we imagine that we owe debts only to other persons and not to other things. This represents a clear difference between our conception of debt and that articulated by Anaximander, a difference with very important consequences, as we will see. This difference is prefigured in Roman law that defines a person as one who has the right to own things, while a mere thing has no such right and thus can be held as property. Essential to the definition of debt, however, is the fact that it is the result of a taking. The nature of the debt thus depends in very important ways upon the nature of that taking. The etymology of the term gives us some insight into this fact. The English term *debt* derives through French from the Latin *debitam,* the "thing owed," itself from the verb *debere,* "to owe," which originally arose from *de habere,* "to have, to seize, or to keep away from someone." We thus incur a debt when we take something from someone else.

The most primordial form of "taking" occurs when we take what is given to us. In the most elementary sense this is our biological being, which is given to us by our parents, although in some sense they are themselves only the penultimate step in an extraordinary cosmological and genealogical process that began about fourteen billion years ago. This bodily "taking" is augmented by sustenance, protection, upbringing, and education that shape us in other important and valuable ways, making us into the kinds of beings we are, giving us language, habits, and the mastery of practices without which we would be quite different and much less capable beings. We do not ask for or demand existence and, for the most part or at least for a long time, we do not choose the manner of our upbringing and education. Without the first, however, we would not be, and without the second we would not be human. For these things we are indebted to our ancestors as well as to our communities, cultures, civilizations, and, some would say, our God or gods. The nature of these debts and manner of repayment has been the subject of an extensive literature stretching from Greek tragedy to the *bildungsroman,* including biography and autobiography, religious narratives, and historical studies, as well as modern film and other forms of popular culture. In these texts and contexts we often see the profound difficulty of determining what is owed to whom, and the clashing obligations that our different debts generate, as the archetypal case of Antigone, for example, so unmistakably demonstrates.

In a certain sense, these debts cannot be repaid or at least cannot be paid off in full. They demand obedience, gratitude, and/or admiration for the giver, but how, for example, can we fully repay our parents for our existence? Or our community for the language we speak? Or all of those faceless artisans who made the incremental advances that produced the many things and practices that make up our civilization?[3] We accept most of these things as given and seldom even reflect on the fact that they are imparted to us by our forebears. The nature of this debt, however, is different from that of the debts we ordinarily enter into because it is not voluntary. After all, we did not ask to be born or to be born into the world in which we came to be, or to be the kind of person we were raised to be. At times we are thus ambivalent about our heritage, and we often feel with some anger that what was purportedly done *for* us was actually something that was done *to* us. And yet while we may not feel the same obligations that would encumber us if we had chosen these things ourselves, we are nonetheless constrained by them.

In the premodern world there was a much greater recognition of the fact that everyone was shaped by the practices and traditions of their families and peoples, and this indebtedness was generally acknowledged as natural and self-evident. This is what Hannah Arendt, for example, calls authority.[4] Moreover, even those who were less willing to recognize the authority of their ancestors and traditions often did not have a great deal of choice in the matter. Resources were largely in the hands of the *pater familias,* and children's professions and marriage partners were generally chosen for them by their father, extended family, clan, or caste. There were no singles bars, online dating sites, banks, venture capital firms, or help wanted listings, and with the exception of the military, the church, and the brothels very few employers were willing to hire workers against the wishes of their families. The limited variety and concrete nature of goods also played an important role in constraining independence. Resources generally included only animals, land, houses, tools, techniques, and slaves. The control and distribution of all of these goods were in the hands of families, states, and guilds, and their transfer to succeeding generations was tightly controlled by law, custom, and parental will. Thus one's life chances were very much in the hands of others, and escaping one's debt to one's family or community was not easy even if one wanted to strike out on one's own.

Another form of debt arises when something is taken from us, including our property, our freedom, our bodily well-being, or our lives. This taking is a form of theft, conquest, torture, or murder. We today imagine that what we owe to the perpetrators of such deeds is obvious, but historically the nature of this debt was more ambiguous. To take just one example, in the case of conquest it seems clear to us that what we owe the conqueror is revenge, rebellion, hatred, or resentment. Many in the past viewed this in a radically different manner. Thucydides, for example, articulates the opposing point of view in his Melian dialogue when he has the Athenian admirals tell the citizens of Melos that they must surrender and that it is right to do so, since it is a law of nature that the strong do what they will and the weak suffer what they must.[5] Hobbes and Hegel, to take two later examples, make similar arguments that obedience is due to those whose power is superior. The justification for this obligation is that they have spared the lives of those whom they conquered; thus these new subjects owe them their lives in the same way children owe their lives to their parents. Subjects consequently are imagined to live at the sufferance of and in service to their masters.

Of course, there is no such obligation for people who suffer such offenses while living under sovereign authority. Under such circumstances it is not the victim who is in debt but the perpetrators of the offense. They have injured other human beings (and the sovereign authority) and can rightly be expected to pay compensation. The debt can then be repaid through the extraction of reparations for the damage, through personal revenge, or through punishment imposed by the state. Even in cases where such repayment is not exacted or where the victim is unable to obtain revenge, we often believe and try to convince others that the perpetrators will be wracked by guilt or will suffer punishment administered by the gods in this life, in an afterlife, or in the person of their descendants.[6] The importance of this notion of debt is evident in the fact that in many Indo-European languages there is a close connection between the terms for "debt" and "guilt."[7] Shakespeare's Macbeth points to this connection with his graphic comment about his own fear of punishment: "Blood will have blood."[8]

A third form of indebtedness occurs in voluntary exchange. The debt here is not associated with the exchange per se but arises when there is a promise to complete the exchange at some point in the future, to abide by the terms of an agreement reached here and now. This form of debt is always voluntary, although there is often an asymmetry in the propensity of the parties to enter into the agreement. It is crucial to this notion of debt that human beings keep their promises and thus earn trust by building a reputation for honest dealing. Given the advantages to be gained by not repaying one's debts and defecting from the initial agreement, it is obvious that such trustworthiness did not develop overnight. Thus, as Nietzsche claimed in his *Genealogy of Morals,* the willingness to act justly must have been achieved over a long period of time by the repeated and terrifying use of violence against those who failed to pay their debts.[9]

The notion of debt that we employ today developed out of these earlier notions of debt but was profoundly transformed by the reconceptualization of man, God, and nature at the beginning of the modern age. Nature ceased to be conceived as an eternal order of forms in a teleologically directed cosmos or a divinely shaped creation and came to be understood instead as an impersonal chaos of matter in motion. God in this context was conceived as distant from his world, a *deus absconditus* available only through revelation. And human beings no longer were imagined to be utterly fallen (and therefore ontologically indebted) creatures, generic descendants of an original sinner, but instead came to be viewed as individual, autonomous, self-moving beings made in God's image, with inalienable rights and quasi-divine powers. Moreover, while they were imagined to have obligations to honor the rights of others, they were not thought to have a similar responsibility to honor, preserve, or protect nonhuman beings. As a result, their indebtedness to their God or gods, their traditions, their family, and the world around them increasingly seemed less significant.[10] In this way the regime of individual rights came to replace the regime of communal virtues and duties.

This new understanding of the natural world opened up the possibility for the development of modern science. This science developed out of an older alchemical tradition that was deeply concerned with the transmutations of one thing into another. The goal of modern science is not essentially different from that of alchemy, although it increasingly depends on methodologies or techniques that allow for the ever more successful control of these transmutations through the growing knowledge of the causes of all things. Natural things in this sense are not conceived as divine creations with a sacred form or end, nor are they seen as embodiments of eternal reason. Rather, they are understood as the accidental agglomerations of stuff that can be manipulated and transformed to satisfy human needs and desires without violating the natural order of the world or sinning against God. The natural world in this context comes to be conceived over time as raw material to be mined, refined, and transformed into something humanly useful that can be either consumed or traded for other goods. As John Locke succinctly put it, God gave the world to human beings in common to use for their preservation, and we can justly remove from this common store anything that is not already owned by another human being.[11] All debts to and constraints on the use of nature thus disappear.

The effective application of scientific techniques to the exploitation of the natural world enormously increased human productivity and prosperity. Thus we have increasingly become able to more effectively and rapidly transmute the things we find in the world into more serviceable objects for our consumption. Knowledge, as Bacon put it, gives us power, and with this power man can become the master and possessor of nature. As a result, a new path to human well-being, or what Thomas Hobbes called commodious living, was opened up.[12]

In the ancient and medieval world, it was broadly assumed that the number of goods was largely fixed by the totality of land and the natural cycles of growth and decline. The only way to significantly increase your wealth was thus to take land or goods away from other human beings, or better yet to conquer and enslave them so they could produce goods for you. The success of an individual or people thus depended upon strength and prowess in war. Modern science and the technology it serves, however, opened up a new path to wealth through the development of new sources of power and the application of this power to the ever more efficient production of goods and services necessary to human well-being. As a result, there has been a general devaluation of the warrior and conqueror, who dominated the ancient and medieval worlds, and an increased recognition of the value of the worker, the entrepreneur, the scientist, the inventor, the bureaucrat, and the manager, who have been the backbone of the modern industrial civilization.

This great transformation was not without its complications. In a way that was not at first recognized, the mastery of nature required not just the transformation of things but also the ever more comprehensive reorganization of humanity into larger political and economic units with a continually growing flexibility to mobilize and maximize the forces of production. The inevitable consequence of this reorganization was the reduction in importance of families, clans, and local attachments, which limit flexibility.[13] This social transformation was reflected in changes in property laws that increasingly conceived of ownership as an attribute of the individual rather than the extended family or community. This new notion of ownership fundamentally changed the time horizon in which humans thought about investments and debts, and it is certainly one of the factors that has led us to focus more often on immediate success and the annual bottom line than on the enduring well-being of our firms, corporations, or societies.[14]

The economic logic of the modern economy was spelled out by Adam Smith, who recognized that the growth in the aggregate wealth of nations and the well-being of humanity depended on (1) an increasing division and specialization of labor, (2) the elimination of barriers to trade, and (3) the formation of what he called stock or capital to make this extension of trade and the division of labor possible.[15] Stock or capital in its most rudimentary sense is needed in Smith's view to sustain those involved in an extended process of production until they can bring their goods to market and exchange them for consumables. To take a simple example, for a company like Dell to produce a PC it is necessary to provide food, clothing, and shelter for everyone involved in the process of production as well as to provide all the materials and equipment involved at many sites around the world until all the various parts of the computer can be assembled and the product can be brought to market and sold. Capital in this sense is the surplus production above and beyond what is needed for subsistence that is used to increase the efficiency of the process of production. Of course, not all surplus becomes capital. Some, and in many cases a great deal, is used to improve human life, to appease the gods, to attain social prestige, to wage war, and so on. Smith suggests that future human well-being depends upon the reduction in the use of this surplus for economically superfluous purposes and an increase in the amount of the surplus used to augment capital and thus to extend the division of labor. It is also crucial to Smith that the surplus be employed, put into circulation rather than being stored in a mattress or secured in a strongbox.[16] Capital is thus that amount of production that is reinvested in further production, that therefore provides the basis for further economic expansion and the ever more efficient transformation of the natural world into humanly useful things. The existence of capital is thus the essential precondition for debt as we understand it.

Debt, in the narrow economic sense, is possible only because there is surplus production, that is, because we produce more than we need to survive. Without such a surplus there would be nothing available to loan to others. Even where there is a surplus, there is no guarantee it will be lent to others. One can always consume it or use it to expand one's own production. Moreover, unless there is a guarantee that a loan will be repaid, the risk of losing the principal clearly reduces one's chances of survival or well-being. The importance of an enforcement mechanism in this context is obvious, whether in the form of collateral or the threat of punishment by the lender or the state. Here the rule of law and the protection of property rights are essential to the formation of capital and indebtedness. Crucial in this context is obviously the protection of property rights by the government and the nature of tax law. The greater the tax on my investments, the more likely I am to consume my surplus. The greater the tax on my consumption, the more likely I am to invest the surplus as capital.[17] While these provisions are important first steps toward facilitating lending, they are not sufficient, since they do not provide any return to the lender for the opportunity cost of loaning his surplus to others. Thus perhaps the crucial fact shaping modern lending practices and the dominant modern notion of debt was the elimination of the prohibitions on usury. As we conceive of debt, it requires not merely the return of the thing (or the value of the thing) lent out, but an agreed-upon amount for the use of the thing over time. Thus debt is entered into only with the expectation that the surplus or capital that is loaned out will increase the effectiveness of the productive process. This can occur, however, only if capital is intelligently used to more efficiently organize human labor to transform the natural world into ever more humanly useful commodities. For debts to be repaid, the objects produced by the use of the capital must thus be worth more than the original amount of capital itself. The surplus that makes capital and thus debt possible must in other words always become greater.

This process is facilitated, but not fundamentally changed, by the introduction of a market governed by supply and demand. Markets make possible the aggregation of subjective preferences for goods and services and thus help determine the appropriate ends of the productive process. In a certain sense consumers thus give direction to the market, and competition among producers to sell their goods forces down prices and promotes the continual improvement of the means of production. While we often refer to this phenomenon as consumer sovereignty, such terminology is at least in part misleading. The process of preference formation is obviously not simply the result of an introspective act by an individual; rather, it occurs in a social environment where interaction effects among individual consumers as well as the efforts of producers to convince consumers to buy their products play a huge role in determining behavior. All of these factors may convince individuals to make choices that are not in their best interests and may induce them to want more than they can afford, but in such an environment consumers can live beyond their means only if lenders make credit available to them. Consumer debt is thus ultimately sustainable only on the same grounds as all other debt. I can overspend today only if my overspending makes me more productive tomorrow (for example, by improving my health or increasing my skills in useful ways). If it does not, I will have to spend less in the future. The facts of the market and the formation of consumer preferences thus do not undermine the essential fact of debt, which is that it is predicated upon increasing productivity and increasing capital.

The introduction and development of money plays a more complicated role. Money in general facilitates exchange by introducing a notion of value that is applicable universally to all products and services and that thus allows the precise comparison of relative values. The total amount of money represents the value of all goods. Money, however, does not merely represent them but homogenizes them, allowing us to treat qualitative differences quantitatively. This has enormous value in enabling us to calculate the relative advantage of investment in one area over investment in another. However, it also depreciates the intrinsic or unique value of individual things in favor of their abstract value. Things that may in times past have had a special or unique value or meaning in this way become mere commodities, just "stuff." As things are increasingly commodified and come to be understood simply in terms of their monetary value, social status also increasingly becomes determined, not by prowess, virtue, beauty, genius, or noble birth, but by the total amount of money in one's bank account. In a disenchanted world where there are few special, let alone sacred, things, quality is everywhere reduced to mere quantity, and greatness comes to be understood in terms of productivity.[18]

While the modern economy depends upon our ability to organize labor and capital ever more effectively for the increasingly efficient production of goods and services, the overall management of this titanic productive enterprise falls to those who determine the allocations of capital and thus the distribution of debt. It is a truism that capital flows to where it can be most effectively used, but while this process may be irresistible (or at least very difficult to control), it is not automatic or perfect. It is crucially dependent upon the decisions of investors/bankers/venture capitalists, who gauge the probable risk and profitability of all the enterprises seeking capital. These managers of the distribution of capital within the global economy are responsible for determining where the investment of capital will bring the highest return, that is, who should be entrusted with capital and thus with debt, or, to put it in other words, which forms of productive activity are most credit- or debt-worthy given the probable demand for specific products. These financial managers thus effectively make judgments about the best ways to use capital to achieve the most rapid growth of "surplus of value." Their prognostications are obviously based upon many different factors and informed by the historical knowledge of past performance and market research as well as empirically based judgments, but they always remain prognostications, and thus ultimately depend upon the transparency of information, the absence of unexpected shocks to the world economic system or sudden unforeseeable shifts in aggregate human behavior.

Many investments obviously are aimed not at fostering the long-term growth of capital but at obtaining short-term profit by taking advantage of the overly enthusiastic or overly pessimistic behaviors of other investors. Investment in this sense always occurs within an environment where an investor has to predict not merely what the market will demand tomorrow and the day after tomorrow but also what other investors will do over that same period of time. Thus there is the possibility for short-term investments based not on estimates of probable productivity gains but simply on guesses about the probable behavior of other investors. Investing in this way is effectively a form of gambling, and while such gambling can increase or decrease an individual investor's wealth, it cannot increase the overall productivity of capital. For this reason investment counselors repeat the maxim that it is not timing in the market but time in the market that is essential to sustained growth. In the short term, some will win and some will lose, but the sums will more or less equal out, with a marginal loss because of transaction costs. Real return on capital is possible only if the value loaned is ultimately converted into greater value. While some short-term bets are inevitable and can be advantageous to the system, it is crucial to the ultimate success of the economic system that investors focus on the longer term and thus on the real growth of capital. Moral risk provides a disincentive to such short-term gambling, but governments also often offer incentives (such as variable tax rates) and disincentives (such as fees on early IRA withdrawals) to encourage longer-term investing.

While this economic system based on capital and debt has produced great wealth, which has benefited almost everyone by raising the overall standard of living, it has not produced, and almost certainly will not produce, a more egalitarian society. In fact, it will probably actually increase inequality, since the process of allocating capital and debt inevitably favors those who have previously been successful in using capital profitably and disfavors those who have not been successful. Thus, while it is not necessarily the case that the rich get richer and the poor poorer, those who have been successful are much more likely to be entrusted with capital and thus with the opportunity to become richer than those who have not. While we might wish that this were not the case, it is hard to see how it could be otherwise, since the managers of capital have a fiduciary responsibility to their shareholders to maximize the return on capital and not to lift up the rest of humanity. Even the most ardent egalitarian would likely be distressed if the manager of his retirement fund chose to loan funds only to the inexperienced and previously unsuccessful.

We thus cannot expect our current practices of capital and debt allocation to improve the chances of the poor relative to the rich. Nor is there any means within the economic system that will bring this about. Reducing the differences between the rich and the poor can be achieved only politically, either by directly transferring funds to the poor to supplement their income or by investing in their training and education to make them more productive and thus more creditworthy. Simply transferring funds is not a long-term solution and in fact will almost certainly only increase the demand for such support without any corresponding increase in productivity. Thus the only real chance of reducing economic disparities in a society is an investment in the training and education of the less productive sections of the population. Investment in the development of human capital is thus more likely to produce a more egalitarian society than any other form of investment. Whether such an investment makes economic sense, however, depends on the conditions of the market and the demand for labor in the different sectors of the economy.

The importance of efforts by the state to create a more egalitarian society notwithstanding, the use of the state to redistribute wealth and opportunity is not as easy as it may at first seem, and any effort to do so on behalf of the less well-off is always in danger of coming to serve the interests of the wealthier portion of the population. Indeed, in democratic states the wealthy almost invariably have significant advantages in the political process that allow them to ensure that most legislation works to their benefit. Thus even programs that clearly help the poor, such as Medicaid, almost always and in quite substantial and often disproportionate ways increase the wealth of the owners of the industries that provide the products or services needed by such programs.

The state can and generally does play an important role in promoting the lending of money and thus the formation of debt by establishing and maintaining a stable currency, as well as regulating exchange to prevent monopolies and to require or at least to promote transparency in all interactions. The stability of the money supply is crucial in this context. Stability does not require that the amount of money should always be the same, but it does require that the amount should increase or decrease with the increase or decrease of available goods and services. The more stable the currency, the more likely investors are to lend capital.

The government's role in the economy, however, is rendered problematic by a number of factors. Chief among these is the cost of government itself, which must support itself by the sale of public goods (such as grazing, drilling, or mining rights), taxes, borrowing, or the printing of excess currency. This problem is exacerbated in democratic governments by the fact that it is almost invariably in the interest of democratic politicians to have the government borrow money rather than raise taxes. They thus can provide benefits to their constituents today while transferring the cost of these benefits to future generations. As children have come to forget their obligations to their parents and grandparents, as we noted above, those same parents and grandparents have effectively voted to live at their offspring's expense by returning such politicians to office.

The government's reliance on debt to fund its activities can be successful or unsuccessful depending on the purpose to which it is put. If it uses the funds it borrows merely to support individuals, families, or enterprises or to pay its own supporters or employees, there will be no return on the investment and the principle itself will be consumed. Such a use of funds is not profitable and does not justify incurring debt. If, however, the government uses the funds to produce public goods, the investment should increase the productivity of enterprises within the state by providing such benefits as lowered costs of transportation. Such promotion of commerce will almost invariably increase the aggregate income of the state and thus expand the tax base, making it possible for the government to repay the debt it has incurred with interest.

The danger, of course, is that states will portray their consumption of resources as forms of investment and thus fall into an unproductive debt spiral that can finally be solved only by drastic cuts in public expenditures with the resulting political dislocations. We have seen the consequences of such behavior in Third World debt crises and most recently in Greece.[19]

Several factors play a role in diminishing the capacity of any investor, however knowledgeable, to make accurate predictions. The changing demand for goods and services by consumers especially in nonsubsistence economies depends a great deal on adventitious changes in style and taste. Herd behavior often leads to unexpected results among both investors and consumers. Investors often use past success as a measure of future productivity, and while this is obviously sensible, if such retrospective judgments were sufficient all the investors in General Motors would still be millionaires. Machiavelli's assertion that even with the best preparation and planning we will fail half the time in predicting the future is probably not unreasonable and is part of the reason so many investors diversify their portfolios and choose to reduce their chances of success in order to reduce their risk of failure. The inherent uncertainty of the future is further exacerbated by the fact that in a world as dependent on capital and debt as our own, individuals, corporations, and countries all have incentives to try to portray their future as rosier than it actually is. Here governments, rating agencies, and accounting firms are needed to improve transparency, and when they fail in their job of ensuring clarity, as we saw in the Enron scandal and in the recent financial crisis, there is the danger that loss of trust will vastly decrease the willingness of everyone to extend credit, leading to disaster.[20]

Despite the best efforts of investors to direct capital and debt to where it can be used most productively, excessive optimism, fraud, a lack of transparency, irrational changes of taste, anxiety, excessive short-term gambles, the failure to maintain a stable currency, excessive government debt, lack of honest accounting, overestimation of values by appraisers and rating agencies, and many other similar factors may foster an overexpansion of debt and thus produce a bubble that when burst leads to a severe economic contraction. With the bursting of such bubbles uncertainty about the future, a lack of trust, an inability to determine realistic values, a chain reaction of margin calls, the inability to meet those calls because of a lack of liquidity, a growing panic, pessimism, and a sense of apocalypse become the order of the day. The reaction thus often proves more exaggerated than the bubble.

In the last few years we have had to deal with the collapse of such a bubble, and it has not been easy, with the government stepping in to both borrow and lend money until the credit markets regained a measure of confidence. We may weather this crisis, but the costs have been high and will be borne principally by future generations. Even if we are successful in dealing with this economic crisis, however, the problem of excessive debt will not go away, for the real debts we have to deal with are not financial but our unrecognized and growing debt to our ancestors and to the natural world.

Debt in the modern world, as we have seen, is inextricably bound up with the use of capital. The use of capital, however, is possible only if it produces more capital, and this can occur only as part of an ever more widespread and ever more efficient organization of production for the transformation of things into commodities. The demand for the continual recycling of capital means that debt must always increase.[21] As we have seen, however, this demand for continual expansion undermines families and communities and leads to the treatment of nature as mere matter in motion.

The wealth of nations that modern science and economics make possible thus depends in the first instance upon the transformation of our debts to our ancestors into a debt to capital. The formation of capital is due to the choices that many of our predecessors made to save and invest the products of their labor rather than to consume them. Everything that was done by them to create the institutions, tools, practices, and surplus that make possible our civilization exists for us only as capital. Our debt to them has thus been transmuted into a generic debt to the current owners (or managers) of capital. While this has had a positive effect in vastly increasing our productive power and in helping to free individuals from the paternalistic structures of authority that characterized traditional society, it has also weakened the social relationships, practices, and institutions that have underpinned society and in many ways have ameliorated the negative consequences of modern individualism. The traditional relationships and responsibilities within families, for example, increasingly become merely financial relationships often mediated by the state. Reciprocal duties of care are replaced by child care at the beginning of life and social security at its end. Our continued well-being thus depends, not upon the vitality of our families and the mutual care we take of one another, but upon our percentage ownership in global capital as individuals and as citizens. In this context the young are increasingly willing to neglect their parents and the old to allow or indeed demand that the government exact payment from future generations to provide for their support. As the relationship between the present and the past becomes ever more abstract and measurable only in financial terms, we increasingly see a diminishing concern with intergenerational justice. This problem may be intractable within the framework of the modern world, and liberal democratic governments have been generally unwilling even to raise this question, let alone address it.

The disruptive effects of modern individualism and a reliance on capital are even more significant when we look at the ways in which modernization and economic development have weakened and undermined long-standing authority structures, religious beliefs, and moral strictures in more traditional societies. The impact has in a number of cases been little short of cataclysmic, provoking a bitterly conservative and at times fundamentalist reaction. As these societies are swept into a world dependent upon capital, the multiple social and cultural practices and institutions that have made life bearable are increasingly dissolved. As we have seen in countries such as Iraq, the ancient webs of social relationships that have allowed communities to live in relative peace and stability cannot be replaced easily by a new web of ever-evolving economic relationships without significant social and political dislocation. This is a problem that is not likely to go away and almost certainly will become more acute with accelerating globalization.

Our modern reconceptualization of what it is to be human also fundamentally changes our notion of what we owe to nature. First, the modern treatment of nature as mere stuff to be used clearly has an effect on our understanding of human nature. While we recognize the unique status of humans as rights-bearing beings, we also increasingly come to measure the value of human beings in concert with the value of all other things in terms of their "price," to use Hobbes's famous characterization, that is, in terms of their labor power, or even their value as raw material that can be converted into something more useful.[22]

Our modern understanding also affects the way we experience the nonhuman world. This is captured in the image of a capitalist who walks through a primeval forest filled with majestic trees but who can think only about how many matchsticks they would make. The nonhuman world in modernity is increasingly transmuted into raw material. In this way our sense of indebtedness to nature disappears. We have come increasingly to see nature as a resource that we can use in whatever way we wish without having to pay for it. Our use of nature, however, is not costless. First, nature is not just stuff, but stuff that has developed over billions of years into the forms it currently holds, forms that are variably useful and valuable to us. In our indiscriminate use of nature we thus often deplete and in some cases completely eliminate these particular natural forms, or species. Even if viewed only from a narrow anthropocentric perspective, this can obviously have grave consequences. Second, every transmutation of a natural thing requires energy and generates unwanted by-products. In small amounts these by-products may be inconsiderable, but as we have learned to our dismay, when produced on a global scale they have inevitable and inconvenient global consequences.[23]

It is likely that we will solve our current economic woes, but I fear, as I have tried to show, that we can do so only by increasing our debt to our ancestors, our communities, and the natural world. We may imagine that the mighty powers of modern science and technology can absolve us from these debts, but in the end I believe that there is no free lunch and that we will be driven to recognize the truth of Anaximander's assertion that all beings must pay their debts for their injustice according to the law of time.

Notes

1. Friedrich Nietzsche, *Philosophy in the Tragic Age of the Greeks* (Chicago: Regnery, 1962), 41–42.

2. Quoted in Simplicius, *Comments on Aristotle's Physics* 24.13.

3. On this point, see Henry Petroski, *The Pencil: A History of Design and Circumstances* (New York: Knopf, 1989).

4. Hannah Arendt, "What Is Authority?" in *Between Past and Future* (New York: World Publishing), 91–142.

5. Thucydides, *Peloponnesian War* 5.17.

6. Raskolnikov in *Crime and Punishment* springs to mind as such an imaginary example, but there are many others.

7. For example, in German "debt" and "guilt" are the same word, *Schuld*. The connection between these two, however, varies considerably. We can gain some insight into this by the different degrees of guilt that are assigned to bankruptcy in different societies. On this point, see David A. Skeel Jr., *Debt's Dominion: A History of Bankruptcy Law in America* (Princeton, N.J.: Princeton University Press, 2003).

8. William Shakespeare, *Macbeth* 3.4.121, Arden edition, ed. Kenneth Muir (London: Methuen, 1951).

9. Friedrich Nietzsche, *Genealogy of Morals*, trans. Walter Kaufmann (New York: Random House, 1967), 57–82.

10. Arendt, "What Is Authority?" Descartes's rejection of all authorities famously stands at the beginning of modern philosophy.

11. John Locke, *Two Treatises of Government*, ed. Peter Laslett (New York: Cambridge University Press, 1988), 286–87.

12. Thomas Hobbes, *Leviathan*, ed. Edwin Curley (Indianapolis, Ind.: Hackett, 1994), 78.

13. The result of this development in our own time is the topic of Robert Putnam's *Bowling Alone: The Collapse and Revival of American Community* (New York: Simon and Schuster, 2000).

14. This problem is further exacerbated by the fact that managers often play a bigger role in controlling corporations than the owners.

15. Adam Smith, *An Inquiry into the Nature and Causes of the Wealth of Nations* (Chicago: University of Chicago Press, 1976), 5–25, 289–398.

16. Here the element of trust is crucial. You are likely to lend your unused hammer to your neighbor only if there is some likelihood you will get it back. If there is not, it is likely to hang uselessly on the wall of your tool shop. It is a form of capital that is not being employed and thus is doing nothing to increase human well-being.

17. The character of taxation also profoundly affects capital formation. The higher the tax on investment, the less likely I am to invest and the more likely I am to consume any surplus. The higher the tax on consumption, the more likely I am to invest the surplus as capital. We obviously need some balance between these two, but attaining such a balance is difficult because every tax system runs the risk of mis-incenting behavior.

18. The exceptions in this case prove the rule. In these circumstances, the few truly unique and irreproducible things such as Rembrandt paintings or da Vinci manuscripts become extraordinarily valuable.

19. While excessive debt can be destabilizing for states, it would be a mistake to conclude that debt as such is politically undesirable. Indebtedness can be a significant advantage especially in relatively weak states, because such debt attaches the interests of the lending class to the fortunes of the state. On this point, see Douglass C. North and Barry R. Weingast, "Constitutions and Commitment: The Evolution of Institutions Governing Public Choices in Seventeenth-Century England," *Journal of Economic History* 49, no. 4 (December 1989): 803–32. Both Britain in the seventeenth century and the United States in the late eighteenth century pursued a conscious policy of borrowing that aimed at shoring up political support for the new regimes. On this point, see Harvey Mansfield Jr., "Party Government and the Settlement of 1688," *American Political Science Review* 58, no. 4 (1964): 933–46. The importance of debt continues to play a similar role today. We see this perhaps most clearly in the improvement of China–US relations, which in no small part is due to the fact that China owns a huge proportion of American national debt.

20. It is almost certainly not sufficient to rely upon states alone to provide such information, since they also have multiple reasons to misrepresent the facts.

21. Smith points out that any attempt to slow down this process or to actually shrink GDP will lead to widespread poverty because it inevitably entails a widespread reduction of the demand for labor and thus in the wages paid for labor. Smith, *Wealth of Nations*, 351–71. This assumes, of course, a stable or rising population. It is not inconceivable that wage rates would remain high in a contracting economy if the population or at least that portion of the population seeking employment were also declining.

22. Here it is not merely a question of labor power but increasingly the question of the ownership of body parts, DNA sequences, etc.

23. Thomas Friedman has pointed out that the earth may have been able to sustain two "Americums" (an "Americum" equals 350 million people with a per capita income of $15,000 per year with a penchant for consumerism) but that it will not be able to tolerate the multiple "Americums" that globalization and economic development are bringing into existence. Thomas Friedman, *Hot, Flat and Crowded* (New York: Farrar, Straus and Giroux, 2008), 88. It is not clear, however, that we can avoid this outcome without developing a more encompassing notion of debt.

5 The Growth Imperative

Prosperity or Poverty

Joel Magnuson

GENERATING A MEASURABLE rate of return for investors is the core element of any capitalist economy. Investors derive their income from percentage returns on stocks, bonds, or other business investments. If investors do not get these expected returns, they will sell their investments and seek returns elsewhere. By disinvesting, or cashing out, investors can drive down the book value of a company, which can ultimately cause the business to fail. To prevent this outcome, the prime directive of a capitalist business is to sustain robust returns and growth of financial wealth for their investors. This is the paramount goal of capitalist enterprise.

To provide these returns for their investors, businesses essentially have three choices. One would be to pay investors with money held in their business bank accounts. This choice, however, would amount to self-impoverishment, as businesses would make themselves poorer by drawing down their bank account balances, just as a person would become poorer by trying to live on a savings account. Another choice would be to generate profits from sales growth gained by taking market share away from competitors. Although the threat of losing market share in a competitive marketplace can force an individual business to be innovative and create new cost-saving technology, one business's gain is another business's loss in a zero-sum strategy. This would ultimately be self-destructive to the interest of the capitalist class as a whole. The third and only viable, long-term choice would be for each business to generate its returns by producing and selling more goods and services for profit.

In other words, driven by the financial necessity of providing investors with a robust rate of return, capitalist businesses must also sustain a robust rate of growth in the production and sale of goods and services. Financial growth is the taskmaster that drives growth in real production.

To sustain ongoing growth in production and sales, businesses must use a portion of their profits for reinvestment in capital stock (plant, equipment, inventory, etc.). With more capital stock, businesses can increase their production capacity to meet the demands of new growth in output and sales. As the funds for making these capital investments are mostly derived from profits on sales, sales growth and investment are locked into a dynamic relationship: profits from current sales provide financing for new investments, these new investments drive future production and future sales, and future sales and profits will finance yet more investments, and so on. Looking at the system in its entirety, keeping the engine of the economic machine running requires a steady flow in real investments that are derived from a steady rise in production and sales. In the other words, the economy has to keep growing.

This growth imperative is systemic and extends beyond merely generating returns for investors. Not only are individual businesses driven to grow, but also the entire capitalist system depends on it. If the dynamic relationship between investment and growth were to break down, the economic system would break down as well. For example, if sales growth were to slow down, the source of funds for capital investment would begin to evaporate and new investments in capital stock would begin to fall. Falling investments would lead to an overall slowdown in production and sales. With falling sales, incomes would fall, and a downward vicious circle of contraction would follow. Contraction or recession, if sustained over time, can turn into a depression, and depression signifies systemic failure of the capitalist system.

As the capitalist machine speeds up or slows down, the changes are felt in every corner of the economy. Every institution within the US economy is connected to every other institution as parts in the machine, and all have evolved to be dependent on the growth imperative. Therefore, if the economy grows, there is a chorus of cheers. Consumers look to growth because it means more goods and services available in markets; workers see growing job opportunities and rising incomes; public agencies receive more money from increased sales and income tax revenue to pay for police, schools, and roads; nonprofits receive more donations and grants from rising incomes; bank loans are repaid; and, most importantly, investors' profits are realized.

When growth turns to contraction (recession), however, trepidation is felt by all. Workers experience layoffs and default on their bank loans; falling profits and share prices in the stock markets deplete the value of pension funds; bankruptcies soar along with government budget deficits and budget cuts. Growth is so centrally important that it has shaped the development of America's most powerful institutions. Without steady growth, the economic system will proceed to wither away like a plant deprived of water and sunlight. For this reason, most observers are very hesitant to question this growth imperative of capitalism.

The acceptance of the growth imperative has become deeply infused in American culture and thought. Most Americans would rather ignore the inevitable environmental damage that ongoing growth causes than question it. As long as people are feeling benefits of growth, and feel that those benefits outweigh the damage it causes, they are likely to accept the idea that ongoing economic growth is benign. If this changes, however, and if it becomes clear that the damage outweighs the benefits, then a crisis in the perception of growth will emerge. This shift in perception is bound to occur at some point because of the scientific fact that *ongoing growth is not possible.* This is perhaps the single most deleterious consequence of the capitalist system. The system is based on a fundamental contradiction that it must continue to grow but that it cannot. Many people seem to be more willing to accept even illusions of growth than to directly face and reconcile this contradiction.

One such illusion of growth is a financial market "bubble." Market bubbles occur when speculators inflate prices far above what would be considered reasonable. A steady rise in stock values or housing prices can make those who own these financial assets feel wealthier. But if growth in the value of financial assets is not supported by growth in the real economy of goods and services, then it is growth on paper only, and the feeling of greater wealth is merely an illusion. Such illusions can suddenly transform into a harsh reality when the bubbles inevitably burst, prices fall, and the paper wealth collapses. For the few who sell prior to the collapse—as top Enron executives did moments before the company famously plunged into bankruptcy—the growth in wealth is real, as they can take their profits and buy real goods or property. But for the majority who lose, their losses are also real as their life savings evaporate. With winners and losers offsetting each other, bubbles in stocks, bonds, gold, or real estate are typically zero-sum situations that do not represent real growth in wealth but rather an upward redistribution of existing wealth. Some real growth can hitch a ride on bubbles such as a booming housing construction industry that rides along with a bubble in the housing market, but these industries also suffer tremendously when the market bubbles burst.

Bubbles aside, capitalism is a money-based system. Growth is tracked and measured in monetary or financial terms such as the dollar value of GDP or securities. For economic growth to be real and not an illusion, increases in these monetary measurements must be anchored to real growth in production. If not, then there will be a fundamental disconnect between the financial and the real, and this disconnect will become a source of instability. In other words, if the stock market shows a steady increase in values of say 7 percent per year but real production of goods and services grows by only 3 percent, then the money wealth represented in stock prices begins to pull away from what one can buy with that money. Money begins to lose its real purchasing power, and a sustained decline in the value of money eventually leads to economic collapse. A key factor in maintaining economic stability is to maintain a stable proportion between monetary growth and growth in the goods that you can buy with that money.

The paramount purpose of capitalism is to provide steady returns to investors. These returns are measured by growth in the value of the financial instruments the investors own, and for this growth to be real and stable it must be supported by real growth in the production and sales of goods and services in the economy overall. A common misconception about the growth imperative is that it is driven by American consumers, who are driven by a deeper impulse to buy and have more things. But the cultural phenomenon of consumerism does not push the capitalist economy to grow; rather, it is a by-product of the capitalist system's growth imperative. Consumers do not push into the malls to buy things as much as they are pulled into the malls by the producers' desperate need to sell more and more.

Consumerism: Nurture, not Nature

The term *consumerism* is used to describe a cultural norm that equates personal well-being with purchasing more and better material possessions. If this were a natural human impulse, then economic growth would naturally follow human nature. At some primal level, we can see that economic growth is in fact necessary for our survival and success as species. Economist Thorstein Veblen asserted that a deeply rooted tendency of human beings is to see that our offspring have a fair chance at a good life. Veblen referred to this tendency as a "parental instinct." Driven by this instinct, Veblen argues, each generation seeks to make its material standard of living better than the last, causing the economy to grow to higher and higher levels of production. If what Veblen tells us is true, then at some level we are by our nature driven to achieve economic growth. This primal instinct, however, has very little to do with the systemic imperative to grow into what is now an already massive $11 trillion economy. In fact, the parental instinct to ensure a good life for our offspring and ongoing growth are actually *contradictory* goals, as endless growth promises to deplete available resources and undermine the welfare of future generations.

Ongoing growth entails using more and more inputs or resources. As these resources are depleted, the productive capacity of future generations is compromised, as will be their chance at a decent livelihood. Moreover, the things people really want for their children—good schools, clean and functional neighborhoods, a healthy and vibrant natural environment, economic stability and security—are those that are least likely to be offered in the growth-driven capitalist system.

Veblen argued that alongside the parental instinct is a "predatory instinct," which is also a deeply rooted human tendency toward certain behavior. Predatory behavior is concerned not as much with caring for future generations as with conquests and self-aggrandizement. Coining terms such as *pecuniary emulation* and *conspicuous consumption*, Veblen was one of the first economists to identify the predatory impulse to achieve social status through owning and consuming more and more goods. In Veblen's view, bigger and better and more goods are consumerist trophies celebrating the prowess and skill of the predator like the taxidermy heads of animals displayed on the hunter's game room walls. For Veblen, the simultaneous existence of these instincts—the parental instinct to care for our young and the predatory instincts of ostentatious consumption and competitive acquisition—stand in an antagonistic relationship and are emblematic of modern life.

Whether their primary impulse stems from a parental or a predatory instinct, the generally accepted view in American culture is that consumers are sovereign in the marketplace. Most proponents as well as critics of capitalism hold the belief that consumer demand is the prime mover in the basic economic processes. That is, consumers express their demands in the markets, and businesses dutifully follow. Proponents argue that growth serves to satisfy the demands of people, and critics argue that people are selfishly, or perhaps unwittingly, creating their own destruction with excessive demands. In either view, the line of causality begins with consumption, and consumption drives production.

We challenge this viewpoint and argue that consumerism is a cultural phenomenon that was created as part of a broader systemic need of the capitalist economy to grow. Profits from sales are the source of returns to capitalist investors, and these returns cannot be sustained if people do not sustain high levels of consumption. The relentless drive for profits created the consumer culture that fuels the economic machine.

If consumerism did in fact stem from a natural instinct of the human species, it was not evident among most Americans in the nineteenth century. One of the problems facing capitalism throughout the nineteenth century was chronic overproduction. Businesses were producing goods for the market, but people tended to be frugal, self-sufficient, and reluctant to spend their earnings on more and more consumer goods. More often than not, people tended to follow the ethic expressed in biblical proverbs, "He that tilleth his land shall have plenty of bread: but he that followeth after vain persons shall have poverty enough" (Prov. 28:19) and "Remove far from me vanity and lies: give me neither poverty nor riches; feed me with food convenient for me" (Prov. 30:8). For many Americans at that time, conspicuous consumption—overtly consuming and buying to display social status—was unseemly.

By the turn of the twentieth century, businesses began searching for new ways to get people to spend more of their earnings on consumer goods. To sell goods in volume, businesses began deploying revolutionary methods designed to entice people into consumer indulgences that had previously been considered frivolous or unnecessary. In his description of America in the early twentieth century as "the dawn of a commercial empire," cultural historian and author William Leach writes: "After 1880, American commercial capitalism, in the interest of marketing goods and making money, started down the road of creating . . . a set of symbols, signs and enticements. . . . From the 1880s onward, a commercial aesthetic of desire and long-ing took shape to meet the needs of business. And since that need was constantly growing and seeking expression in wider and wider markets, the aesthetic of longing and desire was everywhere and took many forms; . . . this aesthetic appeared in shop windows, electrical signs, fashion shows, advertisements, and billboards."[1] To satisfy the growth imperative of capitalism, the marketing and advertising industry was born. By the "Roaring 'Twenties," consumerism, molded by the nascent advertising industry, was in full swing and had established itself, not as a fad, but as a permanent and central feature of American culture. Today advertising is a several hundred-billion-dollar industry, which is about ten times the entire gross domestic product (GDP) of the US economy at the turn of the twentieth century when the industry began.

Capitalism has a systemic need to sell things. If people show no inclination to buy these things, then the capitalist machine will break down. To survive, capitalism must find ways—manipulation and seduction if necessary—to get people to buy more and more things that potentially have little or no relevance to their physical or spiritual well-being or to that of their offspring. Consumerism is a product of modern market-ing techniques that stimulate deep psychological impulses to consume, not because it makes people better off, as consumption may or may not make them better off, but because the growth imperative of the capitalist machine requires it.

Ongoing growth in production and consumption is not just some haphazard thing that people do by chance; it occurs deliberately in response to the capitalist sys-tem's requirement to produce and sell ever larger amounts of goods and services. The roots of this requirement run very deep, and the requirement has exceeded the planet's ability to sustain it.

Throughput and Limits

The production process draws from available resource inputs to produce final goods, or outputs. It is logical to assume that continuous growth on the output side of the production process must necessarily draw more resources from the input side. This process is limited by the availability of resources of our planet. It is for this limitation, more than any other reason, that ongoing capitalist growth is not sustainable.

Parallel to this input/output production process is the process of *throughput*. Throughput is a one-directional process in which usable resources and energy are con-verted into unusable waste. For example, a wooden match is a usable resource, and when it burns it eventually is converted into ash, which is waste and is no longer usable. The immutable laws of matter and energy govern throughput and all other physical and economic phenomena. In a sense, matter is the substance of physical reality, and energy determines how that substance will act. Without energy, matter would be life-less, motionless, and inert; without matter, energy is like a ghost with no medium through which it can become manifest.

Any serious consideration of matter and energy should include the laws of thermodynamics. The first law of thermodynamics informs us that the quantity of all available energy is constant, and the second law states that this energy is continuously transforming from a usable state to a nonusable state. The rate of throughput and the rate at which this one-directional transformation takes place will vary with various rates of economic production. The faster the economic machine turns resources into products, the faster people turn usable resources into unusable waste.

The capitalist growth imperative is not the only force behind throughput. Population pressures obviously play a role, and ongoing growth is evident in noncapitalist systems as well. But these other factors do not take away from the fact that capitalism is driven by a growth imperative, and this growth imperative is a major force behind throughput.

Biologist Mary E. Clark describes the process of hastening throughput as analogous to running up a balance on a credit card that will have to be paid in the future:

> We have been—and are—living on a one-time "bank account" of fossil energy and mineral deposits both formed over eons of geologic time. To have become as dependent on them as we now are is singularly imprudent. Not only are we using up these one-time resources at a galloping rate, we are also living far beyond our day-to-day income of potentially renewable resources—of soil, of water, and of other living species. Instead of husbanding them so they will last forever, we exploit them. We are borrowing from the future.
>
> We are not paying our way at all. We are living off past and future natural capital that we have suddenly learned to exploit. Like irresponsible credit card users, we live high today by borrowing from tomorrow.[2]

Not only are we borrowing from tomorrow, we are doing so at faster and faster rates. Clark's analogy is perhaps more literal than she thought, as the need to use up resources stems from the underlying need to sustain returns to financial investors. As we argued above, steady growth in the value of financial assets drives growth in real production. Mathematically, if investors expect to receive a relatively constant rate of return on their investments, the value of the investment must grow *exponentially*. No matter how small, any fixed rate of return must grow at an exponential rate. A 2 or 3 percent growth rate means that every year the value of the investment must be 2 or 3 percent greater than it was the year before. Using the "72 rule," we can calculate approximately how long it will take for something to double in size by dividing the number 72 by the percentage growth rate. An $11 trillion economy growing at 3 percent annually would double to a $22 trillion economy in approximately twenty-four years (72/3 = 24). That is, in twenty-four years, the US economic machine will be cranking out $22 trillion worth of goods and services. If the growth rate continues at 3 percent for an additional twenty-four years, national output will climb to $44 trillion. Driven by this internal mathematical logic of exponential returns, capitalist production is being pushed beyond the carrying capacity of our planet, or, in the language of thermodynamics, pushed toward "heat death," the ultimate state in which all usable energy is turned to waste.

Physicist and mathematician Albert Bartlett refers to those who believe in the possibility of perpetual growth as members of a "New Flat Earth Society." Bartlett argues that a belief in the ability to grow into perpetuity is logically consistent with believing that the earth is flat. If the earth is flat, then mathematically it exists as a plane in two-dimensional space and is therefore boundless. Only something that has no bounds as such can grow to infinity. If one envisions the earth as a sphere, however, then it is contained in three-dimensional space and is finite. Bartlett's conclusion is:

> If the "we can grow forever" people are right, then they will expect us, as scientists, to modify our science in ways that will permit perpetual growth. We will be called on to abandon the "spherical earth" concept and figure out the science of the flat earth. We can see some of the problems we will have to solve. We will be called on to explain the balance of forces that make it possible for astronauts to circle endlessly in orbit above a flat earth, and to explain why astronauts appear to be weightless. We will have to figure out why we have time zones; where do the sun, moon and stars go when they set in the west of an infinite flat earth, and during the night, how do they get back to their starting point in the east. We will have to figure out the nature of the gravitational lensing that makes an infinite flat earth appear from space to be a small circular flat disk. These and a host of other problems will face us as the "infinite earth" people gain more and more acceptance, power and authority. We need to identify these people as members of "The New Flat Earth Society" because a flat earth is the only earth that has the potential to allow the human population to grow forever.[3]

Bartlett touches on a point that is important for the discipline of economics. When presented with the factual and indisputable mathematics of limits to growth, as well as resource depletion and ecological ruin caused by endless growth, most economists slip into vague and clichéd references to scientific or technological fixes. For over two hundred years, the discipline of mainstream economics has been tailored to fit the logic of capitalism and is not equipped to deal with a world without perpetual growth. Scarcity and economic growth are fundamental tenets in virtually every mainstream economic textbook. Yet in these same textbooks the contradiction between these two tenets is universally ignored. Mainstream economists, it would seem, are full-fledged members of "the New Flat Earth Society."

The Growth Imperative and Global Warming

One of the major consequences of unchecked growth is global warming. An important feature of the earth's atmosphere is that it is kept warmer than would otherwise be allowed given its distance from the sun. As heat radiated from the sun enters the earth's atmosphere, some of it is absorbed by the planet and some of it is reflected back into the atmosphere in the form of infrared radiation. As carbon dioxide and other greenhouse gases accumulate in the atmosphere, heat energy that would otherwise radiate back out into space is trapped and the ambient temperature of the planet rises—global warming. The Intergovernmental Panel on Climate Change (IPCC)—a body of hundreds of scientists brought together by the United Nations, as well as the World Meteorological Association and the National Academy of Sciences—has concluded from their analysis of data on carbon dioxide emissions and the historic temperature changes that the earth's temperature is warming and that the primary cause is the accumulation of atmospheric carbon dioxide and other greenhouse gases.

Carbon dioxide emissions have been growing exponentially for the last two hundred years.[4] This last two hundred years also precisely coincides with the exponential growth in real US GDP based on industrialization and the extensive use of fossil fuels.[5] Throughout most of the period between 1800 and 2000, there has been a slow but steady climb in global temperatures. The largest increase has occurred in the last fifty years, during which both national output and carbon dioxide emissions have recorded gigantic increases.

In their report *Climate Change 2007: The Physical Science Basis,* IPCC scientists conclude that the planet is getting warmer and that the cause is very likely to be an increased amount of greenhouse gases emitted by human activity. The report specifies that the planet will get progressively warmer by 3.2 to 7.1 degrees Fahrenheit over the next hundred years. Although the evidence of global warming and its causes is conclusive, it is still uncertain what exactly the consequences of global warming will be, how severe those consequences will be, and when they will occur.

The IPCC report outlines a possible sequence of events such as a rise in seawater levels of anywhere from seven to twenty-three inches; flooding of coastal regions, including many highly populated urban areas; changing weather patterns; warmer ocean temperatures; arctic conditions developing in some temperate climates; drying trends; falling crop yields; and drought. The report adds that human-made emissions of greenhouse gases are already identified as the cause of intense heat waves, hurricanes, and tropical storms.[6]

Melting of polar ice caps is at the center of the global warming problem. As the ice continues to melt, several inches of additional fresh water will continue to flood into, and disrupt, the Gulf Stream, which carries warm air northward from the tropics. The result will most certainly be a sharp cooling trend in western Europe and eastern North America, causing their temperate climates to change into arctic climates similar to those of present-day Alaska and Siberia. Changing climate conditions could also create deserts within the interiors of large landmasses. The Pentagon has raised concerns that these changes, combined with depleting fuel sources, will result in food shortages and that food shortages could easily develop into national security problems. Melting ice caps will also raise sea levels, which threaten to submerge coastal urban areas, causing immeasurable property damage and displacing hundreds of millions of people.

Warming seawater and melting frozen tundra, or permafrost, will release methane that has been trapped in ice for thousands of years. Methane is also a major contributor to global warming. Methane release acts as a kind of global warming supercharger because it does not come from burning fossil fuels; it is simply released into the atmosphere as the planet gets warmer. This sets in place an unstoppable vicious circle—as the planet gets warmer, more permafrost will melt, more methane will be released, and with an increased amount of methane comes more global warming, and so on.

Although the Defense Department has raised concerns based on IPCC reports, the US government under the leadership of President George W. Bush chose not to participate in international efforts to reduce greenhouse gases such as the Kyoto Protocol in 1997 and the UN Climate Change Conference held in Bali, Indonesia, in 2007. The administration argued instead that such steps would cripple the economy. In other words, the official government position was that the growth imperative of capitalism overrode serious natural disasters caused by global warming. Political appointees at the Environmental Protection Agency and the Departments of Interior and Agriculture are tied to powerful oil, mining, and forest products industries and have been methodically removing information or concerns about global warming from their reports. Moreover, as political favors to their corporate supporters, these agencies are overturning regulations and relaxing enforcement actions directed at reducing air pollution. Yet as callous as this may seem, government officials and industry leaders are doing precisely what they ought to do in a capitalist system: ensuring a steady flow of returns to investors.

Efforts are being made to reform the capitalist system to bring about reductions in greenhouse gas emissions. The most commonly suggested proposal from both business leaders and environmental groups is to enact mandatory reductions in carbon emissions using a combination of taxes, markets, and investment incentives. In these proposals, the core institutions of capitalism would remain intact but would be modified to make the system more environmentally friendly. One suggestion is to levy a tax on fossil fuel consumption and use the revenue generated from the tax to subsidize investments in alternative energy research and development. Such a policy promises to achieve two goals: a forced reduction in the burning of fossil fuels by making it more expensive and, simultaneously, the development of more energy-efficient alternatives.

The logic of these proposals is sound, and undoubtedly they would achieve some level of success, yet the root problem of the growth imperative would remain unchanged. Up to now, energy-efficient technology has not curbed growth in energy consumption. Motor vehicles, for example, have been made more fuel efficient, but fuel consumption has increased as growth in the auto industry has resulted in more cars and larger vehicles such as SUVs and minivans, and people are driving more miles than ever before. Oil production and distribution technology has become more efficient as well, and the result has been growth in output, decreasing production costs, and growth in consumption. As long as capitalism remains as the dominant system, it will continue to find ways to grow, and growth will inevitably give rise to more greenhouse gas emissions.

Another problem lies with the regressive nature of the fossil fuel tax. Any consumption tax is regressive, which means that it puts a disproportionately heavier burden on low-income households, individuals, or societies than on the wealthy. As a result, those at the bottom of the income scale are fleeced in order to deal with environmental problems caused by a capitalist system that primarily benefits those at the top. Globally a tax on fuel consumption would pose a greater hardship not only on poorer individuals but also on entire societies that are strapped for cash. This would exacerbate a growing gap between the wealthy and poor—another innate feature of capitalism.

One variation on this proposal is to make the fossil tax "revenue neutral." This would entail establishing a more complex tax levy/tax credit structure such that there would be no net increase in the tax burden by extending tax credits by the same amount as the levy to those who reduced their consumption. Those who reduced their fuel consumption or converted to renewable energy sources would benefit from the credit, and those who continued to burn fossil fuels would pay more, and there would be no net increase in tax revenues to the government.

The fossil tax/credit proposals have serious shortcomings. They are based on the assumption that consumers choose to burn fuels in certain quantities rather than by necessity. It is true that people choose to buy vehicles and homes of a certain size, and if buying and operating larger vehicles and heating larger homes were made more expensive, people would have an incentive to downshift to smaller, more fuel-efficient sizes. But fuel consumption faces an inelasticity problem. In other words, people are not very flexible in their consumption of gasoline and other fossil fuels, particularly with transportation, as the infrastructure is built in a way that offers very few alternatives. What is more likely is that people would simply be stuck paying higher prices, and although they might cut back their consumption, the actual reduction would not be statistically significant enough to overcome problems of global warming, which would require far more dramatic changes in energy consumption habits. Also, the proposals make no provisions about what people would do with the tax credits once they received them. In the United States, chances are that people or businesses would spend the money, which would mean more consumption, more production, and more burning of fossil fuels.

Another proposed strategy to reduce greenhouse gases is a *carbon trading system*. This is a system designed to use a global marketplace to cut carbon emissions by a specified amount. Under the carbon trading system, each business or government would be given a certain allowable, but reduced, quantity of carbon emissions. Those who voluntarily adopted better methods and technology and thereby fell below the allowable amount of emissions could sell their carbon surplus on the open market as an emission credit. The buyers of these credits would be businesses or governments that found it too costly to reach their mandated targets and had to pay for their excess pollution. The results are predicted to reward financially the carbon good-doers at the expense of the carbon bad-doers. The good-doers could further invest and gain more tradable credits and become stronger competitors. The bad-doers would find that their higher costs made it increasingly difficult to compete in the marketplace, and if they had to continue to pay for their carbon emissions, they would eventually be forced to either clean up their plants or cease operations. On the basis of the familiar Darwinistic logic of free markets, it is believed that the bad-doers would eventually be weeded out of the global economy. After years of attempts to use this program to make businesses greener, the results are, according to industry insiders, dubious.[7]

The carbon trading system has been implemented at local levels and up to now has failed to reduce overall carbon emissions. The main problem with this system is that most of the major polluting industries do not operate in competitive market environments and are not facing such pressures to survive. Moreover, most of these industries are also very profitable, and the businesses have deep pockets from which to pay for a seemingly endless quantity of carbon credits. There has been no indication that businesses will voluntarily reduce carbon emissions as long as it is more profitable for them to buy the credits and continue polluting.

The most obvious problem with these tax/credit/market proposals is that they do not address the core problem of the growth imperative of capitalism. The use of energy credits is mere "window dressing" to make companies look greener and therefore improve their standing with the public.[8] Any policy that does not specifically address this root problem is doomed to fail to achieve its goals in the long run. It takes a long stretch of imagination to envision that capitalist institutions of for-profit enterprises and markets, which have been a major driving force behind the problem of excess fossil fuel consumption in the first place, will suddenly be a central part of the solution. Using capitalist institutions to solve problems created by capitalist institutions is proving to be as futile as training a lion to become a vegetarian—they are simply not programmed to work that way.

Tax/credit/market reform proposals at best will result in small and temporary reductions in carbon emissions and lack resonance as lasting earth-friendly solutions. Such a system is as dubious as trying to make slavery more human-friendly by taxing slave owners who mistreat their slaves and giving credits to those who do not. By their very institutional natures, the growth imperative of capitalist economies prevents them from being earth-friendly, just as the fundamental violation of human rights inherent in slavery prevents slave systems from being humanitarian.

It is a scientific reality that the supplies of oil and natural gas are being depleted. It is also a scientific reality that the planet is warming and climates are changing. Yet the growth imperative of capitalism continues unabated and largely unquestioned, even depleting resources that are considered renewable through overuse.

The Growth Imperative and the Overuse of Renewable Resources

To the extent that oxygen, trees, plants, fish, and topsoil are continually reproduced in nature they are considered "renewable." But although they are considered renewable, they are not without limits. The limit on renewable resources is time. These resources can be considered renewable only if they are used at a rate such that they can be naturally replenished and sustained. With endless economic growth, however, the pace of renewal is slow compared to the rate at which they are being used or destroyed. In every category, renewable resources are being exploited to extinction. Here we will explore the impact growth is having on just a few of the more critical resources—topsoil, water, and forests.

Topsoil

Topsoil is a renewable resource in the sense that it has the capacity to regenerate itself. Like oil and other resources, however, it is being used up and destroyed at a rate faster than it can be restored. As capitalism demands more growth, this growth is fed by the throughput process of transforming usable land into unusable waste. Continuous and accelerated economic production involves destructive agricultural practices—overgrazing, land and water pollution, deforestation, and strip mining—all of which accelerate topsoil ruination.

According to one estimate, over the last millennium humans have transformed about ten billion acres of productive farmland into unproductive wasteland, and about 11 percent of the planet's topsoil surface has suffered from moderate to extreme soil degradation in the last fifty years.[9] Since the end of World War II, about three billion acres (1.2 billion hectares) of usable land has either been significantly degraded or destroyed.[10] The rate of topsoil ruination has accelerated from 25 million tons per year in the eighteenth century, to 300 million tons in the nineteenth and twentieth centuries, to 760 million tons in the past fifty years.[11] In other words, two hundred years of exponential economic growth has come at the cost of two hundred years of exponential and irreversible increases in wasteland.

The economic imperatives to grow, sustain higher profits, and expand market share have also driven farmers into agricultural practices that are not sustainable. The necessity to grow overrides attempts to conserve the integrity or fertility of soil, and capitalist agriculture strives to use whatever combination of land, water, and chemicals is required to yield maximum output on a short-term basis.

Farmers generally do not have much control over the prices of the crops they produce for the market. Prices are set in global commodities markets and seem to be chronically low. Farmers must therefore get the maximum yield from their land during the growing seasons to maximize revenues and profits. Each season farmers face increasing pressure to borrow funds in order to purchase the latest version of patented seeds, chemicals, fuel, and water to avoid losing their places in the market. To pay back their loans and make their interest payments, they must get the highest yield possible on a short-run basis. Yet the following season the soil worsens, requiring more water and chemicals, and so on in a downward spiral of topsoil degradation. Many farmers have not survived this process financially, and the result has been a steady rise in bankruptcies, particularly among the smaller family farms. Compared to large corporate farms, small farms must pay higher interest rates on their credit and have the least purchasing power to pay for increasingly expensive chemicals and seeds. To increase their profitability, farmers are allowing for shorter and shorter fallow periods in which land is allowed to rest and regenerate from cultivation.

Historically, agricultural technology has succeeded in multiplying the output per acre. Since the beginning of the application of the internal combustion motor to agriculture and the use of tractors, combines, and other heavy machinery, agricultural output and productivity have increased dramatically. The extensive use of petrochemical fertilizers and pesticides began in agriculture about fifty years ago and was heralded as a "green revolution," as it contributed to significant increases in productivity and output. Yet the destruction caused by this technology remains largely hidden. Topsoil is being hardened from the compaction caused by the heavy machinery. Hardening decreases the rate of water absorption, causing problems of water runoff and inadequate drainage and increasing the occurrence of erosion. In Nebraska, for example, wind erosion removes about 186 tons of soil per acre every year, a rate far above natural rates of soil erosion.[12] As we shall see in the next section, fresh water is another resource that is being depleted. As the water tables fall, and as farmers use petroleum-based chemical pesticides and herbicides, the soil is becoming dryer and more susceptible to wind erosion.

Fresh Water

Fresh water is considered renewable as it is restored continuously by the natural hydrologic cycle of evaporation, condensation, and precipitation—all of which are driven by energy from the sun. If fresh water were used at a rate equal to the rate it is restored by the hydrologic cycle, water supplies could be sustainable into perpetuity. Unfortunately, this is far from the case, as fresh water is being consumed or polluted much more quickly than it can be restored. Water is the most basic and necessary resource for sustaining life on the planet, but is being used up as if its supplies were limitless, and like topsoil fresh water is used as a sink into which wastes are dumped.

Approximately 70 percent of the planet's fresh water supply, or "wet gold," is used in agriculture for irrigation of crops.[13] The rate of water consumption is not equally distributed around the planet. The fastest rates of consumption are in predominantly growth-oriented capitalist economies in western Europe, North America, and Japan, where per capita water consumption ranges between 80 and 150 gallons per day. In most of the rest of the world, people consume about 2 to 5 gallons per day.[14]

Throughout most of human history, water was directed from rivers, stored in small dams, and channeled into farmland by canals. This changed after the development of industrial capitalism, when wells were sunk deep in the ground so that high-quality fresh water that had seeped underground into porous soil and sand and had collected in pools could be brought to the surface by diesel or electric pumps and used for human consumption. At upper levels groundwater has higher saturation rates, and millions of shallow wells sunk throughout the world have tapped into virtually all available supplies. As the demand has increased, and with the development of pumping and drilling technology, deeper wells have been sunk, providing access to larger underground reservoirs that have formed naturally in much deeper geological basins known as aquifers. Like oil drilling and extraction, groundwater stored in aquifers is being pumped out at a rate faster than it can be replenished.

The United States is fortunate compared to many places in the world, as it is blessed with much rainfall. About 25 percent of the water used in the United States comes from groundwater pumping—about twenty-eight trillion gallons a year—and the rest comes from surface water from precipitation.[15] Nonetheless, all of the major aquifers in the United States are being depleted. In the arid southwestern states, the groundwater levels, water tables, have dropped as much as 110 feet in ten years.[16] As water tables drop, previously productive wells go dry and farmers must either dig deeper wells, drawing down water tables even further, or drill new wells where the process of depletion starts anew. In Arizona's Santa Cruz basin, water tables are being depleted by a half million acre-feet (an acre-foot equals about 326,000 gallons) every year. California's San Joaquin Valley, a rich agricultural region, depletes its groundwater supplies by 1.5 million acre-feet annually.[17] Also, falling water tables cause spring-fed rivers, lakes, and wetlands on the surface to dry up. This, in turn, causes ground surfaces to sink, creating lifeless sandboxes.

The most dramatic instance of groundwater depletion is the Ogallala aquifer, which spans several states from west of the Mississippi River to the Rocky Mountains, and from South Dakota to Texas. This huge 225,000-square-mile aquifer was created millions of years ago. Snow runoff from the Rocky Mountains has not fed into the Ogallala in over one thousand years, and since then the aquifer has been largely cut off from any significant replenishing source. Most of the water in the Ogallala is considered "fossil water," as it is melted ice that dates back to the last ice age. For decades, over 170,000 wells scattered throughout the Ogallala region have been pumping out millions of gallons every year. The rate of pumping increased by 300 percent between 1950 and 1980, and this rapid increase is, in part, due to the fact that the water is relatively accessible to the surface—about three hundred feet on average. From the time that pumping from the Ogallala began in the 1930s to about 1950, the levels drawn out remained fairly constant. Between 1950 and 1985, the Ogallala water table dropped by about 160 feet. Although the rate of depletion has slowed down in recent years, the water table continues to fall. As aquifers like the Ogallala are stocked mainly with fossil water, once they are pumped dry they will become extinct, and populations that have depended on them will either have to make do with rainwater, suffer health problems, or migrate.[18]

A 1997 United Nations report entitled *Comprehensive Assessment of the Freshwater Resources of the World* drew the following conclusions: "About one-third of the world's population lives in countries that are experiencing moderate to high water stress partly resulting from increasing demands from a growing population and human activities. By 2025 as much as two-thirds of the world population would be under stress conditions. Water shortages and pollution are causing widespread public health problems, limiting economic and agricultural development, and harming a wide range of ecosystems. They may put global food supplies in jeopardy and lead to economic stagnation in many areas of the world."[19] The report stresses not only that water is being used up but that it is being spoiled with contamination, rendering it useless for human consumption. Heavy use of petrochemical pesticides and fertilizers not only kills soil-dwelling insects and microbes and sterilizes the soil but also contaminates groundwater. In the 1980s, concern about groundwater contamination led to a federal government investigation and report entitled *Protecting the Nation's Groundwater from Contamination*. This report found that some 245 toxic substances were contaminating groundwater and that about a fourth of those came directly from compounds used in herbicides and pesticides.[20] About thirteen thousand square miles in Mississippi contains a body of dead water in which chemical runoff and soil erosion has killed virtually all aquatic life.[21]

According to UN projections, at current levels of population growth and per capita demand growth a severe water shortage will occur before the end of the twenty-first century.[22] As that time approaches, water, like oil, will become steadily more scarce and expensive. The economic burden of expensive water will affect poorer countries most severely. Water shortages will reduce food production, causing famine in addition to an increase in diseases associated with contaminated drinking water. Scarcity of water and other resources is closely linked with the growing inequality of living standards around the world.

Forests

Like topsoil and fresh water, forests are renewable resources in the sense that they can self-regenerate through natural processes. Also like topsoil and water, forests are being depleted. The economy's need for profit making and accumulation causes forestry to be practiced in ways that are highly destructive and unsustainable. The most profitable way to harvest lumber and wood fiber is to extract it in a manner similar to strip mining—clear-cutting—in which huge swaths of forest land are razed to the ground. Clear-cut logging permanently drives forests to extinction by destroying the fragile and complex ecological systems on which forests depend for their existence. Forests that remain in their original pristine state, untouched by logging, are known as "old-growth" forests, and only a very small percentage of them have survived.

Some of the world's most magnificent old-growth forests are located in the Pacific Northwest. The earliest records of logging in the United States' Pacific Northwest forests date back to around 1875 in what is now the Willamette National Forest. Since that time about 90 percent of the old-growth forests in the region has been logged; only a very small fraction remains in preserves and parks.[23] These old-growth forests are not merely stands of trees; rather, they are complex systems made up of living trees and plants, fungi, bacteria, decomposing matter and detritus, animals, and a delicate balance of shade and sunlight. If any of one of these elements is significantly disrupted, the forests are irreversibly transformed. Physicist Vandana Shiva explains similar complex relationships in the food chain: "It is precisely because these essential links in the food chain have been ignored and destroyed by 'developed' and 'scientific' agriculture that the croplands of the world are rapidly being destroyed. . . . The little earthworm working invisibly in the soil is actually the tractor and fertilizer factory and dam combined."[24] Most old-growth forests have been logged, transformed into tree farms and managed by the profit-driven wood products industry. Tree farms are not forests but planted crops to be harvested like fields of corn or wheat. Modern agriculture creates huge land areas planted with a single species of crop, or monocultures, that require high doses of chemical fertilizers and pesticides. Chemicals are used to generate high yields and fight against locusts and other biological imbalances associated with monocultures. The same is true of modern forestry. Clear-cut logging results in loss of soil fertility and erosion, and in response the forest products industry turns to chemicals to boost yields and industry profits.

The destruction caused by clear-cut deforestation extends far beyond damage to the land. Biological diversity and natural biological processes that have sustained forests for thousands of years are also being permanently destroyed. Erosion associated with logging causes excessive siltation of streams and riverbeds in which fish attempt to fertilize and hatch their eggs. The fish population thus declines in areas affected by clear-cuts. Moreover, clear-cuts cause floods and drought as rainwater is no longer absorbed and controlled by tree roots. Destruction of forests means the destruction of the habitats for over half the species of plants and animals that live on the planet.[25]

Forests absorb carbon dioxide from the atmosphere, which, as we have seen, is one of the primary causes of global warming. Deforestation destroys the planet's natural ability to moderate climate, and rather than absorbing carbon dioxide it releases more into the atmosphere. Deforestation also depletes soil nitrogen, an essential element for all forms of plant life.

To replace the lost nitrogen, foresters began using expensive nitrogen fertilizers. Most nitrogen fertilizers are chemicals derived from oil. Once the practice of chemical nitrogen fertilization has been adopted, the natural process of nitrogen-fixing in plants is suppressed. Forest management will be forever dependent on chemicals made from increasingly scarce and expensive petroleum. The only alternative to this permanent chemical dependency would be to abandon the logged areas as wasteland that will take generations to bring back to life.[26] According to forest ecologist Elliot Norse, "Even this cursory nitrogen budget suggests that intensive timber management is not renewable resource management, the stated aim of most kinds of commercial forestry. It is not even farming. It is mining."[27]

Although mining forests for wood fiber is not sustainable, it is very profitable. Capitalism does not reward prudent, forward thinking regarding resource conservation.

Its goal is profit maximization, and clear-cut logging is the most direct way to achieve this goal. A single high-quality, old-growth conifer in the Pacific Northwest contains as much as $10,000 worth of wood fiber. A small stand of one hundred such trees can be worth about $1 million, and its clear-cutting requires little in the way of harvesting costs. Given its profitability, it would be virtually impossible to convince any profit-maximizing enterprise that long-term sustainability would be a better use of forest resources. This is particularly true of large, publicly traded corporations that have shareholders who never see, or know, or even care about the long-term, irreversible damage the company they own is doing.

The long-standing practice of depleting vital resources such as fossil fuels, topsoil, water and forests for profit will necessarily end. Either by conscious and mindful changes in our economic institutions, or by calamity, a change in our practices is inevitable. Of course, if we wait for calamities to arrive before making meaningful changes, it will be too late.

It is uncertain how much longer the US capitalist machine can remain on this path before experiencing dire environmental consequences. In *Collapse: How Societies Choose to Fail or Succeed* (2004), evolutionary psychologist Jared Diamond predicts that we will continue to misuse our resources mindlessly to a point where the foundation of our collective existence inevitably disintegrates. Society, according to Diamond, will undergo a cataclysmic event such as violent political upheaval, warfare, or some other form of self-destruction. Diamond asserts that it seems easier for people to indulge in collective denial about such outcomes than to face them.

As most of us go about our daily lives, we tend not to think of such extreme events as predicted by Diamond. When confronted with warnings, most are inclined to dismiss them as paranoia or pointless ruminations on distant future possibilities or, if taking them at all seriously, to seek comfort in a technological solution.

The Fallacy of the Technological Fix

The belief in technology pervades economic thought. It is seen as the ultimate solution to virtually every economic problem, from poverty to growth limits. This is true of most economists whether they are proponents of capitalism or critics. In 1848, Karl Marx and Friedrich Engels wrote glowingly of the technological wonders associated with capitalism: "[The capitalist class] has created more massive and more colossal productive forces than have all preceding generations together. Subjection of nature's forces to man, machinery, application of chemistry to industry and agriculture, steam navigation, railways, electric telegraphs, clearing whole continents for cultivation; . . . what earlier century had even a presentiment that such productive forces slumbered in the lap of social labor?"[28] In the twenty-first century, David Korten, author of *When Corporations Rule the World*, echoes a similar sense of technological awe and wonder: "A mere fifty years ago . . . many of the things we take for granted today as essential to a good and prosperous life were unavailable, non-existent, or even unimagined. These include the jet airplane, . . . computers, micro-wave ovens, electric typewriters, photocopying machines, television, clothes dryers, air conditioning, freeways, . . . chemical pesticides—to name only a few."[29] Korten is correct, as were Marx and Engels a century and a half before him, to point out the many positive aspects of technology. Technology provides hope. Not many people would advocate that we allow our productive technology to regress to premodern standards. Yet without a critical perspective belief in technology becomes an irrational faith that every problem we face will always have a technological fix. Like a secular religion, blind faith in technology provides comfort and reassurance that perpetual growth is possible.

Like a religion, belief in technology provides comfort to people. It allows people to believe that they can continue doing things in the same way, that they will never have to change their behavior, beliefs, or institutions. Technology allows people to have confidence that the growth imperative of capitalist economies can continue uninterrupted by resource limitations. By analogy, the irrational belief in technology instills a sense of confidence in perpetual growth much as if a doctor reassured a heavy smoker that he could continue smoking because medical science would always provide a technological solution to any health problem. Like heavy smoking, perpetual growth has consequences, and those consequences become more severe over time. Technology can provide short-term remedies, but long-term solutions require behavioral and institutional change. Perhaps most importantly, they require an end to the belief that perpetual growth is possible.

Perpetual growth under capitalism is inseparable from the technology that allows growth to continue. Technological development is not random and is always fostered within a specific environment. There is very little by way of technological development that is insulated from the demands of our economy or political environment. The cotton gin, steam-powered locomotives, petrochemicals, the guillotine, and nuclear warheads are all instances of technology that did not develop in a vacuum. These technological developments came about as ways to solve immediate economic and political problems. One of the biggest problems capitalism is facing is the simultaneous need for ongoing growth and the limitation of available resources to power that growth. To solve this problem, the capitalist system turns to technological fixes. Yet just as much as a technological "fix" remedies an immediate problem of scarcity, it can give rise to new and perhaps deeper problems.

For example, as mentioned above, the problem of agricultural productivity was met with the application of chemical technology. Yet this technological fix gave rise to a host of other and deeper problems, such as environmental damage and dependency on increasingly scarce and expensive oil. And the proposal to fix the problem of energy shortages with nuclear technology will set a framework for the most dangerous and toxic input to growth that the world has ever encountered.

Prosperity or Poverty of Growth

One of the greatest ironies of capitalism is that perpetual growth is heralded as the ultimate solution to the problem of poverty, yet its future is bleak with poverty caused by resource depletion and environmental destruction. Economic growth as a solution to poverty has always been popular among the affluent, for it suggests that the problem can be solved by expanding wealth, not redistributing existing wealth from the rich to the poor. John F. Kennedy popularized this sentiment in his political adage "A rising tide lifts all boats." Kennedy's message was misleading, however, for anyone who has visited the ocean knows that tides ebb and flow and that a rising tide will eventually give way to a receding tide. When this happens, the receding water will not lift boats but ground them. Just as there is no such thing as a perpetually rising tide, there cannot be a perpetually growing economy.

Any serious reflection on the capitalist growth imperative will lead to the conclusion that available resources will be exploited to the point of exhaustion and thus that growth cannot be sustained. As resources are exhausted, people's ability to produce goods and services will be undermined, and prosperity will eventually turn to poverty. A mindless belief in technology as a panacea for chronic resource shortages will only hasten this inevitability.

Technology cannot change the immutable laws of nature and physics any more than it can bring a dead person back to life. Scarcity of resources that are used to sustain growth is an immutable scientific reality—as real as the fact that our planet is not flat but rather three-dimensional and finite. Oil and natural gas are resources that have definite limits, and once they are depleted they will never be brought to life again. As coal, fresh water, topsoil, and other finite resources disappear or become filled with waste, they will become increasingly scarce and more expensive, and the cost of finding new usable replacements will also rise. Rising scarcity and costs of resources are tightening their grip on the throat of capitalist growth and—technology notwithstanding—will eventually bring centuries of exponential growth to an end. And then where do people go? Do we wait for the calamitous scenarios of poverty as envisioned by Jared Diamond, or do we become proactive and work for institutional change while there is still time?

Technology can and does lead to good solutions, and this should not be ignored, but technology is always fostered within a specific institutional context, and this should not be ignored either. If our institutions are warlike, then we will develop weapons technology. If they are oriented toward growth for growth's sake, then we will develop growth-oriented technology. But if they are oriented toward survival and sustainability, then we will develop survival- and sustainability-oriented technology. Mindful institutional change, away from the capitalist growth imperative, will allow for a rising tide of new and appropriate technological developments.

Notes

1. William Leach, *Land of Desire: Merchants, Power and the Rise of a New American Culture* (New York: Random House, 1993), 15, 9.

2. Mary E. Clark, *Ariadne's Thread: The Search for New Modes of Thinking* (New York: St. Martin's Press, 1989), 99.

3. Albert A. Bartlett, "The New Flat Earth Society," *Physics Teacher* 34, no. 6 (September 1996): 34243, www.hubbertpeak.com/bartlett/flatearth.htm.

4. T. A. Boden, G. Marland, and R. J. Andres, *Global, Regional, and National Fossil-Fuel CO₂ Emissions* (Oak Ridge, Tenn.: Carbon Dioxide Information Analysis Center, Oak Ridge National Laboratory, U.S. Department of Energy, 2010), doi 10.3334/CDIAC/00001_V2010.

5. U.S. Bureau of Economic Analysis: www.bea.gov/bea/dn/gdllev.xls.??

6. Intergovernmental Panel on Climate Change, *Climate Change 2007: The Physical Science Basis*, contribution of Working Group I to the Fourth Assessment Report of the Intergovernmental Panel on Climate Change, ed. S. Solomon et al. (Cambridge: Cambridge University Press, 2007), www.ipcc.ch/publications_and_data/publications_ipcc_fourth_assessment_report_wg1_report_the_physical_science_basis.htm.

7. Ben Elgin, "Little Green Lies," *Bloomberg Businessweek*, October 29, 2007, www.businessweek.com/magazine/content/07_44/b4056001.htm.

8. Ibid.

9. UN Environment Programme, *Farming Systems Principles for Improved Food Production and the Control of Soil degradation in the Arid, Semi-Arid, and Humid Tropics* (Patancheru, India: International Crops Research Institute for the Semi-Arid Tropics, 1986), 7.

10. Thomas Prugh, *Natural Capital and Human Economic Survival* (Solomons, Md.: International Society for Ecological Economics, 1995), 75.

11. B. G. Rosanov, V. Targulian, and D. S. Orlov, "Soils," in *The Earth as Transformed by Human Action: Global and Regional Changes in the Biosphere over the Past 30 Years*, ed. B. L. Turner et al. (Cambridge: Cambridge University Press, 1990), 203–14.

12. Clark, *Ariadne's Thread*, 109.

13. Bill McKibben, "Our Thirsty Future," *New York Review of Books*, June 2004, 58.

14. Ibid.

15. Ibid., 59.

16. Clark, *Ariadne's Thread*, 107.

17. Ibid.

18. For statistics on Ogallala, see Kathryn Hilgenkamp, *Environmental Health: Ecological Perspectives* (Sudbury, Mass.: Jones and Bartlett, 2006), 151–55.

19. UN Report of the Secretary General, *Comprehensive Assessment of the Freshwater Resources of the World*, E/CN.17/1997/9 (New York: United Nations Commission on Sustainable Development, Fifth Session, April 7–25, 1997), paragraphs 2 and 3, www.un.org/esa/documents/ecosoc/cn17/1997/ecn171997-9.htm.

20. As cited in Chris Maser, *The Redesigned Forest* (San Pedro, Calif.: R & E Miles, 1988), 17.

21. Donella Meadows, Jorgen Randers, and Dennis Meadows, *Limits to Growth: The 30-Year Update* (White River Junction, Vt.: Chelsea Green, 2004), 65.

22. Ibid., 36.

23. Elliot Norse, *Ancient Forests of the Pacific Northwest* (Washington, D.C.: Island Press, 1990), 6.

24. Vandana Shiva, *Staying Alive: Women, Ecology, and Development* (London: Zed Books, 1989), 108.

25. Edward O. Wilson, "Threats to Biodiversity," *Scientific American*, September 1989, 108.

26. Norse, *Ancient Forests*, 218.

27. Ibid., 219.

28. Karl Marx and Friedrich Engels, *The Manifesto of the Communist Party* (1848; repr., New York: Verso Press, 1998), 40–41.

29. David Korten, *When Corporations Rule the World*, 2nd ed. (Bloomfield, Conn.: Kumarian Press, 2001), 27.

6 Democracy's Debt

Capitalism and Cultural Revolution

Stephen L. Gardner

SINCE THE FRENCH Revolution, writers Left and Right have famously lamented the nihilism of bourgeois society. Take the *Communist Manifesto* for example: "Constant revolutionizing of production, uninterrupted disturbance of all social conditions, everlasting uncertainty and agitation distinguish the bourgeois epoch from all earlier ones. All fixed, fast-frozen relations, with their train of ancient and venerable prejudices and opinions, are swept away, all new-formed ones become antiquated before they can ossify. All that is solid melts into the air, all that is holy is profaned, and man is at last compelled to face with sober senses, his real conditions of life, and his relations with his kind."[1] Thus Karl Marx channels Joseph de Maistre. Tellingly, though, the sentiment of this famous passage is conflicted. Marx's scandal at bourgeois society betrays sacred terror of its revolutionary drive, suggesting even that it may be more radical than its socialist rivals. The specter of communism wants to rob the "bourgeois epoch" of its revolutionary genie, perhaps in order to stuff it back into the bottle at the same time. In any case, Marx reveals more than he realizes here. Even when he misses the point he sometimes has an uncanny ability to put his finger on it. What is revolutionary about the epoch is that it makes revolution itself its driving principle. There has always been but one revolution in modernity, and that (*pace* Marx) is the bourgeois one. Relentless and irresistible, it has accelerated mightily since Marx's time. The substance of its principle is equality, and its form is the market—things Marx elsewhere protests as not revolutionary enough. What his ambivalence perfectly crystallizes, though, is the Jekyll-and-Hyde character of modernity, revolutionary and counter-revolutionary at the same time, split into warring personalities.

Like Marx, other critics moderate or radical, from Tocqueville and Kierkegaard to Nietzsche and Heidegger, have criticized nihilism or cognates such as leveling, alienation, or decadence. They variously ascribe these to equality, democracy, capitalism, liberalism, or technology, but their reaction unites them despite their differences. The nihilist lament is also a fixture of conservative and communitarian social criticism of the loss of capacity for greatness or for awe and wonder, the desecration of tradition, the destruction of community, or the ethos of hedonism. What its critics ignore, though, is just how efficacious nihilism is in the social mechanisms of liberty, how indispensable to the moral economy of equality. They fail to describe its functionality within the democratic universe as a cultural means of mediating the exigencies of a world transformed by equality—or at least seeming to mediate, since all it may really do is defer insoluble dilemmas of modern life. Even so, the culture of nihilism is, alas, very far from being stale, flat, and unprofitable.

To describe the functionality of nihilism, its debt to debt, and how it intimates the mortal limits of democracy, is the aim of this paper. Democracy generates a teleology of nihilism, but one it cannot do without, even if in the end it is fatal. Democracy strives to replace what once appeared as a "natural" or "divinely legislated" order with a "cultural" or "aesthetic" one in which individuals are free to invent themselves, a virtual reality predicated on individual will or imagination. The revolution in debt affords critical leverage in this. If not the cause of it, the exponential expansion of debt (especially since World War II) is at least joined at the hip to a wholesale revolution in democratic culture driven by the market at least since the Jazz Age. The spiritual economy of democracy seems unable to sustain itself without a vast amplification of credit, personal and national. This affords the possibility of the privatized utopias of consumerism. Sooner or later, of course, the bill comes due. In the meantime, though, this economy operates by a dual action projecting the future—partly by conjuring up an imagined tomorrow and partly by fending it off. In a word, it keeps the future open and ongoing in ostensibly perpetual postponement. Within this context, debt is not a peripheral liability of economy but its foundation, the "material" equivalent of a future that must never arrive. Ostensibly it affords an instrument by which reality itself may be kept at bay.

This is not simply bad policy; it is anthropological necessity. All social orders have cultural means for dealing with conflicts, containing the violence of rivalries that might destroy society were they permitted to get out of hand. Democracy, though, inhabits a peculiar dilemma. It abolishes traditional means of damping down social conflict by means of hierarchy or rank order, upheld by religion and tradition. Simultaneously, it increases the potential of conflict by forcing citizens into greater psychological proximity, removing the cultural distances between them. It cranks up the agonistic anxieties among those who are, in each other's eyes, on the same moral plane. Equality is not just a right; it is a burden, as individuals must demonstrate to themselves and their contemporaries that they are not inferior but just as good as anyone else or even better.

"No one is better than me," declares the ambiguous ethic of equality. The definingly democratic passion is humiliation, real or imagined, actual or feared. Its proper emotion is a sense of nothingness experienced in self-comparison with others.[2] That is, it is an existential inferiority complex, and no one should underestimate its motivating power. Apparently the only way to hold one's own, psychically speaking, is by proving—as much to oneself as to others—that one is "free," the author of one's destiny. To show oneself as "equal" or better, one must also show that one is autonomous, independent, or self-determined, if not self-created. In this context, democracy's addiction to debt, personal and sovereign, may be understood as a strategy of deferral that underwrites myths of freedom of popular culture. Dangerous as this might be for the long-term health of the economy or polity, this structure of postponement can scarcely be avoided as a condition of democracy, at least one that has nearly doubled its population and vastly expanded civil and privacy rights in the past sixty years or so. The subject of this essay is the "apocalyptic" teleology this entails.

Drawing on René Girard, Philip Rieff, Daniel Bell, Karl Polanyi, and others, I develop the first part of what is properly a two-part argument. The argument as a whole consists in two pairs of propositions forming an "apocalyptic" progression. Space prevents me from doing justice to the second (and equally indispensible) part of the whole, which I can only touch upon here and again at the end, as a likely continuation.

In the first place, capitalism is democracy; markets are democracy in motion, an emancipatory contagion of equality; money is the tangible expression of equality, the object and symbol of democratic desire. The egalitarianism of money is by no means inconsistent with scandalous inequalities of wealth; to the contrary, equality generates its own inequalities, just as it generates the desire for inequality. The money-driven economy affords a social mechanism by which the passions unleashed by equality, negative passions usually destructive of society such as envy or resentment, can be turned into sources of prosperity.[3]

In the second place, capitalist markets are revolutionary, but their revolutionary nihilism makes them all the more effective both as contagions of democratic desire and as means by which its social conflicts are mediated and deferred. Capitalism does not just spread the gospel of equality; it also makes it socially workable, within limits. But it does so only by means of a cultural revolution that transforms all traditional moral understandings, especially in the region of personal life and the relation of the public and the private. However effective this may be in servicing the exigencies of the democratic psyche, though, it threatens the cohesiveness of society. Thus the paradoxical productivity of capitalism: the more creative it is of democratic wealth and culture, the more it disintegrates social order. Capitalism serves to postpone antagonisms within civil society, the envies and jealousies of democratic men and women, but only by intensifying antagonism between itself and social order as a whole.

This brings me to the latter half of the argument, which will be developed more fully at the end of the essay. As capitalism cannot perform its function of discharging or deferring the antagonisms of democracy without attacking the communal order of society, it provokes a collision between its two primal drives, the sacred and the profane. According to Durkheim, the social order is founded on the dichotomy of the sacred and the profane, respectively the ritual and symbolic expressions of communal identity and the everyday dealings with things that sustain life.[4] Social order is not to be confused with "politics" and "economics," which always presuppose it. Order is not forged from politics and economics; rather, the latter emerge from social order, even if they attack it. But modernity is not "secularization," the progressive reduction or elimination of religion by the disenchanted worlds of politics and economics. As if returning to primeval Durkheimian origins, it entails an antagonism between the sacred and the profane and between its conjugations, the modern and the archaic, the secular and the religious. Traditionally, both are equally necessary but not equal in rank. In the modern world, though, the sacred and the profane become rivals, enemy brothers—as if the profane demanded equality with the sacred. The secularizing impulses of modernity—more precisely, of the market, as the principal force of profanation—only stiffen the sacred resistance of social order (and of the individual personality too, for this constitutive distinction is the basis of character, a structure of the psyche). To the secularizing mentality, the reaction of the sacred must seem like an inexplicable attack of Hitchcockian birds from out of the blue. It cannot understand why the sacred keeps reappearing irrepressibly to scourge it, even growing in strength as the profane thinks to ply its way to "emancipation."

In the fourth place, finally, modernity does not diminish the power of the sacred but only debases it. Sacred order, both socially and individually, defends itself against the depredations of the market, even if to do so degrades the sacred at the same time. In debased form, sacred order can return only as a cult of violence, an idolatry of the once hidden source of the sacred itself, inasmuch as the sacred is originally founded in sacrifice. In the modern context, the return of the sacred—like the decomposing resurrection of the living dead in the movies—cannot save social order but can only hasten its destruction. It no longer enjoys the innocence of its operations in archaic religion, an ignorance that made it effective. The emancipatory freedom of the market both provokes and corrupts the sacred reflex, which serves to accelerate rather than deter communal disintegration. In this scenario, reality is experienced traumatically, as the apocalyptic revenge of the sacred in the collapse of the illusions of popular culture. This is not just a cinematic conceit, though. The sacred immune system of the body politic becomes a threat to that body itself. A critical aspect of this debasement is the politicization of society by means of the culture wars. Modern politics is incapable of resolving cultural divisions, yet it cannot resist the temptation to think that it can. And so those who believe they are the ones to save order are the ones who consummate its destruction.

The crux of this argument runs on two axes, that of René Girard and that of Philip Rieff. The final works of Rieff (best known for his classic books on Freud and "therapeutic culture" in the 1950s and 1960s) imply that modernity is a fraternal rivalry of two orders, a world divided against itself.[5] Rieff implies this without actually stating it, though, because he is so caught up in the culture wars himself that he cannot entirely see the kinship that its rivals intimate, a kinship constitutive of the modern world.[6] He presents as two distinct cultural types what are in fact two cultures in one, a single culture whose unity is its schizophrenia. Effectually, though, this schizophrenia is what he reveals. Rieff's later thought, published just before and after his death in 2006, is more polemical than theoretical. But it does offer a theory of social order in terms of sacred order, a Durkheimian notion paradoxically leavened with Judaic (and Christian) elements, which he contrasts with a culture of "transgression" that is "modern" in the narrow sense of the term. His thought is an intuitive reflection on the implicit fraternity of these enemies, their tacit bond in their antagonism. An "apocalyptic" thinker (not his term), Rieff is a thinker of order in decline, order in the process of decomposition. Evidently he offers no solace that this is reversible.

If Rieff expresses the vertical axis of social order, Girard lays out its horizontal, the human level of interaction, or "mimetism." According to Girard, human desire is "mimetic," acquired by reciprocal imitation of human beings. Not only do human beings acquire objects of desire from each other, but the distinctively human behavior of desiring is itself picked up by contagious reciprocity. Paradoxically, Girard argues, the mimetic nature of desire entails not just conformity or social comity but rivalry and violence, as individuals cannot but find themselves in competition for the same things. These conflicts are especially intense when the object of contention is human "being" itself, personality or individuality or freedom, some image of an authentic existence of a "self" of one's own, wrested away from others, as it were. In a universe predicated on equality, the "self" so devoutly desired is always, on closer analysis, the self *of someone else*. One's neighbor secretly supplies one's model and thus is doomed to become a rival.

Girard's theory of mimetic desire is, I suggest, really a theory of democratic desire, in effect a theory of democracy itself, as an anthropological phenomenon. Equality transparently reveals the nature of desire as mimetic. Nowhere is this so clear as where it is so insistently denied, in consumer culture, where everyone is afforded the illusion that he is author of his desire. Conversely, desire is the natural mode of existence of equality, a relation of individuals who measure the being they crave in terms of each other. Democracy is not just a political regime but a modality of human relations in which individuals relate to each other psychically as "equals," same in their difference and different in their sameness. Anthropologically speaking, democracy is desire itself, stripped of all traditional limits. As Pierre Manent argued in *Tocqueville and the Nature of Democracy*, equality generates almost a new species of human being, "democratic man": he and "aristocratic man" think and feel the same emotions but in radically different ways.[7] This is where the real dynamic of modern life is to be sought. It exists most profoundly on social, cultural, and psychological levels (which "anthropology," as I use that term here, tries to grasp in their identity), at a depth that simply escapes the merely political or economic, which abstract from the total social fact.[8]

My argument weaves together Girard and Rieff. Girard hypothesizes a burgeoning "mimetic crisis" in the modern world, as equality breaks down boundaries and barriers erected to differentiate individuals, separate their desires, and keep them at some salutary distance so as to dampen their propensity for violent conflict. Rieff theorizes culture as *culture war*, sprouting from the implacable rivalry of the holy and the hedonistic under modern conditions. The "mimetic crisis" that unfolds in the profane dimension of the market feeds a larger collision between the profane and the sacred, as what Friedrich Hayek calls "catallaxy," the order of the market, encroaches on social order. The apocalyptic crisis of the modern world is not just the mimetic rivalries intensified by the emancipation of desire, as Girard tends to say, but the rivalry of the sacred and the profane as these assume political form.

Daniel Bell and Karl Polanyi, the social critic and the economic historian, afford us important clues to the apocalyptic teleology in question. Bell's notion of the "cultural contradictions of capitalism" suggests a moral schizophrenia of advanced liberal democracy. Such schizophrenia is not just a recent phenomenon, though; it divides the modern world from the beginning, into Left and Right, economics and politics, and the other divisions that constitute the human sciences, especially sociology and psychology. Bell's own criticism, partly sociological and partly moral, reflects the split personalities of modernity. Polanyi seeks to diagnose the political cataclysms in European history in the first half of the twentieth century through the antagonism that emerged in the century preceding World War I between laissez-faire capitalism and social order. Like the cultural schizophrenia of democracy described by Bell, what Polanyi describes is an insoluble political and economic crisis—a conflict between the political and the economic—brought on by the catallaxy of the free market and society's inevitable, but aggravating, defensive reaction. His diagnosis of past events, though, might in some way serve as a prognosis of our condition. With him I will conclude.

In making this argument I am neither defending nihilism nor attacking democracy, just describing the structure and teleology of the modern equation of equality and liberty from an anthropological point of view. Contrary to the Left, capitalism or the "free market" as we know it is not (for all its inequalities) the antithesis of democracy but its most potent form (on the level of culture). It is a veritable contagion of democratic desire, of appetites shaped by the anxieties of equality. The more its scandalous disparities grow, the greater the force of its democratic contagion and egalitarian appetite. As it awakens these desires, it also affords them an avenue by which to discharge themselves, to "satisfy" themselves after a fashion, in the production and possession of wealth, in the quest for status, in the satisfactions of self-image. This forestalls potential conflicts that might otherwise spin out of control, as long at least as it is prosperous. Contrary to the Right, though, capitalism and markets are a radical force of moral and cultural revolution. In fact they are the principal engine of the wholesale transformation in social and personal mores across the last century, especially in the relations between the sexes and within the sexes—the sexual revolution supposedly brought about by the counterculture of the sixties, the flashpoint of the "culture wars." With its double embrace of the free market and moral traditionalism, American conservatism is a Trojan horse in which cultural revolution is gift-wrapped in moral nostalgia—as if "free market principles" were like a return to the 1950s, the halcyon childhood of today's market, before we actually had a Fed chairman devoted to Ayn Rand. Or perhaps we should describe it as the wolf disguised as grandmother in the fairy tale. Just as the ideology of the Left is designed to disown the effects of democracy by blaming them on capitalist economics, the ideology of the Right is designed to disown the moral and cultural effects of capitalism, by blaming them on the political democracy of the Left. A final question, then, is how the internal division of democratic modernity into Left and Right in the first place and the consequent blind spot at the center of the vision of each facilitates the operation of the whole, though only within mortal limits.

Daniel Bell and Democratic Schizophrenia

In his 1976 classic of social and cultural criticism, Daniel Bell argued that twentieth-century American capitalism undermined its own generative ethic: "The breakup of the traditional bourgeois value system, in fact, was brought about by the bourgeois economic system—by the free market, to be precise. This is the source of the contradiction of capitalism in American life.["][9] "*The* contradiction of capitalism in American life"—that is a pretty bold claim. The phrase rings Marxian, but Bell rejects the materialist theory of a collision between relations of production and forces of production. Bell's thesis is the profound contradiction between the Protestant or Puritan ethic that generated modern capitalism (along the lines of Max Weber's famous analysis and that of R. H. Tawney) and the culture antithetical to it that capitalism itself generates.[10] Bourgeois economics subverts bourgeois values; the effects of the capitalist dynamo undo the virtues that created the dynamo. Like Penelope's web, all the self-discipline and productivity of the hard work of day are undone by the hedonism of night. Modern society thus succumbs to moral schizophrenia, warring personalities into which it is divided. Social order, roughly corresponding to the demands of everyday life in the family, at the workplace, in civil society, and in government, generates a "postmodern" culture antithetical to social order itself, even to any social order at all. Culture versus society, culture versus economics, culture versus politics—all are pairs of fraternal enemies. This schizoid effect is the effectual truth of a consumer's utopia created out of new kinds of debt. Expanded for the sake of personal consumption, "buying on the installment plan" is the real muse of postmodernism, a culture based on fantasy, desire, and the narcissistic cult of the "self."

Bell's picture of the ethical reversal that took place in the course of the twentieth century owes a great deal to Max Weber's classic account. Originating from Puritanism but emancipating itself from its theological roots, what Max Weber called "worldly asceticism" was the moral backbone of American wealth and power. This was the so-called Protestant work ethic in its most emphatic form, one driven by the need to accumulate wealth as evidence of one's self-discipline: not to assert personal autonomy, to be sure, but just the opposite, to show that one was an instrument of God. This was to be accomplished by the methodical subjection of the milieu to rational (or better, rationalizing) control and organization. Originally, Weber argued, the accumulative drive was motivated by the need for proof of one's own election, according to the Calvinist doctrine of predestination. Its psychic motive lay in the profound solitude of the Calvinist, cut off from the rest of the human race by the preordination of salvation and damnation. But it freed itself of theological dogma, taking on a life of its own, to become a psychological drive in the contest of social recognition in democratic capitalist society. That could be just as morally isolating as the theological dogma of election, though. While Bell doesn't say so, as modern equality forced human beings into greater *psychological* proximity by removing the traditional roles, "formalities" (Tocqueville), and hierarchies that separated (and protected) them, it also introduced the greatest *moral* distance between them, an abyss of alienation (think here of Kierkegaard). The Puritan devoted to proving himself God's instrument gave way to the "self-made" man who sought to indemnify himself against "the look" of "the others" (as Sartre might say) by showing that he was the author of himself.

What broke the backbone of Puritan asceticism, according to Bell, was that most ingenious of capitalist inventions, easy credit, or buying on the installment plan. This simple expansion of liberty and equality in the realm of buying amounted to a moral revolution transforming the whole society: "The Protestant ethic was undermined not by modernism but by capitalism itself. The greatest single engine in the destruction of the Protestant ethic was the invention of the installment, or instant credit. Previously one had to save in order to buy. But with credit cards one could indulge in instant gratification. The system was transformed by mass production and mass consumption, by the creation of new wants and new means of gratifying those wants."[11] This leads Bell to his problem, the cultural revolution of modernism that ensued from the "double-bind" of American capitalism:

> What this abandonment of Puritanism and the Protestant ethics does, of course, is to leave capitalism with no moral or transcendental ethic. It also emphasizes not only the disjunction between the norms of the culture and the norms of the social structure, but also an extraordinary contradiction within the social structure itself. On the one hand, the business corporation wants an individual to work hard, pursue a career, accept delayed gratification—to be, in the crude sense, an organization man. And yet, in its products and in its advertisements, the corporation promotes pleasure, instant joy, relaxing, and letting things go. One is to be "straight" by day and a "swinger" by night.[12]

This schizophrenic revolution thus split culture from social order and social order from itself by the "spread of installment buying, which, more than any other social device, broke down the old Protestant fear of debt."[13] It directly reversed the traditional moral order, in which debt had signified ties to the past or its burdens rather than the promise of a new and better present, predicated on the future. The other media and instruments of the cultural revolution of the last century—the silver screen, the automobile, cosmetics and celebrities, electronic communication and entertainment, and so on—would perhaps never have gotten off the ground to create popular culture as we know it today without the vast expansion of personal credit, now evidently the foundation of our economy and of our political system as well. "None of this would have been possible without that revolution in moral habit, the idea of installment selling."[14]

The crux of this contradiction, according to Bell, is the invention of installment buying and its kin, such as the credit card. If postmodern culture is predicated on fantasy, as Bell claims, its "objective" foundation is debt, especially that generated by a rapid expansion of personal credit extended for the sake of consumption, less and less collateralized. Such inventions as the credit card thus produced a moral revolution. Eviscerating the traditional fear of debt and the ethic of delayed gratification, they legitimized instant gratification, a sense of entitlement, and, one might add, a gambling attitude, living predicated on an imaginary future. Traditional common culture disintegrated into one increasingly devoted to self-affirmation, a cult of the "self," under the auspices of self-expression, sexual liberation, the psychology of self-esteem, and the like. Late modernism and postmodernism are the flip side of the advanced economics of modern debt, cultural siblings of the new order of finance.

Democracy and Desire

Tempting though Bell's picture is, it is limited. Bell sees the installment plan primarily in terms of hedonism, removing the delay in gratification, reversing the moral order of traditional consumption: "Earn first, then enjoy" gives way to "Buy now, pay later." But the system driven by the accumulation of personal debt has more far-reaching implications than just old-fashioned hedonism. The revolution in the attitude and instruments of debt was not just an economic one but a phenomenon of democracy. If it broke down the Protestant work ethic, it did so in the name of an even more fundamental value, that of "equality of conditions." To sustain this, it marked an evolution in a social imaginary ostensibly able to detach itself from reality almost completely.

Modern equality rests above all on the notion of "equality of conditions" (Tocqueville) or vocational choice—the notion that accidents of birth such as blood should not stand in the way of one's social ambitions or desires. At first applied to aristocratic rank or the lack of it, the story of the modern world has been its ever more consistent expansion, irresistibly it would seem, to race, gender, ethnicity, religion, sexual orientation, and so forth (not necessarily in that order). As Tocqueville observed, the principle of equality (demanded by justice) unfolds with an "awesome Providence." Modern equality is unlike the *isonomia* of the ancient polis, since it links equality to liberty, so that to be equal one also has to be free. Above all it applies to individuals in their personhood or "self," not just to groups of population (if to those at all). It is, at least in inspiration, an emancipation of the individual from whatever group he or she may belong to—his or her class, race, or sex, for instance. On the cultural level, this generates various "myths" or symbolic images of freedom (such as those imparted by works of art, novels, movies, philosophies, and—not least—advertisements) that are not just political, economic, or juridical (the standard fare of political philosophy) but "metaphysical" or "ontological" (in a sense broadly connected with the meaning associated with these terms by nineteenth- and twentieth-century thinkers, especially Continental thinkers). Freedom is not just a legal condition (for which we may reserve the term *liberty*) but an envisioned state of being, a mode of "authentic" existence— even an aura, if you will, a charisma, such as the divine gift of sex appeal. Or at least it is imagined to be, in the symbolic of popular culture. Equality does not just banish accidents of birth from the political and economic realms, as Tocqueville had mainly in mind. It also generates myths of its own, especially those of self-image.

Bell argues that capitalism undermined the Puritan ethic, but the Puritan ethic may well undermine itself, in two ways. First, the Calvinist ethos described by Max Weber (seeking signs of God's election in the rationalizing and productive discipline of the will) morphs into narcissism far more naturally than theology alone would lead one to expect. Calvinist guilt expressed in existential solitude (fueling the need for certainty of election so well described by Weber) already reflects a morally egalitarian world in which human beings see each other as models and rivals, a world in which the old spiritual bonds of society have largely lost their meaning. The Calvinist doctrine of the depravity of man, through the correlative doctrine of election, is the flip side of self-divinization. As Christopher Lasch argued, the narcissistic self is a mark not of existential fullness but of poverty; one seeks self-confirmation or even self-aggran-dizement out of an irrepressible sense of deficiency. The modern economy readily lends itself to this requirement and is enhanced by it.

The deification of the self in American culture is a logical outgrowth of its Puritan roots, even prior to the capitalist revolution. But further, though Weber concentrates on the need of the Puritan or capitalist for signs of election, whether this-worldly or otherworldly, he doesn't do much justice to the importance of what Calvin called the "reprobates" in this economy of salvation—or what in this context might be described as modern consumers not able to live within their means. Those who are not saved are those who do not save, and they are just as necessary in the scheme of things as those who do. Just as in theology they lend themselves to setting off the glory of God in the elect by their own profligacy, so in economics they lend themselves to the glory of the omniscient and omnipotent Market by showing its infallible effects. Though advertising and popular culture are designed to tempt them, if they fall they alone are responsible for it. For every successful entrepreneur, then, there must be a crowd of consumers willing to sacrifice their own health and well-being and that of their fami-lies for the utilitarian good the economy as a whole. The Calvinistic capitalist does not go into incurable debt because so many others do. The distinction of the industrious and frugal capitalist requires not just the indiscipline of others but the cultivation of their indiscipline. They must fall so that he can display his merit.

What Bell's account leaves out is the pressure of equality in generating the cultural revolution of capitalism. The nihilism of popular culture is not just a hedonistic revolt against traditional constraints or an indulgence of infantile narcissism, as so many critics have seen it.[15] More interestingly, it is a consequence of—that is, a reaction to— the *loss* of traditional constraints, the collapse of the older order. Nihilism does not so much cause that collapse as express a defensive reaction against it. Equality places demands on the individual to prove himself not just to his contemporaries in a (supposedly) disenchanted world but also under the gaze of a modern public, all the more intense for being anonymous and indefinable. The struggle for signs of election, which divides society into "producers" and "consumers," is a reflection of this pressure. The difference between them, though, is bound to blur. As the quest for signs of election generates an economy, that economy liberates those signs from the conditions of its emergence. Bred in the marketplace, postmodern culture is devoted to fantasy (which is not to say it doesn't have its moments of reality). But above all, that is the fantasy of divine election, cast in aesthetic (quasi-literary) rather than religious terms. Consumerism makes the signs of election available to anyone.

This is the site of a revolution, the emancipation of desire, the destruction of traditional mores, most significantly registered in the transformation of relations between the sexes and within the sexes. The cultural revolution of modernity is primarily a moral and cultural, not a political or economic, revolution. It pertains to private life primarily, not the political or economic. The establishment of liberal political and economic institutions is not the summit of its achievement but the precondition and instrument of its complete unfolding. The catalyst of this revolution is the market, which generates a new kind of public and popular culture as it evolves in the twentieth century, through mass media, technology, and mass production. In this new public, the old "vertical" authorities of church and state disappear, and the traditional division of public and private and the hierarchical relation between them is effaced or inverted. In the new public, the individual and his or her affairs become the dominating theme, even in politics. This does not just dissolve the old, authoritarian notion of the public (rooted in religious and political sovereignty); it also radically transforms the private itself, traditionally associated not with the detached individual but with the family. It presupposes an anonymous and decentralized public, in contrast to the *authoritatively* structured *res publica* of the premodern world, presided over by throne and altar. It also assumes an *aesthetic*—rather than religious—order of society, what came to be called "culture" in a relatively recent sense (since the Enlightenment). A new kind of social phenomenon utterly unprecedented in history, modern publicity, creates a virtual reality, an aesthetic universe of the commodified imagination, of material yet disembodied signs and images that freely circulate and are increasing impossible to distinguish from the economy itself. These images appear to be the more individualized the more social they are. This new social "order" (if it can be called that) is predicated not just on individual fantasy but equally on the fantasy of the individual.

Only within this context can consumerist dreams flourish. This is a universe of ideas, signs, and "representations" freely circulating in the ether of the economy as objects of individual possession and consumption. Signs and ideas in an aesthetic (rather than religious) sense are the lingua franca of modern society. Material yet disembodied, these "representations," as structuralists and postmodernists sometimes call them, are detached from traditional religious and political institutions and customary rituals, simply existing on their own. They bear social myths, but mostly not communal ones. They are symbols and images with "lives and loves," as W. J. T. Mitchell adroitly puts it, of their own.[16] As images they do not refer, like holy icons or Renaissance masterpieces, to a transcendent or natural reality but are themselves realities, simply as images. Our democratic "selves" are played out through the "lives" of such aesthetic things.

The expansion and legitimization of debt and its instruments, as Bell's own account of postmodern expressivism suggests, corresponds to the rise of the "self" and its "narratives." For that mythic invention of modern culture, the "self," is constituted by the "stories" in which it casts itself, typically as the main hero if also as a victim, both sacrifice and savior. It is essentially a form of advertising. And just like advertising, its theological underpinnings, its intimations of immortality, are unmistakable. Like the Puritan ethic of Weber, its organizing genius is a charisma of divine election. It is not just that the self is self-advertising or self-advertisement. The "self" itself is a kind of credit card; don't leave home without it.

The twentieth-century reinvention of debt interpolates between reality and life an imaginary realm, a seemingly interminable deferral of reality. What philosophers sometimes call the "social imaginary" here acquires its fullest meaning, a fantasy world of supposedly self-casting individuals predicated on mutually shared illusions. Originally, the social contract of classical liberalism was conceived to be a fiction, albeit a kind of legally or politically necessary one. Here, though, fiction itself, calculated illusion, is the substance of the social contract, a reciprocal consent to share mutual fantasies, to act out roles in each other's dreams, to keep shared secrets. It creates the conditions for the democratization of what Alexander Nehamas found in Friedrich Nietzsche, "life as literature."[17] That, at least, is the promise of life above the tree line, an invitation not everyone is obliged to accept. The credit card makes "existence as an aesthetic phenomenon" (Nietzsche) possible for everyone, possible as a world, if at a certain cost. It is the democratization of Nietzsche, the realization of democratic man already at the core of the Nietzschean enterprise.

The rise of equality dismantles traditional forms that mediate human relations, especially those based on religion, tradition, hierarchy, and the like. The more consistently these relations are structured by equality, the more interceding elements that

Tocqueville called "formalities" are reduced or removed. Human relations in their immediacy, though, are inherently self-subverting and conflicted. Psychological proximity tends to destabilize them, rendering them uncertain and volatile in the absence of clear roles.[18] Though often arbitrary if not unjust, conventions of manners and mores (such as sex roles) may all the more effectively give a grammar and syntax to human interactions. Girard explains this volatility through "mimetism," the crystallization of the desires of individuals through reciprocal imitation or "mimesis" (an unconscious reflex) and the rivalries (as well as comities) that it induces. "External mediation," in which individuals emulate models not directly present to them or on the same level, gives way to "internal mediation," in which individuals directly take each other as models—and so as obstacles and rivals too, of a particularly intense sort. The tendency of equality is to collapse differences and so to heighten the antagonisms of human relations. As it levels, it intensifies the need to differentiate oneself, to set oneself apart. It is within this context of "indifferentiation" (a notion that may be partly traced to Durkheim) that capitalism plays a role in mediating—that is, deferring and delaying, not removing—the psychological contradictions of democracy. What equality diminishes in the way of psychic difference, the aesthetic animism of consumerism with its reassuring things and signs can to some extent restore (or seem to). Within this spiritual economy, it is easy to see a propitious role for an expansive notion of debt as a "material" form or basis of the temporization so essential to social existence. For debt funds a virtual reality in which individuals can maintain a self-image in relative peace and insularity.

The great paradox of the modern world is that the rise of equality actually aggravates the violence of human relations, physical or psychological, political or personal. Girard has shown with devastating clarity just how this is in his classic analysis of the modern novel.[19] In the aftermath of the French Revolution, but anticipating the subsequent upheavals not just of the July Revolution of 1830 but of European history *tout court* down to 1945 or even 1991, the endlessly vexed character Julien Sorel (of Stendhal's *The Red and the Black*) acts out the psychological toils of equality, in a context in which impassable social barriers have been, not liquidated by the French Revolution, but to the contrary petrified. Aggravated by a sense of egalitarian entitlement culturally crystallized in the legend of Napoleon—the original self-made man, a man from nowhere who became lord of the world on the basis of his own will—but scandalized by the class obstacles of the time, Sorel, with his insatiable jealousy, envy, and rage at real or imagined humiliations (in a social context that does not permit them a serviceable catharsis), portends the eventual explosions that destroyed Europe in the twentieth century, the petty bourgeois resentments mobilized in the catastrophic collisions of the Left and the Right.

But in 1830 in France, laissez-faire capitalism had not yet created a social alternative. Using Flaubert's novel *Madame Bovary* (a novel Girard also treats), Girard's former student and anthropological theorist Eric Gans shows how the beginnings of consumerism in the Second Empire, the setting of Emma's tragedy, hold open the possibility of some sort of solution to the contradictions of Julien's world a generation earlier.[20] The only thing that can really overcome the Old Regime and satisfy the cravings of democratic desire is the circulation of commodities. It is not an ideal solution, but it is better than none at all. And however tragic Emma may be, it seems inhuman to deny her "right" to desire; it is her only defense, even if in her case it is fatal. Though Gans is far too optimistic (in my view) about the finality of this solution, he rightly sees in the early consumerism emerging toward the end of the nineteenth century the properly modern form of democracy, realized in America before it could be established politically in Europe. This is not just an economic event but a cultural one, inasmuch as culture offers symbols to mediate human relations, interpolating signs and images and their exchange into relations of individuals, but also substituting them for them.[21]

Democratic desire by its very nature is conflict driven. It is by nature bound up with scandal; desire is awakened by obstacles; it is always in the end the desire of *someone else*—someone imagined to be or actually standing in the way of one's own desire. Thus Julien's fascination with those whom he pretends to despise, his social betters. His eternally wounded pride perpetually binds him to them as he seeks to trump them in virtually every relationship in which he engages. This propensity for rivalry, though, conceals (from him if not from us) the extent to which he depends on them, taking them secretly as his models. His animosity toward his social rivals dissembles his abject envy of them. His jealousy hides from him how he sees himself through their eyes. In Julien's world, the psychological proximity of human beings, coupled with their moral distance or isolation (what other thinkers might call their "alienation"), predisposes him to become pathologically obsessed and fascinated with others. In a world in which equality has vastly diminished if not removed the old orthodoxies of tradition and religion, without necessarily transforming the outer social environment (of ossified classes), "men become gods to each other," as Girard puts it—would-be gods who, emulating each other's divinity, are openly or secretly in constant warfare with each other. This "underground psychology," whose moral climax was described for Girard by Dostoyevsky, is the cultural precondition for the disasters of the twentieth century—the twin totalitarianisms and two world wars. Europe was not able to solve this hidden schizophrenia in its version of the modern world, split by implacable rivalry between the new and old regimes.

Within this context, the rise of economics and aesthetics and their fusion in popular culture and consumerism play their role. "Aesthetics" is essentially a modern invention, a reflex of the rise of a universe that is itself composed of aesthetic things, images and signs, a somewhat organized chaos of autonomous "representations" that do not actually represent anything other than themselves. Aesthetics in this sense is the flip side of economics. A central trait of the revolution of the twentieth century, in this connection, is the (ostensible) privatization of the imagination, its isolation from what Emile Durkheim called the *conscience collective,* the communal representation of a social whole active in the mind of the individual member. That is, the individual appears as a psychic being in contrast to the social whole to which he belongs.[22] The modern public, technology, and commodities make possible an individual's acquisition of his "own" representations or ideas, as if the imagination were primarily a private, personal, interior phenomenon, an inner world an individual inhabited by himself, a realm of freedom in which an individual could be the genius of his own "story." This conceit of the "self" as a "narrative" structure is the reflex of a commodity culture and of advertising ("See yourself in this picture"). Commodities in the consumerist sense are especially things that (seem to) enable one to imagine oneself, to "create" one's own virtual reality, or to have a self-image at all.[23]

Ironically, though, as imagination becomes ostensibly individualized and interiorized with the fragmenting of the body politic into consumers, a new kind of "mechanical solidarity" emerges in effect, that of the market itself, and the popular culture it generates. Originally, Durkheim contrasted the "mechanical" solidarity of primitive and archaic societies to the "organic" solidarity of more complex societies, especially those of the modern world. In archaic societies, he claimed, individuals did not see themselves as radically different from each other, did not see themselves and each other as independent "individuals." In the "organic" solidarity of modern society, a complex articulation of individual functions occurs in which the unity and order of the social whole disappears from view, exposing the individual to the "anomie" of not knowing what his (social) purpose or teleology is. In Durkheim's view, this elicited the "infinity" of desire, the inability of human eros (in a broadly Platonic sense) to discover a satisfying, because limiting and definitive, object. The complexity of modern society is disorienting and vertiginous, since it masks any manifest order that might give direction to the individual. The pathologies of romantic desire, such as motivate the statistical phenomena Durkheim studies (divorce, suicide, murder, addiction) or such as Girard studies in literature, are the "positive" phenomena of "anomie."

Individualism, though, gives rise to a new "mechanism," as René Girard calls it, of those who imagine themselves to be "free and equal," who believe that they are the creators of their "selves," the eros or ambition that defines them. It is a community of those who believe themselves to have nothing in common except their difference—a community in which everyone is "unique." A basic paradox of modern equality is that it compels individuals to establish and display their difference from each other, their "individuality" (in order to sustain their self-esteem, as we would say today), just as it becomes harder and harder actually to show any such difference. The differences themselves are effaced by the very economic means by which individuals seek to display them. In the fashions and myths of popular culture, the market creates a perverse new kind of solidarity in the seemingly personal but actually mechanical identity of the individual who imagines himself the free author of himself.

Most scandalous about popular culture is not just its nihilism but the productivity of nihilism, its vital contribution of our prosperity. It is key to the economic metabolism. Democracy amplifies the violent passions, envy, jealousy, resentment, rage, social passions that all other forms of order sought to contain and channel by means of rank or hierarchy. It not only unleashes them; it legitimizes them in what might be called a culture of endless scandal, provocation, and insulted pride. Given that these are profoundly destabilizing if not destructive outright, equality can emancipate them only because it turns them at the same time into engines of prosperity. And it does this by means of the market. Ingeniously, capitalism transmutes what all prior orders rightly regarded as the greatest dangers to social well-being into the creative dynamo of the wealth of nations. Wealth and its inequalities cathartically discharge the negativity of social collisions, humiliations, and resentments of democratic men and women that might otherwise destroy society. Far from being inconsistent with it, market "order" generates a wholly new kind of inequality, one generated by the frictions of equality itself. Founded on fungible wealth rather than accidents of birth, this kind of inequality is itself a function of equality. After all, the need for inequality—to prove that one is different—is the most democratic of desires.

But the productivity of nihilism is not just that popular culture is an exportable commodity that makes us rich and so affords us some compensation for the deficiencies of bourgeois existence. Democracy's nihilistic conceits are crucial to its spiritual economy, too. Salvific myths of consumerism mediate its psychological exigencies, but this is possible only by means of aesthetics, in the virtual world of popular culture, where, to speak with the postmodernists, reality is image, a sign that signifies itself. The material economy of democracy rests on this spiritual one, at least when it reaches a certain age. In the virtual reality of popular culture, democracy finds the imaginary space to replace the psychic distance between individuals lost with the collapse of traditional rank order. This compensates for the mortifications of modern life, the slings and arrows of outrageous fortune and the proud man's contumely, by enabling individuals to entertain for themselves some degree of an imaginary reality, a fantasy self-image. If democracy emancipates desire, it ostensibly requires an individualization of the imagination, so as to guarantee (apparently) a future to democratic dreaming. It needs an aesthetic of illusion, of open horizons, a world without limits, and that is what consumerism and popular culture deliver, technology and media. As geographical spaces close off, mental and technological spaces open up. The objectified image is not meant to satisfy; it is meant to enable us to indulge our imagination, for democratic men and women are essentially creatures of self-image. It enables us to live in the ambience of desire. Democratic man must above all be able to desire. Without expansive personal debt, however, this illusion of limitlessness would be difficult to maintain.

Karl Polanyi and the Collision of Sacred and Profane

The cultural revolution of democracy cannot but weaken social bonds, but it doesn't follow that social order or its sacred reflexes simply evaporate. The economic historian Karl Polanyi anticipates this kind of social crisis, on the economic and political level, rather than the cultural or moral one that we have been pursuing here. Still, his account of the "political and economic origins of our times" provides a template for the enmity of the sacred and the profane that is the inevitable outcome of market society.[24]

In his usage, a "market society" is one in which the market in its necessarily illusory manner embraces society as a whole, dissolving all social relations into itself. It is well instanced by Friedrich Hayek's notion of "catallaxy," or "market order."[25] The freedom of the market is not just the notion that "a" market should be "free" to follow its own "internal" logic without the distorting interference of the state. Rather, as the two Viennese-born economic thinkers (explicitly and implicitly, respectively) suggest, it is the right of markets to extend over, dominate, and absorb *every* aspect of human life and communal order. Society, the common good, communal life, have no rights against a "free" market. Family, institutions of civil society, government, even religion must bow to it. It is the market that has absolute rights against individuals and their forms of community.

There is no doubt that modern life and its liberties would not be possible without markets or capitalism. Polanyi's account, however, poses a problem to which there is evidently no solution. The market does not solve the problem of modern society, as free-market ideologues believe, but expresses it in its most acute form. Marxists in reverse, they are like their opposite numbers the ideologues of "diahistomat," who embraced the equally absurd notion that a state can create society out of itself. Each of these apparent antipodes buys a fundamental illusion of modern ideology, the idea that society is exhaustively divided into "economics" and "politics"—markets and legal institutions—rather than constituting a cultural dynamic of human relations that exceeds either the rule of things or the rule of men. Social order, like society itself, precedes and underwrites whatever political and economic order one has; it is not created out of them but is the condition of their existence. Diahistomat and Ayn Rand are each ideologies of radical freedom, alternately applied to the two sides of the political economy of the modern world, but with comparable results, the destruction of social order. Whether markets can actually constitute society without destroying society itself—that is, whether "market society" is not actually an illusion, a self-destroying contradiction—is the question.

In making his analysis, Polanyi set out to explain the self-destruction of Europe between 1914 and the end of Word War II (his book was published in 1944), following the most prosperous and peaceful century of European history—the triumph of laissez-faire capitalism—between the fall of Napoleon and the start of World War I. In Polanyi's view, the free market cannot but destroy society the more successful and prosperous it is. In so doing, it drives society and government into a defensive reaction by its attempt to commodify what can never be just another commodity, namely nature, humanity, and the medium of exchange itself, money. "Land, labor, and money" are "fictitious commodities," by which Polanyi meant they naturally resist being reduced to commodities by a spontaneous reflex grounded in life itself, social and natural. This defensive reaction typically makes the situation worse, however, especially when it takes strongly statist forms, crippling the market even further in blind response to catastrophic economic crisis. There is no simplistic resort to socialism as if that had all the answers, nor does Polanyi reject the Hayekian description of the market as a price-determining mechanism that facilitates productive organization most efficiently. What he does, in effect, is point to a dilemma that is characteristically modern, a constitutive collision between market and society, market and communal institutions. This fatal impasse laid the groundwork for political apocalypse, the rise of the totalitarian twins and the world wars, by which Europe nearly committed suicide in the first half of the twentieth century. The modern world could not make its peace with the market then any more than it has made it now. It cannot live without a free-ranging market but doesn't know how to live with it, either, without attacking its own social and natural conditions. This volatile tension, not just between economics and politics (the conventional view) but between either or both of these and society itself (social, cultural, and we may add, natural order), is the unstable core of modernity. Social order can never be reduced to economics, politics, or their combination. It can never be replaced by the catallactic "spontaneity" of the market, however indispensable the latter may be. The Left has some recognition of the dilemma posed by the market to society but misguidedly reacts (usually by means of a bull-in-a-china-shop use of the state) in such a way as to hamstring the only mechanism that can generate prosperity and so recover from economic crisis. The state can be as much a threat to social order as the economy is. The Right understands this well enough but is utterly incapable of seeing the danger of the market, at least in this country. It still blames "government" as if that were the omnipresent source of evil in modern life, even in the midst of market catastrophe. The Left invented modern "ideology," but the Right, though beating the Left at its own game, becomes its abject slave.

Daniel Bell's theme or variations on it (the moral self-subversion of democratic capitalism) have been echoed by a number of other postwar cultural critics before and since him, most of them, like him, culturally if not politically conservative—thus, for example, Philip Rieff, Christopher Lasch, Leszek Kolakowski, and, more recently, Andrew Bacevich. Unlike today's ideological (or "movement") "conservatives," their moral and cultural conservatism precludes them from being politically or economically "conservative" in the partisan sense. Judged by contemporary usage, these writers would have to be called "socialistic" (though they certainly don't reject market economics or private property) inasmuch as they recognize in capitalism—not just intellectual modernism or the 1960s counterculture—a primary if not the primary drive of the moral transmogrification of the twentieth century. But this shatters the ideological structure of modern politics even as it concedes its inevitability.

Political ideology is structured by the division into Left and Right, which reflect the constitutive drives of democratic modernity, but in such a way as to mask their origin, their common root, and their mutual complicity. The war of the wings reflects, but also conceals and distorts, another, more fundamental, "anthropological" one, that between the sacred and the profane. In previous social orders, the profane is embedded within a sacred order—much as, in Louis Dumont's account, Eve is embedded within Adam, who is simultaneously distinct from Eve, equal to Eve, and encompassing of Eve. "Man" is both the whole and a part within the whole. This "logical scandal," as Dumont calls it, is the basic relation of "hierarchy," which fundamentally is a relation not of power but of order. The sacred is not just different from the profane, it is the *difference* of the sacred and the profane itself, in all its irreducibility. In the modern order, this "analogical" relation of parts to the whole is reversed, as the profane seeks to encompass the sacred in political economy—for example, by the privatization of conscience. This creates the opposite of an analogical relation, though, a "dialectical" one—not just a difference but an antithesis—in which the sacred and the profane cannot but become rivals, combatants who can't agree about their proper order and are endlessly contesting their rights. For however equally necessary they may be, they can never simply be equal. The modern gambit of founding social order on economics can only generate antagonism between society and economy. This antithesis is the common element in each of the wings, yet their opposition dissembles it, as if the one or the other held the secret to social peace and prosperity.

The opposition of the wings involves another constitutive distinction, between economics and politics, which throws a shadow in the middle of the field of political vision. This makes possible the blind spot of modern ideology, the identity of capitalism and democracy. The distinction between economics and politics, Polanyi argues, already presupposes "market society" or the autonomy of the economic. Within the framework of this distinction, conventional political philosophies—conservatism, liberalism, social democracy, even socialism and fascism—appear plausible. However sophisticated these alternatives may be in the hands of their proponents, they are "ideologies," since they assume blindness to the conditions of their own existence. In reality, they are not "alternatives" at all, either because, like liberalism or conservatism, they are (practically) only relative ways of accenting policy or because, like fascism or communism, they would lead to outright destruction of social order. Conservatism and liberalism both pretend to stand on their own and so to displace their opposite number, but in reality they make sense only because they form a relative pair that can never be dissolved without catastrophe. This pairing makes them practical, though only within limits, since neither is an "absolute." The paradox is that this pairing is possible only because they deny and exclude each other—they pretend to be absolutes, not relatives. Dividing economics and politics, one creates the impression of an ordered division, a complementary opposition, where the only remaining question is how, exactly, to allocate the prerogatives of each, how to limit and harmonize them. How they should be parsed, however, is a completely pragmatic issue that cannot be decided in definitive terms. The alternatives of liberal versus social democracy, for example, are far less a matter of "principle" than of culture and history and exigency.

All the same, the dialectical antagonism of Left and Right structures modern political systems. Roughly, these were in (European) origin parties of modern secularity and of the archaic—the parties of Enlightenment versus religion, reform versus tradition, equality versus privilege, rights versus duty, economic interest versus patriotism, universal justice versus sacred nation, and humanity versus national particularity. One side sees the whole as a class antagonism in which a particular "victim" class represents universal humanity. The other sees itself as representing the whole in the face of outsiders and enemies. Disaster strikes when one side thinks it alone ought to be the whole, that is, when it loses its allegiance to the constitution, the social whole represented through its political institutions. This happened in the 1930s and earlier in 1917. The breakdown of European political systems between the wars and the triumph of profoundly tyrannical parties signifies an inability of society to maintain the irritable balance of sacred and profane—or better, a fragile modus vivendi between drives pitted directly against each other. The battle between political parties became a "culture war" in which the stakes were all or nothing. When cultural war directly becomes a political battle, the political system is destroyed, even as politicization of culture rots the remnants of cultural order. The proper aim of modern politics, as the French political sociologist and critic of ideology Raymond Aron best understood, is to prevent modernity from annihilating itself—that is, to prevent the two sides from thinking they can get by without the other. It is to avoid the revolutionary temptation.

The critique of nihilism is the mask behind which the total complicity of the Left and the Right, joined at the hip, deceives itself about itself. The more the cultural revolution of market equality aggravates the social bond, the more it compels the wings to dissociate, blame each other, and displace each other definitively within the political economy. The more compromised they are, the more must they deny it. Neither of the "wings" can come to terms with the quandary that is democracy. Both are incoherent, simultaneously demanding the imposition of limits while advocating their denial. The Left wants to expand equality yet contract capitalism; it wants open horizons yet no impact on the environment. The Right wants unfettered capitalism yet traditional morality; the divorce rates and sex scandals of conservative evangelicals, though, give this the lie. The Left cannot acknowledge that the market is equality in motion, the most potent form of it ever, while the Right refuses to admit just how revolutionary it is, just because it is the truest form of democracy. The Left wants equality but not the market, the Right wants the free market but not the revolution it inevitably generates. The ideologies cannot see the whole because they are always trying to slice it in half, the better to disown what one does not like and to render invisible the connection of the two sides, their mutual complicity. All the same, nihilism is one of the secrets of democracy's astonishing success—though scarcely proof of its immortality. Our terrifying dilemma is that the abolition of nihilism would be tantamount to the end of democracy itself.

The problem of this essay could be described as a synthesis of Polanyi and Bell on the plane of culture and social order, by means of Rieff and Girard. "Equality of conditions"—the demand that accidents of birth, such as rank, race, ethnicity, sex, orientation, may not be permitted to determine one's social role a priori—is a demand of justice. But the less discerning advocates of equality fail to understand that justice is not a social bond and does not make social life or, for that matter, integral community. Nor does justice render the conflicts of personality easier or smoother (consider, for example, the novels of Dostoyevsky). Equality may be morally necessary, but it is not a solution to anything—on the contrary, it is on the plane of equality that the human problem first becomes fully transparent, where human beings confront each other without any excuses. According to Girard, human order cannot sustain itself without violence, without innocent victims to fuel its moral economy. An ineliminable component of arbitrariness is required to leaven or lubricate its justice. Human beings cannot deny or overcome violence; they can only channel and differentiate it into good versus bad, licit versus illicit violence. That is what is called religion, law, morality, and the like. But if that is so, then equality, especially the modern sort based on liberty or the market, either must be the enemy of *human* order in the name of justice, like an avenging angel of the Lord, or must be a supreme cataclysm of violence, the destruction of all justice, as a world driven by endless conflicts that can only intensify in the long run—the war of all against all. Either way, the result is the same. The problem with egalitarianism is not that it is morally wrong (at least short of Leninism) but that it is philosophically obtuse, hopelessly imperceptive to the apocalyptic implications of its own relentless teleology.

Notes

1. Karl Marx and Friedrich Engels, *The Communist Manifesto*, trans. Samuel Moore, reprinted in Robert C. Tucker, ed., *The Marx-Engels Reader*, 2nd ed. (New York: Norton, 1978), 476. A commentary on the ambiguous dynamisn of modernity in this passage may be found in Marshall Berman, *All That Is Solid Melts into Air: The Experience of Modernity* (New York: Penguin Books, 1988), ch. 2.

2. The philosophy of Sartre probes this democratic sensibility, the experience of nothingness of the self in the face of the other.

3. Eric Gans, like other neoconservative or neoliberal writers, links capitalism, markets, and democracy, and also recognizes the "deferential" role it plays. My view here, though, is not finally a neoconservative one. Gans's deeply perceptive and original view nevertheless does not do justice to the apocalyptic implications of democracy thus understood. Eric Lawrence Gans, *Signs of Paradox: Irony, Resentment, and Other Mimetic Structures* (Stanford, Calif.: Stanford University Press, 1997).

4. Emile Durkheim and Karen E. Fields, *The Elementary Forms of Religious Life* (New York: Free Press, 1995).

5. Philip Rieff, *Freud, the Mind of the Moralist*, 3rd ed. (Chicago: University of Chicago Press, 1979); Philip Rieff, *The Triumph of the Therapeutic: Uses of Faith after Freud*, 40th anniversary

ed. (Wilmington, Del.: ISI Books, 2006). These books were originally published in 1959 and 1966, respectively.

6. See especially Philip Rieff and Kenneth S. Piver, *My Life among the Deathworks: Illustrations of the Aesthetics of Authority*, Sacred Order/Social Order 1 (Charlottesville: University of Virginia Press, 2006); Philip Rieff, *Charisma: The Gift of Grace, and How It Has Been Taken Away from Us* (New York: Pantheon Books, 2007).

7. Pierre Manent, *Tocqueville and the Nature of Democracy* (Lanham, Md.: Rowman and Little-field, 1996).

8. As Marcel Mauss calls the structure of reciprocity that constitutes a social order. Marcel Mauss, *The Gift: Forms and Functions of Exchange in Archaic Societies* (Glencoe, Ill.: Free Press, 1954), 78.

9. Daniel Bell, *The Cultural Contradictions of Capitalism*, 20th anniversary ed. (New York: Basic Books, 1996), 55.

10. Max Weber, *The Protestant Ethic and the Spirit of Capitalism*, Routledge Classics (London: Routledge, 2001); R. H. Tawney, *Religion and the Rise of Capitalism* (New Brunswick, N.J.: Transaction Publishers, 1998).

11. Bell, *Cultural Contradictions of Capitalism*, 21.

12. Ibid, 71–72.

13. Ibid., 66.

14. Ibid, 69.

15. Such as Philip Rieff or Christopher Lasch.

16. W. J. T. Mitchell, *What Do Pictures Want? The Lives and Loves of Images* (Chicago: University of Chicago Press, 2005).

17. Alexander Nehamas, *Nietzsche, Life as Literature* (Cambridge, Mass.: Harvard University Press, 1985).

18. Think of Richard Sennett's critique of the so-called "culture of intimacy" that evolved in the nineteenth century. Richard Sennett, *The Fall of Public Man* (New York: W. W. Norton, 1996).

19. René Girard, *Deceit, Desire, and the Novel; Self and Other in Literary Structure* (Baltimore: Johns Hopkins Press, 1965).

20. Eric Lawrence Gans, *Madame Bovary: The End of Romance* (Boston: Twayne, 1989).

21. Marx's oft-cited criticism of the "fetishism of commodities" fails to do justice to the fact that human relations *require* the mediation of things to be *human* at all. The economic romanticist conjures up a world of "individuals as such" (as he puts it in *The German Ideology*), where individuals relate to each other directly and immediately, without the interpolation of class distinctions and other social "fetishes." It is precisely this sort of direct relation, though, that renders social relations volatile and unstable.

22. Here again one might think of Kierkegaard's notion of subjectivity as the classic instance, though it begins earlier with the "faculty psychology" of the eighteenth-century thinkers and then the Romantics.

23. This is supported by the history of literature, in which the rise of "self-image" corresponds to the rise of the novel and of readily available, easily readable books, as studies like those of Gans and Girard show. The greatest modern novels expose the extent to which the novel itself is the key to modern self-image, according to Girard. To which Gans replies, yes—but that is the great achievement of economic aesthetics. In Emma Bovary's case it may not end well. But the democratic self may not have any other alternatives.

24. Karl Polanyi, *The Great Transformation: The Political and Economic Origins of Our Time*, 2nd ed. (Boston: Beacon Press, 2001).

25. Friedrich A. Hayek, *Law, Legislation, and Liberty*, vol. 2, *The Mirage of Social Justice* (Chicago: University of Chicago Press, 1976).

7 Is Debt the New Karma?

Why America Finally Fell Apart

Morris Berman

THE AMERICAN WAY of Life—which can be basically characterized as the union of technological innovation and economic expansion—has been mythologized or romanticized in various ways, and one of these is in terms of the story of Prometheus, a god of great energy who stole fire from Zeus and passed it on to mankind. It is a powerful image, and one that feeds the notion of American exceptionalism. What Americans tend to forget, however, is that there was a debt involved in this transaction. For Zeus was angry at Prometheus and had him chained to a rock, where an eagle or a vulture would come every day and eat out his liver. Since Prometheus was a god, the liver would regrow during the night, only to be devoured again the next day. Unfortunately for the United States, and contrary to popular belief, the country is not divine, and so its liver is now being devoured without possibility of regeneration. We can thus summarize the story as follows: first hubris, then nemesis—a fair portrait of the rise and fall of the American empire. Hubris incurs the debt; nemesis is the collection agency that comes to get the money back. A second allegory of the American Way of Life is the story of Dr. Faustus, who made a pact with the devil. "A Faustian bargain," writes the Canadian author Margaret Atwood in her book *Payback,* "is one in which you exchange your soul or something equally vital for a lot of glitzy but ultimately worthless short-term junk."[1] Your soul, in other words, is the debt that has to be paid at the end of the day.

In effect, the American Way of Life has been a Faustian bargain, and this is true both domestically and in the arena of US foreign policy. Alistair Cooke, who used to host a *Letter from America* program on the BBC every week, once said that the essential idea of America was to regard as necessities those things that the rest of the world regarded as luxuries. This attitude manifests itself in the fact that although the United States comprises less than 5 percent of the world's population, it consumes 25 percent of its energy—a situation that was condemned by only one American president, Jimmy Carter, and Americans did not take kindly to him as a result. The dark or debt side of the notion that life is about unlimited material goods shows up in the data on bankruptcy: whereas 8,600 Americans filed for bankruptcy in 1946, more than 2,000,000 did in 2005. Put another way, in 1946 one in 17,000 Americans declared bankruptcy; in 2005, one in 150 did.[2] By 2006, the total public debt stood at $9 trillion, or 70 percent of the GDP, and personal bankruptcy filings for 2007 increased 40 percent over the figure for 2006. Journalist Chris Hedges reports that as of 2009, American consumers were $14 trillion in debt. As for the activity of the US government in this arena, Hedges notes that the Obama administration "has spent, lent or guaranteed $12.8 trillion in taxpayer dollars to Wall Street and insolvent banks in a doomed effort to reinflate the bubble economy, a tactic that at best forestalls catastrophe and will leave us broke in a time of profound crisis. [In addition, the Obama administration] has allocated nearly $1 trillion in defense-related spending and the continuation of our doomed imperial projects in Iraq, where military planners now estimate that 70,000 troops will remain for the next 15 to 20 years."[3] In fact, the bailout did not stay at $12.8 trillion for very long; it soon turned into $13.3 trillion, then $17.5 trillion, and, at one point, $19 trillion. Meanwhile, we are expanding the war in Afghanistan, a land that has traditionally been called "the graveyard of empires." But "America's most dangerous enemies," writes Hedges, "are not Islamic radicals but those who sold us the perverted ideology of free-market capitalism and globalization. They have dynamited the foundations of our society."[4]

The best example of these domestic radicals is the Wall Street firm of Goldman Sachs (GS), the world's most powerful global bank. In a 2009 article in *Rolling Stone*, journalist Matt Taibbi documents how GS played a key role in the crash of 2008 and how it has been doing this repeatedly since the crash of 1929.[5] Their formula, he says, is to position themselves in the middle of a speculative bubble and sell investments they know to be worthless. They then make huge amounts of money, and when the bubble bursts they reposition themselves to begin the process all over again in a different sector of the economy. In the case of the housing crisis, GS created financial vehicles to package bad mortgages and sell them to insurance companies and pension funds, the failure of which wiped out the savings of millions of older citizens. This created a "mass market for toxic debt." GS hid these in collateralized debt obligations (CDOs), which turned junk-rated mortgages into AAA-rated investments. They then convinced companies such as AIG to provide insurance (known as credit default swaps) for the CDOs, by means of which they were actually betting that home owners would default. Meanwhile, the government, which at any time is typically staffed with Goldmanites or ex-Goldmanites, was persuaded to change the rules of the banking game to make all of these grossly unethical transactions technically legal. Nomi Prins, a former managing director of GS, characterizes this incestuous relationship as "Government Sachs"; Taibbi notes that GS contributed nearly $1 million to the Obama election campaign.[6]

In the case of the subsequent bailout, says Taibbi, former GS CEO Henry Paulson (G. W. Bush's last Treasury secretary) took trillions of dollars and funneled them into the pockets of his friends on Wall Street. So Robert Rubin (at GS for twenty-six years and Clinton's former Treasury secretary) moved to Citigroup, which then received $300 billion from Paulson; John Thain, who moved to Merrill Lynch, also got a multi-billion-dollar handout; and AIG received $85 billion, which enabled it to repay the $13 billion it owed GS. "Gangster elite" is the appropriate phrase for these people, I would think, although Taibbi himself favors the phrase "vampire squid." He points out that after playing a key role in four historical bubble catastrophes, helping $5 trillion disappear from the NASDAQ, and pawning off thousands of toxic mortgages on pensioners and American cities, GS paid a total of $14 million in taxes in 2008, an effective tax rate of 1 percent.[7]

As a former GS insider, Nomi Prins makes it abundantly clear that her ex-colleagues care absolutely nothing about the country and everything about their own private wealth and power. They believe, she writes, that their privileged position is their destiny, and they regard themselves as being completely "above explaining their actions to the public or expressing anything that might look like contrition or humility."[8] This proved to be true in April 2010, when the Senate finally dragged some of these executives to a hearing on GS business practices. The list of accusations was quite extensive: you stacked the deck against clients in the market slide of 2007; you set up your company's own securities to fail, secretly bet against those securities, and never told your buyers what you were doing; you dumped toxic mortgage assets on unwitting clients; and so on. Several senators read aloud internal GS documents, in which these men boasted of how they had helped GS profit from the declining housing market or described the firm's subprime deals in scatological terms. No matter; the Goldmanites refused to show any regret for their actions and would not admit that they had behaved irresponsibly or that they had anything to do with the crash of 2008. A few argued that they were actually the victims of this financial debacle. In fact, GS's behavior continues much as before, as the subsequent Greek economic crisis, in which they played a key role, demonstrates. Meanwhile, as Paul Krugman and several other leading economists have argued, indicators are that our economy, given the historical record of downturns, is not likely to recover from the crash of 2008 for a very long time, and that we can actually expect worse crises to come, since no significant change of mind-set, financial practices, or even personnel has surfaced on Wall Street or in the US government.[9] Indeed, with the possible exception of the millions of unemployed, most Americans seem to believe that the "glitch" is over, that we dodged a bullet, and that we can keep doing what we've always been doing without having to "really" pay the subsequent debt.[10]

Somewhat atypical of the American Faustian pattern was our seventh president, Andrew Jackson, whose farewell address of 1837 eerily predicted these kinds of events. In fact, his speech comes off as a pretty good characterization of GS. Jackson's focus was on the behavior of banks, who (he said) think only of themselves, and never of the community. "These banks may and do operate injuriously upon the habits of business, the pecuniary concerns, and the moral tone of society," he declared. Their bent for speculation, he warned, "will foster this eager desire to amass wealth without labor; it will multiply the number of dependents on bank accommodations and bank favors; the temptation to obtain money at any sacrifice will become stronger and stronger, and inevitably lead to corruption which will find its way into your public councils and destroy, at no distant day, the purity of your Government." The danger, Jackson went on, is that "the Government would have passed from the hands of the many to the hands of the few; and this organized money power, from its secret conclave, would have dictated the choice of your highest officers. . . . The forms of your government might, for a time, have remained, but its living spirit would have departed from it."[11]

"The temptation to obtain money at any sacrifice," "this organized money power," a "secret conclave"—these are indeed key elements of our Faustian bargain, ones that have, as Chris Hedges asserts, dynamited the foundations of our society. I believe, however, that we need to put all of this in a larger perspective, a social and even spiritual context, if you will, because it can be argued that these foundations were not all that solid to begin with. The real debt incurred by the United States took place very early in its history, and it involved choosing a way of life that was ultimately not viable and was even self-destructive. In that sense, outrage at GS may be misplaced, because from this broader perspective they were just doing what all good Americans are supposed to be doing—*hustling,* as the historian Walter McDougall characterizes the American Way of Life.[12] McDougall argues that this way of life can actually be dated from the late sixteenth century, but let me turn to the late eighteenth instead and follow the analysis of Joyce Appleby in her book *Capitalism and a New Social Order.* According to Appleby, the colonial understanding of social organization turned on the concept of virtue. Following the European model, virtue was defined as the capacity of individuals "to rise above private interests and devote themselves to the public good."[13] Free men realized their human potential in service to the commonwealth, in other words, and this was the dominant definition of virtue in the colonies for much of the eighteenth century. By the 1790s, however, this began to change, and by 1800 it had undergone a complete inversion: virtue now meant the ability to look out for oneself and one's family, nothing more. It meant personal success in an opportunistic environment.

Appleby locates the source of this change in the impact of the English industrial revolution and the French and Scottish Enlightenment. The liberal concept of freedom was individualistic, based on self-interest, and lay at the heart of the new market economy. For Adam Smith, every man was basically a merchant, and a proper society was a commercial one. Through the so-called "invisible hand" of the market, the collective result of individual selfish actions would supposedly result in the greater good. These ideas fell on receptive ears on the other side of the Atlantic. While the Federalists held on to the classical definition of virtue, the Jeffersonian Republicans were strongly attracted to the notion of laissez-faire. Thus during the 1790s in particular, the new nation began to shed its European ethos, and the organic model of society, which saw virtue in terms of reciprocal rights and obligations, began to dissolve. Literature during this period extolled the search for new commodities, and Thomas Cooper, in *Political Arithmetic,* wrote that "consumers form the nation."[14] Competition, not cooperation, would be the order of the day, and Thomas Jefferson was only too happy to distribute Cooper's work as election campaign material in 1800. With his victory, the communitarian vision of the Federalists, which gave primacy to public over private interest, was eclipsed. The result, wrote the historian Richard Hofstadter, was "a democracy of cupidity."[15]

But it didn't have to be this way. Marginalized though it was, America had an alternative tradition, dating from John Winthrop's sermon on the *Arabella* in 1630. Ronald Reagan was fond of quoting the part about the "City on a Hill." What he failed to add was the part that came after that, in which Winthrop told his flock that "the care of the public must oversway all private respects."[16] If it was a maverick tradition (although it may have included President Jackson among its ranks), it was nevertheless a vibrant one. From Emerson and Thoreau to Frederick Law Olmsted and Lewis Mumford to Vance Packard and beyond, the argument of this alternative tradition was that the dominant tradition, the so-called American Way of Life, was flawed and misguided. As opposed to the pursuit of Frederick Jackson Turner's "outer frontier"—the geographical or material one—the alternative tradition focused on an "inner frontier" that reflected the values of craft, quality, and community. All this was rejected as "elitism" by the dominant culture, however, and got pretty much repressed very early on. Historian Sidney Mead tells us that as a result there was a loneliness and remorse in the frontier adventure, expressed in sad folksongs and gospel hymns, but that this was "a minor refrain, drowned in the great crashing music of the outward events that mark in history the conquering of a continent and the building of a great nation." This conquest, he goes on, has been "told and retold until it has overshadowed and suppressed the equally vital, but more somber, story of the inner experience."[17] In his book *How Cities Work,* Alex Marshall argues that we could have chosen the community solution over the individual one time and again in every area of American life but that we almost never did that. The result, he says, is that "we live in one of the loneliest societies on earth."[18] Indeed, between 1985 and 2004 the number of Americans who said they had no one in whom they could really confide tripled. The U.S. Census for 2000 revealed that 25 percent of American households consisted of only one person; the figure for New York City was nearly 50 percent.[19] No other society is as isolated as ours. There is a debt here, in other words, in terms of "shadow" material—material that is now knocking at our door. In his recent book *Come Home, America,* William Greider writes that "the sacrifices demanded by the engine of American capitalism" are not only "the small grace notes of everyday life, like the ritual of having a daily dinner with everyone present," but, more substantially, "time—time to experience the joys and mysteries of nurturing the children and other fulfilling obligations. People forfeit the small pleasures of idle curiosity, of learning to craft things by one's own hand, and the vital satisfactions of friendships and social cooperation. . . . If we could somehow add up all the private pain and loss caused by the pursuit of unbounded material prosperity, the result might look like a major political grievance of our time."[20] And, I would add, a major social and psychological debt. Indeed, it goes way beyond this: the data of ignorance and violence for the United States, for example, are astounding. Nearly 25 percent of all the prisoners in the world are incarcerated in American prisons, and 24 percent of the adult population says it is acceptable to use violence in the pursuit of one's goals.[21] Two-thirds of the global market in antidepressants is purchased by Americans, and in 2008 164 million prescriptions were written for these drugs.[22] Nearly 60 percent of the population is sitting around waiting for the "Rapture" and the Second Coming; 48 percent believe that extraterrestrials have visited the planet during the past year.[23] Twenty percent think the sun revolves around the earth, and another 9 percent say they have no idea as to which revolves around which.[24] Eighty-seven percent cannot locate Iran or Iraq on a world map.[25] The United States ranks thirty-seventh among developed or developing nations in quality of health care.[26] And so on. As *New York Times* columnist Roger Cohen once put it, if we wish to talk about American exceptionalism, we should take note of the fact that the number of our prison inmates is exceptional, the quality of our health care is exceptionally bad, the degree of our social inequality is exceptionally acute, and public education has gone into exceptional decline.[27]

The arena of US foreign policy is also a classic study of spiritual debt—of oppressing, torturing, and massacring other peoples until they finally couldn't take it anymore. What else was 9/11 about, really? Not hard to figure out, if you study the record of our political and military interference in the Middle East. The media suppressed any real coverage of Obama's disavowed pastor, the Rev. Jeremiah Wright, back in 2008, but in fact the man was no fool: "When you terrorize other people," he declared, "eventually they are going to terrorize you." This is not rocket science; it's just Newton's Third Law of Motion—action and reaction. *New York Times* reporter Stephen Kinzer said much the same thing in his book *All the Shah's Men* when he asserted a direct line from what the CIA did to Iran in 1953—overthrowing a democratically elected government and replacing it with a torture regime—to the destruction of the World Trade Center.[28] Even Henry Kissinger understands this, having pointed out, a year before the 2003 invasion of Iraq, that "hegemonic empires almost automatically elicit universal resistance, which is why all such claimants have sooner or later exhausted themselves."[29] In his book *The Broken Covenant,* the sociologist Robert Bellah looked around at what constituted daily life in America—this in the seventies, when it was significantly better than it is today—and suggested that there was something karmic about it all: "Our material success," he wrote, "is our punishment, in terms of what that success has done to the natural environment, our social fabric, and our personal lives."[30] In the early years of the republic, the Phila-delphia physician Benjamin Rush predicted that the nation "would eventually fall apart in an orgy of selfishness."[31] The crash of 2008; the subsequent, actual unemployment rate of nearly 20 percent; the payout, by Wall Street firms, of $18 billion in bonuses in the wake of that crash; the ranks of the former middle class lining up at food banks and soup kitchens—all of this suggests that that day has arrived.

"We will," writes Nobel Laureate Joseph Stiglitz, "emerge from the crisis with a much larger legacy of debt . . . and more vulnerable to another crisis."[32] In fact, if you look closely at the 2010–11 federal budget, the projected deficit for that fiscal year is nearly 11 percent of the country's entire economic output, and by Obama's own projec-tions, US deficits will not return to what are generally regarded as sustainable levels over the next decade.[33] It's not likely that they will ever return to those levels. We are a nation, in short, that cannot and will not get our collective head above water. In his book *Reinventing Collapse,* Dmitri Orlov writes: "We're in hospice care. The bailouts can be viewed as ever bigger doses of morphine for a patient that's not long for this world."[34] The truth is that in a whole variety of ways—social, cultural, financial, and spiritual—our liver is now being devoured, and Mephistopheles has returned to collect his due. Karma, after all, is about reaping what you sow.

Notes

1. Margaret Atwood, *Payback: Debt and the Shadow Side of Wealth* (Toronto: House of Anansi Press, 2008), 163–64.

2. Jill Lepore, "I.O.U.," *New Yorker*, April 13, 2009, 34.

3. Chris Hedges, "Buying Brand Obama," May 3, 2009, *truthdig* website, www.truthdig.com/report/item/20090503_buying_brand_obama.

4. For up-to-date tallies of the bailouts, see Nomi Prins's website, www.nomiprins.com/reports/; Chris Hedges, *Empire of Illusion: The End of Literacy and the Triumph of Spectacle* (New York: Nation Books, 2009), 151.

5. Matt Taibbi, "The Great American Bubble Machine," *Rolling Stone*, July 9, 2009 (also posted online April 5, 2010), www.rollingstone.com/politics/news/the-great-american-bubble-machine-20100405.

6. Nomi Prins, *It Takes a Pillage: An Epic Tale of Power, Deceit, and Untold Trillions* (Hoboken, N.J.: John Wiley and Sons, 2009), 80; Taibbi, "Great American Bubble Machine."

7. Taibbi, "Great American Bubble Machine."

8. Prins, *It Takes a Pillage*, 82.

9. Paul Krugman, "Debunking the Reagan Myth," *New York Times*, January 21, 2008, and Paul Krugman, "All the President's Zombies," *New York Times*, August 24, 2009.

10. Peter S. Goodman, "Despite Signs of Recovery, Chronic Joblessness Rises," *New York Times*, February 20, 2010.

11. Andrew Jackson, "Farewell Address," March 4, 1837, *The American Presidency Project*, www.presidency.ucsb.edu/ws/?pid=67087.

12. Walter A. McDougall, *Freedom Just around the Corner: A New American History, 1585–1828* (New York: Harper Collins, 2004).

13. Joyce Appleby, *Capitalism and a New Social Order* (New York: NYU Press, 1984), 9.

14. Thomas Cooper, *Political Arithmetic II* (1798), reprinted in *New York University Journal of Law and Liberty* 4, no. 2 (2009): 432.

15. Richard Hofstadter, *The American Political Tradition and the Men Who Made It* (1948; repr., New York: Vintage Books, 1989), xxxvi.

16. John Winthrop, "A Model of Christian Charity," sermon delivered aboard the *Arabella*, 1630, The Winthrop Society website, /www.winthropsociety.com/doc_charity.php.

17. Sidney E. Mead, *The Lively Experiment* (New York: Harper and Row, 1963), 5, 8.

18. Alex Marshall, *How Cities Work: Suburbs, Sprawl, and the Roads Not Taken* (Austin: University of Texas Press, 2001), 190.

19. Cited in Jacqueline Olds and Richard S. Schwartz, *The Lonely American: Drifting Apart in the Twenty-First Century* (Boston: Beacon Press, 2009), 79.

20. William Greider, *Come Home, America: The Rise and Fall (And Redeeming Promise) of Our Country* (New York: Rodale, 2009), 262.

21. Adam Liptak, "U.S. Prison Population Dwarfs that of Other Nations," *New York Times*, April 23, 2008; Jeremy Rifkin, *The European Dream* (New York: Tarcher/Penguin, 2004), 31–32.

22. Barbara Ehrenreich, *Bright-Sided: How Positive Thinking Is Undermining America* (New York: Henry Holt, 2009), 3; and Louis Menand, "Head Case," *New Yorker*, March 1, 2010.

23. CNN/Time Poll conducted by Harris Interactive, June 19–20, 2002, www.pollingreport.com/religion3.htm; Sci Fi Channel / Roper UFOs Poll 2002, www.ufoevidence.org/documents/doc989.htm.

24. Steve Crabtree, "New Poll Gauges Americans' General Knowledge Levels," Gallup News Service, July 6, 1999, Gallup website, www.gallup.com/poll/3742/new-poll-gauges-americans-general-knowledge-levels.aspx.

25. 2002 National Geographic / Roper Poll Survey, as cited in Michael Mann, *Incoherent Empire* (London: Verso, 2003), 102.

26. Andrew Moravcsik, "Dream on America," *Newsweek International*, January 31, 2005, citing World Health Organization (WHO) data.

27. Roger Cohen, "America Unmasked," review of *The Myth of American Exceptionalism*, by Godfrey Hodgson, *New York Times*, Sunday Book Review, April 24, 2009.

28. Stephen Kinzer, *All the Shah's Men: An American Coup and the Roots of Middle East Terror* (Hoboken, N.J.: John Wiley and Sons, 2008).

29. Benjamin Schwarz and Christopher Layne, "A New Grand Strategy," *Atlantic Monthly*, January 2002, 38.

30. Robert N. Bellah, "75 Years," *South Atlantic Quarterly*, special issue on September 11, 2001, February 2002. Bellah is referencing a point he made in his book *The Broken Covenant: American Civil Religion in a Time of Trial* (New York: Seabury Press, 1975).

31. Gordon S. Wood, *The Radicalism of the American Revolution* (New York: Vintage Press, 1993), 327. The quotation is Wood's.

32. Joseph Stiglitz, *Freefall: America, Free Markets, and the Sinking of the World Economy* (New York: W. W. Norton, 2010), 57.

33. David E. Sanger, "Deficits May Alter U.S. Politics and Global Power," *New York Times*, February 1, 2010.

34. Dmitri Orlov, *Reinventing Collapse* (New York: New Society, 2008), 29.

8 Measures of Time

Exploring Debt, Imagination, and Real Nature

Julianne Lutz Warren

"Without memory there is no debt," writes Margaret Atwood in her 2008 book *Payback*—a series of lectures that explores debt as an imaginative construct. If the construct of debt requires memory, Atwood reasons, "debt [also] involves a plot line," that is, a string of actions occurring over time, beginning with a handshake and heading toward a due date.[1] It is increasingly evident that the human economy is reversing some of Earth's long-term trends. Modern conventional measures of a successful human economy have taken little account of the harmful consequences of such reversals. Many storytellers, however, have tried to incorporate nature's realities into their understandings of what it means for a human economy to be truly profitable for the long run. What might we learn, then, from such stories about the give-and-take between humans and Earth? Might they be helpful in reconceiving notions about debt in ways that are mutually beneficial to all life?

Divergence

Beginnings—of Earth and of humanity—are a good place to start, to briefly trace what turn out to be their diverging stories of progress and measures of time and of debt.

Earth is a 4.5 billion-year-old planet. Earth's life appeared about 4.0 billion years ago. Our species *Homo sapiens* has been around for only about two hundred thousand years.

Nature may seem to humans, looking backward from the point of our own existence, to move with infinite slowness. Across time—beyond what we can ever imagine—Earth's geological foundations formed. With sunlight streaming down to the seething, partially molten, watered body of this globe, photosynthesizing life began mysteriously. Since then, Earth's interdependent biological diversity, complexity, and fertility have increased, helping generate, along the way, a planetary atmosphere and climate conditions to which life is adapted.

Since at least the 1920s, Western ecologists have conceptualized nature as a multidimensional pyramid with layers from foundation to pinnacle connected by a circuitry of food energy flows.[2] In simplified form, on the bottom of the ecological pyramid are waters and soils created from bedrock and teeming underground life. Above ground are multitudes of photosynthesizers: the primary producers, making food from sunlight, water, and soil nutrients—everything from algae to sequoias. On top of the primary producers are numerous primary consumers—the herbivores, like deer or leafhopper insects. On top of the herbivores are a smaller number of secondary consumers—the carnivorous predators like sharks, wolves, and eagles. (Humans, as interdependent omnivores, naturally fall somewhere above the herbivores and below the top carnivores—alongside bears, raccoons, and squirrels). Nutrient atoms weathered from bedrock and captured from air by soil bacteria cycle upwards through such pyramids, which are filled with countless such intricately interconnected food-web relationships, and then are released back down to the soil or water—via defecation and death—to be taken up again by other life-forms, and so on. The more biologically diverse a pyramid or, in other terms, an ecosystem is, the more likely it is for nutrient atoms to be recycled indefinitely and retained within it before being carried downhill via rain, wind, and gravity to rivers and eventually the bottom of the ocean.[3] On balance the gain of nutrient fertility taken up by life and cycling through ecosystems has tended to be greater than the loss over long ages. Similarly, over evolutionary time, more life-forms have been created by natural selection than have gone extinct, for a net gain in diversity. Meanwhile, increasingly diverse and fertile interconnected pyramids of plants and animals exchanging carbon dioxide, oxygen, and other gases link bedrock to atmosphere, fostering a dynamic global equilibrium over the long term.

Over billions of years, Earth's nature has generated capacities for its own self-renewal. "Endless forms . . . have been and are being, evolved," in Charles Darwin's words. Functioning together, they have been collectively promoting what the twentieth-century ecologist and conservation thinker Aldo Leopold termed nature's integrity, stability, and beauty—or in other words, its health.[4] For those concerned with a broad range of life's values, vibrant health is a measure of ancient nature's perpetual progress.

It is difficult to say exactly when in the two-hundred-thousand-year history of *Homo sapiens* our species embarked on a different trajectory of progress, going forward to the present world-dominating human economy—the way multitudes have come to manage feeding, clothing, sheltering, reproducing, and amusing themselves. The starting point might be the point at which we *Homo sapiens*, taking our first breath, realized we could expand our power over the world from mind to hand to tool. Or it might be when we began gathering in groups to plow soil and grow food. It might be when we considered ourselves "enlightened"—believing nature to be nothing more than physical matter for us to manipulate in order to improve our condition. Or perhaps it was when the "enlightened" brought their ambitions to improve the world to bear on a fresh new continent they named America, which was both a reality and a symbol of the riches of the good life many people longed for. Or it might be when our species numbers reached the one billion mark fewer than two hundred years ago and unbridled capitalism combined with industrialism and a belief in Earth's inexhaust-ibility—physical and biological laws aside—further accelerated human population growth, which has required an increasing stock of resources from across the globe. The prodigious powers of technology and industry have helped the human population burgeon to over 7.0 billion today.[5] Whatever time we may take as our starting point, relative to the Earth's long history, *Homo sapiens* have developed their present, mas-sively complex, world-encompassing economy in an incredible flash.

Indeed the swift pace of the rise and ongoing growth of humanity's current global economy defines it as much as anything and drives its expanding spatial scale. To measure its success, modern Western society—with Americans most recently leading the pack—has also established a different standard of progress than the health of the Earth. Our present economy, writes author and climate change activist Bill McKib-ben in *Eaarth* (2010), "is like a racehorse, fleet and showy. It is bred for speed. . . . The thoroughbred, like our economy, has been optimized for one thing only: pure burning swiftness. (Also, both are now mostly owned by sheikhs)," he adds.[6] Aided by scientific discoveries, modern society seeks by controlling nature to progress rapidly toward the lure of infinite wealth. Wealth has been not so much simply a destination, though, as an object of worship. "There is no country in which so absolute homage is paid to wealth" as America, wrote nineteenth-century poet Ralph Waldo Emerson.[7] Progress American-style has "no goal," believed Massachusetts governor Edward Everett back in 1840, "and there can be no pause; for art and science are, in themselves progressive and infinite. . . . Nothing can arrest them which does not plunge the entire order of society into barbarism."[8] This society invents ways to get its economic horse to cir-cle the track faster and faster, without rest, churning nature into money and using that money to churn more nature into more money and so on. With the blessings of increasing wealth, its members believe, comes freedom—freedom from insecurity, from fears of hunger, hard labor, and poverty. Rising GNPs and more and more bushels of wheat, barrels of oil, bathtubs, iPods, and SUVs have become the measure not only of economic progress but even of human success.

Accounting

It wasn't until 1878—a little more than a century after the American Declaration of Independence—that the US government, now self-entitled proprietor of one of the world's most fertile regions, published its first *Official Statistical Yearbook* to keep track of the nation's economic progress. Until then, nature was so abundant on the vast North American continent that the new Americans had not found it necessary to keep accounts of their expenditures and production, let alone attend to the health of the earth, which was vibrant indeed.

In fact, so easy was the American farmer's lot with "nature in her prime" in the late eighteenth century, as Pennsylvanian farmer Richard Peters explained in a letter to British agricultural author Arthur Young, that there was no need for individuals to make "nice calculations" about profits.[9] The land's wealth was there for the taking, and there was more than enough for everyone, so why bother with figures? Indeed, in 1792 George Washington humbly confessed his own share of ignorance when he could not answer "how many sheep an acre of woodland pasture would support."[10] Likewise, Thomas Jefferson admitted that he had not thought of calculating "what were the profits of capital invested in Virginia agriculture." And almost a quarter of a century later America still did not yet have "metallic measures of values" for land or a "stable index of real value."[11]

Washington, more clearly than most, understood that such lack of land-use accounting might eventually have risky repercussions. Because land was so much cheaper than labor (especially because of slavery and indentured servitude), the nation's farmers, "if they can be so-called," he noted disparagingly, tended "not to make the most they can from the land; . . . the consequence of which has been, much ground has been *scratched* over and none cultivated or improved as it ought to have been."[12] Farmers tended to "cut down" and keep "a piece of land under constant cultivation," he explained, ". . . until it will yield scarcely anything; a second piece is cleared and treated in the same manner; then a third and so on."[13] Washington doubted that the "wretched" land-use habits of Americans would be conquered by anything "short of necessity."[14] The easiest and most frequently chosen option for ongoing economic improvement was to substitute quantity of acres farmed for quality of farming, spreading the destruction of land and propelling migration westward.[15] Already by the last decade of the eighteenth century, the speed of expansion into the regions west of the Potomac River was "beyond all conception," to Washington's mind. He could glimpse that a future in which the land would be filled up with people and scratched over with plows might be quickly approaching.[16]

It was difficult for many, though, to reconcile the reality of rapid land exhaustion with impressions of North America as a vast, practically inexhaustible continent. Thanks to that "powerful enchanter, Time," in the words of Charles Dickens, a future in which good land had run out appeared far distant, or at least could be pushed off into an unforeseeable age by buying up more space and inventing better methods of land management.[17] Jefferson—the visionary principal author of America's *Declaration* and the nation's third president—could see, as did Washington, that American agriculture was impoverishing land. In severe cases, he recognized, it would take a long course of years for recovery. Indeed, some of his own Virginia fields by the 1790s had been "completely exhausted by perpetual crops of Indian corn and wheat alternately."[18] Yet Jefferson also believed that the country's original soil was so fertile that with better management it would exhaust only slowly, if ever. Better management would become more important as population increased until there was more labor than land, he understood. But in 1793, in his home state of Virginia, it was still cheaper to buy an acre of new land than to add manure to replace depleted fertility on an old one.[19] And, thinking in terms of democratic economy, Jefferson implied that the problem of the still-distant future would be overproduction, not land depletion: he wrote even before the Louisiana Purchase that there were "now lands enough to employ an infinite number of people in their cultivation" and thus that "our citizens will find employment in this [farming] line, till their numbers, and of course, their productions become too great for the demand, both internal and foreign. This is not the case as yet, and probably will not be for a considerable time."[20]

With far less thoughtfulness than Jefferson, the Pennsylvanian farmer Richard Peters was at least as sanguine about America's landed future. When people's families outgrew their properties or when they were simply tired of their own farms, Americans could and did simply sell them and move to fresh land. A burgeoning population would, in fact, make land increasingly valuable on the market, Peters understood. Because of this he boasted to Arthur Young that if the latter were to sell his English farm and invest his capital in American territory he could turn a 500 percent profit on it in ten years. And while Peters too could imagine that new land might eventually run out and old land be worn out, the end of easy, sure, and fast profit making was, in his view, "far distant." In line with Washington's observation that only necessity would bring landowners to better land use, Peters was content to leave to future generations "the toil, calculation, and expense of renovating lands exhausted by bad tillage." When the need arises, Peters wrote, "the proprietors of old lands will adopt better systems of agriculture, which are now fast advancing."[21] Who could really say, though, which would advance faster—exhausted lands or better farming methods?

Meanwhile, between the period of the earliest European settlement and the nineteenth century, among the most obvious changes in the American landscape were that millions of bison had vanished from the North American plains and that virtually all of the salmon had been wiped out south of Maine. America had also lost almost half of its original forests and considerable amounts of once-fertile soil. In 1847, Vermont intellectual George Perkins Marsh pointed out that in his home state, "for want of foresight," Americans had abused the forested hillsides. Stripped of trees, soils eroded into waterways and rains flooded them. Lush stream valleys were turning into "broad wastes . . . of gravel and pebbles, [becoming] deserts in summer, and seas in autumn and spring."[22] And while it had taken centuries for the ancient Romans to devastate their landscape, he later argued, it had taken Americans mere decades.[23] "The changes, which these causes have wrought in the physical geography of Vermont," Marsh continued, "within a single generation, are too striking to have escaped the attention of any observing person, and every middle-aged man, who revisits his birth-place after a few years of absence, looks upon another landscape than that which formed the theatre of his youthful toils and pleasures."[24]

Marsh was one of the first to speak out on the matter of humanity's debt to the land and to future generations who would require fertile places to live. In 1864, about forty years after Jefferson's death, Marsh published his major work, *Man and Nature*. In this book, Marsh argues that though humans are like all other forms of life in depending upon "the table of bounteous nature," yet they are "a power of a higher order."[25] Humans, in fact, he wrote, were distinguished from all other animal life by their tendency to unbalance nature by taking more of her provisions than they needed and more than they paid back. Man, he pointed out, "has too long forgotten that the Earth was given to him for usufruct alone, not for consumption, still less for profligate waste."[26] With mounting evidence and personal insight, Marsh built his case that it was prudentially responsible and morally right to repay "to our great mother [Earth] the debt which the [swift-footed] prodigality and the thriftlessness of former generations have imposed upon their successors—thus fulfilling the command of religion and of practical wisdom, to use this world as not abusing it."[27]

A decade and a half later, however, the first US *Statistical Yearbook* did not include a column for Marsh's kind of morality. Its ledger included listings for finance, coinage, commerce, immigration, shipping, imports and exports, railroads, agricultural crops, and coal produced. There were no records for how many trees, fish, tons of minerals, or acre-feet of fresh water remained. There was no attempt to account for the native people expelled, soils eroded and exhausted, plant and animal species missing, or waters polluted. There was no tally of what had been not merely used but wasted and consumed, compromising nature's capacity for self-renewal.

American efforts to calculate what was required for Earth's ongoing health and how much of that capacity remained would come later and with them a rising understanding of how difficult such calculations were to make. The formalized concept of maximum sustained yield reaches back at least to German forester Georg Ludwig Hartig's 1795 decree that "not more and not less may be taken annually [from state forests] than is possible on the basis of good management."[28] But this principle proved a battleground for the different measures of short-term market demands versus the long-term realities of nature's regenerative capacities.[29] On the one hand, it was more economically profitable to take all you could as fast as you could, turn it into money capital, and reinvest it to make more—even if it meant drawing on nature's capital, its fertility and diversity. Nature's long-term well-being didn't count in these calculations of sustainability.[30] On the other hand, it was morally responsible to life on the planet and also to future generations of humans to limit the speed and quantities of take to nature's interest, leaving its capacities resilient and productive for ages to come. This was the overriding concern of America's first German-trained US Department of Agriculture / US Forest Service chief forester, Gifford Pinchot. In view of a looming timber famine, he urged the Progressive Era conservation ideal of better managing natural resources for the maximum good of the maximum number of people for the long term.

The sustained-yield concept was theoretically appealing to a range of twentieth-century scientists, policy makers, managers, and economists. Calculating proper limits for sustained yields of particular so-called "natural resources" was, however, confounded by the vast complexities of interrelationships of nature. By the later 1930s, the well-known forester, father of wildlife management, and ecological conservationist Aldo Leopold realized that management for maximum yields of singled-out resources often ended up at cross-purposes. For example, a game manager might kill wolves believing that he was protecting deer for hunters while inadvertently creating a forest manager's nightmare of burgeoning deer herds overbrowsing vegetation that would take many years to regrow. Leopold turned his attention away from resource-by-resource management to a holistic ideal that incorporated nature's interconnectedness. Ahead of his time, he came to understand that healthy nature was the only valuable nature in the long term, developing a new standard for good land use measured in terms of nature's health. A few decades later yet, fisheries biologist P. A. Larkin concluded in a 1977 review article that the whole sustained-yield concept was dead and required an epitaph. He didn't know what would take its place, but he was sure that optimizing sustainable yield of resources had no guaranteed outcome. It could be "a recipe for achieving heaven or hell," in Larkin's words, depending on where you stood or how fast you ran in relation to nature's realities.[31]

Continuing into the twenty-first century, however, the concept of maximum sustained yield has hardly gone away, though it has taken on a few new manifestations in a world where buying more space largely is no longer feasible and intensifying management has taken on greater urgency. Nobel laureate Norman Borlaug, for example, father of the "Green Revolution" in agriculture, in the 1940s began promoting around the world a cropping system involving monocultures, irrigation, fertilizer and pesticide applications, new machine technologies, and credit for farmers so they could pay for these inputs and economic markets so they could sell their harvests. His goal was to help balance the land-food-population equation by maximizing yields of food. With rising hundreds of millions of people hungry, in 2000, on the thirtieth anniversary of his award, Borlaug implored agricultural researchers to improve "maximum genetic yield potential"—the capacity of cereal crops to produce as much seed as possible—in order to sustain a maximum global human population that was continuing to expand. "Imagine the benefits to humankind," he pressed.[32]

It is increasingly clear that this kind of accounting, which takes the satisfaction of humanity's rapidly rising demands as its measure of progress while it largely disregards nature's time-proven, health-generating processes, overlooks a rising indebtedness and an impending due date. As humans hone methods of rapidly taking from nature more than they repay, it is easy to reimagine McKibben's metaphor of the current, world-spanning, modern, sleek racehorse economy now running on a treadmill instead of a track. And as it does so, it turns a small, toothed gear in faster rotations against a larger, slower-cycling one. Wealth circles quickly forward, forcing nature's momentum into accelerating reverse. In modern times we've seen, rather than an increase in biodiversity, a rapid acceleration of global extinction outpacing speciation at a rate that may result in Earth losing as many as 75 percent of its long-evolved species over the geological eyeblink of a few hundred years.[33] To name just a few: great auk, passenger pigeon, Las Vegas leopard frog, Sexton Mountain mariposa lily. Extinction debt—the sometimes centuries-long delayed death response of species to habitat fragmentation and loss—may have already set future losses into irreversible motion. Human economy has also reversed the ancient trends of building soil fertility. Recent studies confirm that agricultural soil erosion substantially outpaces soil production worldwide and is several to a thousand times greater than preagricultural rates. Upwards of a third of the world's potentially farmable land has been lost to erosion since the dawn of agriculture—much of that in the past forty years.[34]

Biodiversity, fertility, and Earth's composition of atmospheric gases are mutually interdependent. In addition to the contribution of carbon dioxide to the atmosphere made by burning fossil fuels—the stored remains of ancient life—as much as one-third of the total greenhouse gas buildup in Earth's atmosphere since the nineteenth century has come from cutting down trees and plowing up hundreds of millions of acres of soils, exposing fresh and long-buried organic matter to air and oxidation, at the same time diminishing ecosystems' capacities to renew their own fertility and biodiversity.[35] Present-day concentrations of carbon dioxide are higher than any that have been observed in the past eight hundred thousand years.[36] This rapid, unprecedented change has contributed to a degree rise (Celsius) in average global temperatures since 1850 and to the destabilization of the planet's climate. This in turn has led to acidifying oceans, rising sea levels, shrinking glaciers, intensifying storms, increasingly frequent droughts and floods, changes in the timing of seasons, out-of-synch predator-prey relationships, further losses in biodiversity, and human suffering—for example, from destruction of homes, diminished food and water supplies, and increased disease outbreaks. Current projections are for temperatures to rise another 2.5 to 4.7 degrees by 2100.[37]

Moreover, the racehorse economy has had inequitable consequences for peoples of the world. While the United States, for example, has produced nearly a quarter of the world's total greenhouse gases, it has ignored its responsibility for doing so, rejecting plans to cooperate globally to cut emissions, with contributions still rising.[38] Meanwhile those already living in poverty—inhabitants of the poles, oceanic small islands, and the global South, who contribute far less to the problem—have been among the first to suffer from the consequences of climate change. These peoples additionally have been left without the option to use the earth as the expanding economy of the West has done. As their familiar environments have been transformed by the actions of others in distant places, they have become creditors in the equation that has been termed ecological debt.

In sum, the capacity of Earth to renew itself and support life has been swiftly altered and impoverished by the urgent and rising demands of the predominating human economy. The accumulation of economic wealth for the good of some has globally outpaced nature's capacities to renew its own health for the good of all. If we are to develop practical strategies to reverse the dominating capitalist-industrial culture's destructive course and redress its injustices, we need, most fundamentally, a transformed mind-set about debt that accepts guilt where it is due and learns respect and care for Earth's whole community of life.[39]

The Witnesses

Earth, if perhaps relatively long-suffering, bears an indiscriminate witness to human responsibility for ecological debt. Bearing witness, too, are a line of justice-minded storytellers—part of Western civilization's conscience—offering to help its members remember that they know they should be acting better. Stories, as Czech author Milan Kundera observes, help us examine what has been in us for a long time and what possibilities remain within us as beings in the world and thus for the world. There are many voices from among whom to choose.[40] I have selected a handful who seem to understand deeply not only about the material imprudence of using short-term wealth as a measure of good life but also about the immorality of neglecting the fuller, fairer measure of nature's enduring health.

Retribution Has the Fastest Horse

In Washington Irving's "The Devil and Tom Walker" (1824), Tom became wealthy by making a deal with the devil and agreeing to make more money by abusing broke, land-ravaging speculators. Legend has it that Tom, in a moment of panicky remembrance of his own growing debt, buried his new horse upside down—one of the fine animals that had pulled his fancy carriage with unoiled wheels squealing like the souls of the debtors he was squeezing. Tom figured that when the devil came to collect on Tom's own debt, sometime in the still-distant future, the world would be turned upside down and his horse thus would be ready for quick mounting. This was a superfluous precaution. For one day—as Tom was in the midst of a usurious transaction—three knocks came on his door. There waiting stood a black man, holding a black horse, who whisked him into the saddle, the "steed striking fire out of the pavement at every bound."[41] In the biblical book of Revelation, the black horse is the one whose rider holds the scales. Indeed, members of a society in which one of its self-proclaimed religious leaders can laugh publicly at the realities of global climate change, exclaiming, "I don't believe a moment of it. The whole thing is created to destroy America's free enterprise system and our economic stability," might do well, as Marsh urged almost 150 years ago, to reconsider its priorities and hubris in light of what its own true faith has always demanded.[42]

We Should Beware of Lightning-Fast Carriages

Charles Dickens was a big fan of Irving's and, like him, mingled insights about debt, nature, and the economy with significance resonant on both sides of the Atlantic. In his *A Tale of Two Cities* (1859), set in late eighteenth-century France and England, Madame Defarge patiently, slowly knits the names of the wealthy who obtained their luxuries by taking from others and from the land itself what was necessary for life and its regeneration. Nothing less than the blood of these rich debtors will be required as repayment by those left poor in whom the desire for a good life still madly burns. Madame Defarge asks her husband, who is impatient for the inevitable vengeance to strike—"How long does it take to make and store the lightning? Tell me."[43] A long time, we might thoughtfully suppose, as did monsieur, a long time in the making. But when it does strike, it does so in an instant and is beyond our ability to predict.

Madame Defarge's slow knitting with mortal implications has parallels in the natural world today in actual, not metaphorical, lightning. "We are in the mega-fire era," says Ken Frederick, a spokesman for the US federal government, referring to the climate change–induced consequence of larger storms over land now creating more lightning-initiated blazes.[44] And, indeed, unhurried as Earth's processes may seem when compared with the human economy, nature's changes may happen in what seems like a flash. A lightning bolt helps make molecular nitrogen in the air available to plants, feeding them and contributing to the long-term fertility building and diversity of their ecosystem, but it may also sear an oak tree, start a blazing fire, and turn a forest and its inhabitants into ashes overnight.

In another scene from *A Tale of Two Cities,* a wealthy marquis riding in a wildly fast carriage drawn by four strong horses runs over a poor man's child—the wheels come to a "sickening little jolt."[45] In response, the marquis tosses a coin out the window to the child's grieving father, intending to pay off in this way his debt of life. But the father hides himself under the carriage, riding amid the dust clouds of the churning wheels. The carriage slowly passes up a long hill through a landscape as stark and withered as the country people enduring starvation, then reaches the green of the marquis's luxurious estate. In the black of night, the father murders the marquis, turning his soft pillow red. Thousands more like him will be dead within a few years. Riders in fast coaches, who offer to pay merely in coin for Earth's treasures, are condemned for incurring inappropriate debts and then denounced and beheaded.

We Should Beware of Fast, Horseless Carriages

It is Dickens's old, familiar, truthful works that quiet the startled mind of Mr. Julian West in Edward Bellamy's *Looking Backward* (1888) as he sits in his hosts' library, trying to get a hold on himself. The privileged traveler, Mr. West, has discovered himself awakening suddenly out of the class injustices of 1887 Boston and into the same city a mere 113 years later, in the year 2000, now characterized by perfect equality. Imagine society in 1887, the narrator suggests, as a "prodigious coach" on which ride only the relatively few wealthy. The coach is pulled not by horses but by the starving masses, who are driven by hunger. In the imagined society of 2000, however, everyone takes turns pulling and everyone takes turns riding. People's wants have become, amazingly, not a debit, but a credit, helping promote an economy that sustains and builds up the earth so that it produces more wealth with a wasteless efficiency that makes it possible to meet everyone's desires and eliminate all fears bred of insecurity. The machinery of the national, globalizing economy in this story is like a "gigantic mill," we learn, "into the hopper of which goods are being constantly poured by the trainload and shipload, to issue at the other end in packages of pounds and ounces, yards and inches, pints and gallons."[46]

This imagined world may be remarkably egalitarian in terms of meeting people's material demands, but independent nature is ended by human control.[47] Whatever has been wild and unpredictable—that perpetual play of forces that kept a diversity of life, in complex equilibrium, humming—has been brought into ultimate submission, conscribed to run its perpetual paces round and round the economic track, fueled by belief in human ingenuity.[48] Yet Bellamy's older contemporary, the naturalist John Burroughs, recognized that it was the long ages of the give-and-take of nature's forces that kept the world alive. "Nature does not balance her books in a day or in ten thousand days," Burroughs writes, "but some sort of balance is kept in the course of ages, else life would not be here. Disruption and decay bring about their opposites. Conflicting forces get adjusted and peace reigns. If all forces found the equilibrium to which they tend, we should have a dead world—a dead level of lifeless forces. But the play of forces is so complex, the factors that enter into our weather system even, are so many and so subtle and far-reaching, that we experience but little monotony. There is a perpetual see-saw everywhere, and this means life and motion."[49] As Leopold would put it later in the next century, "Too much safety seems to yield only danger in the long run. Perhaps this is behind Thoreau's dictum: In wildness is the salvation of the world."[50]

One person's utopia can be another's nightmare—indeed, a whole world's nightmare. We know with increasingly high certainty today that humans embedded in an ecologically and evolutionarily interconnected world are not smart enough to manipulate the "useful" parts of nature piece by piece to maximize benefits for themselves for the long term. Moreover, controlling nature's wildness seems to go hand in hand with subjugating human liberty. In *Looking Backward,* for instance, Dr. Leete, Mr. West's twenty-first century guide, apparently unwittingly compares the humans laboring in this imagined economy to a "disciplined army" under the one head of money capital as "under one general—such a fighting machine, for example," Bellamy wrote, "as the German army in the time of Von Moltke."[51] As Lewis Mumford recognized in his *The Story of Utopias* (1922), Bellamy's imagined world already was all too real.[52]

There Is Wisdom in Walking

According to literary scholars, since at least the later part of the twentieth century—parallel with rising detrimental effects of human economy on nature's health—there has been a decline in the quality and quantity of Western utopian literary works and an upsurge in dystopic visions.[53] Their authors—and readers—are not sure if perhaps a consequence of destroying so much of our own species' habitat might not require our own extinction to pay our debt to nature. We don't know how long we might have to try to make amends, or whether it is even worth making the effort. In these dark stories are signs, though, that the deeper, intuitive parts of us still have not have entirely forgotten, after all, the truth of where our breakfasts come from and still realize that measuring goodness with money and not abundant, healthy life is not only imprudent but morally untenable. Moreover, "That the situation is hopeless should not prevent us from doing our best."[54]

One of these dark stories seeded with conscience's light is told in the ashen landscape of Cormac McCarthy's *The Road* (2006). The human economy and Earth's capacities for self-renewal have been leveled by a fiery disaster. They now walk together at the same slow pace. There are no carriages, no racehorses, no plants, no animals, nothing growing at all that we can perceive. A tattered remnant of humanity turns cannibal. A smaller fragment still struggles to cling to virtue and to resurrect memories of its past—colors, the names of birds, things to eat—which are quickly fading, as is its future. These answer the urge to live, and to live decently, even in the worst of times by delving into earthen cellars for the remains of stored foods in an economy of absence.

The heart of the story is told in spare conversation between a father and son on a journey downhill toward the ocean, where all life eventually finds its end . . . and its beginning. A few simple and slow pleasures remain—a sip of water, a surviving can of peaches—but what has been gained, in the end, is the wisdom of slowness:[55] "No list of things to be done," thinks the father to himself as he lies in the dark, resting in the hours between days of walking. "The day providential to itself. The hour. There is no Later. This is later. All things of grace and beauty such that one holds them to one's heart have a common provenance in pain. Their birth in grief and ashes. So, he whispered to the sleeping boy, I have you."[56]

On Earth there remains bedrock, water, wind, and fire. "The fire," asks the little boy: "Is it real?" His dying father answers yes: "It's inside you," he says, "It always was there. I can see it." A short time later, goodness in the form of a motherly woman finds the boy, now orphaned, and she talks to him sometimes about God. The boy tries to talk to God, "but the best thing was to talk to his father," the boy thought, "and he did talk to him and he didn't forget. The woman said that was all right. She said that the breath of God was his breath yet though it pass from man to man through all of time."[57]

McCarthy's story is a grave reminder. Perhaps among the most important things of all that are being lost in the bargain between the human economy and Earth's health is the "wisdom of slowness" and slowness's "pleasures," in the words of Czech novelist Milan Kundera.[58] In the haste of the modern human economy we are losing the greater meaning of nature, in Thoreau's sense—the sense in which walking on footpaths through grasslands and forests recalls to us the reality that the smallest unit of health is that of the community of nature, of which we are interdependent members with all of Earth's life. In subduing wild nature in a rush, trusting to the mighty steed of our economy, we are also losing our memory of nature as it was before we changed it. "It might be wise," wrote Leopold ironically in the 1940s, "to prohibit at once all teaching of real botany and real history, lest some future citizen suffer qualms about the floristic price of his good life."[59] Without memory—without witnesses—there is no debt, no story, no imagination, and no fresh possibility.

Repacing

It may be, concludes McKibben in his *The End of Nature* (2006), that the key environmental fact of our time is "the contrast between the pace at which the physical world is changing and the pace at which human society is reacting" to the consequences of those changes.[60] We might also say that the contrast between the pace at which we have been changing the world and the pace at which nature is responding is a vital factor in shaping future world conditions. Much may be regained by putting the economic horse out to pasture. Give it a rest. Much may be regained, on balance, for life, paradoxically, by slowing down the global economy as quickly as possible—slowing down human reproduction rates, slowing down the time it takes to craft a product and the time between possessing it and throwing it away, slowing down the ways we gather food, slowing down the time it takes to cook and to eat food, slowing down to a walk on a path through the woods and the fields or from our homes to our offices, places of worship, parks, and pubs. Walk more. See more. Save more. Buy less. Shrink our overbearing consumer-driven economy's presence on Earth. For like Lewis Carroll's Alice, when the magic cake wears off, we too have discovered that growing fast also makes us dangerously big—so big that we tip things over and are forced to leave Wonderland. In slowing down, society's members may regain much by spending freed time in humbly remembering that wide range of deep-seated, very old human values that—given that lightning doesn't strike quite yet—may carry us beyond the worship of short-time wealth to embrace the possibility of Earth's—and our own species—vibrant, dynamic, long-term health. Imagine the truth. Ask for forgiveness. Hope for mercy. For, if we can't pay off our debt, at least we can die trying. We have it in us.

Notes

1. Margaret Atwood, *Payback: Debt and the Shadow Side of Wealth* (Toronto: Anansi Press, 2008), 81.

2. Charles Elton, *Animal Ecology*, new introductory material by Mathew A. Leibold and J. Timothy Wootton (Chicago: University of Chicago Press, 2001). First published in 1927, *Animal Ecology* introduced Elton's "pyramid of numbers." Nature may be conceived as a pyramid based

on body size and food relationships, as well as energy losses in transfers from lower to higher trophic levels. "The animals at the base of a food-chain are relatively abundant, while those at the end are relatively few in numbers, and there is a progressive decrease in between the two extremes" (69). The small animals closer to the base tend to reproduce very quickly and become numerous, and those higher up, which eat those lower down, tend to be larger and slower at reproducing and thus fewer.

3. Based on Aldo Leopold's essay "Odyssey," in *A Sand County Almanac* (1949; repr., New York: Oxford University Press, 1987), 104–7. Leopold drew on the work of animal ecologist Charles Elton.

4. Charles Darwin, *On the Origin of Species* (1849; repr., London: London Folio Society, 2006), 388; Leopold, *Sand County Almanac*, 221–25.

5. Steven Stoll, *The Great Delusion: A Mad Inventor, Death in the Tropics, and the Utopian Origins of Economic Growth* (New York: Hill and Wang, 2008), 164. Stoll discusses the history of economics in relation to the history of physics, noting that "[nineteenth-century] economists seized upon physics without understanding the full implication of the categories they clumsily translated into human action" (145). And it has become increasingly clear that at some point it is not tools for mining "natural capital," like certain fish, for example, that is the limiting factor in take, as Adam Smith might have it, but how many fish there are remaining to catch (if any) (155).

6. Bill McKibben, *Eaarth: Making a Life on a Tough New Planet* (New York: Times Books, 2010), 103.

7. Ralph Waldo Emerson, *The Complete Essays and Other Writings of Ralph Waldo Emerson*, ed. Brooks Atkinson (New York: Modern Library, 1950), 604.

8. Quoted in Stoll, *Great Delusion*, 19.

9. See "Richard Peters's Observations and Criticisms on Mr. Young's Letter of January 15, 1793," in George Washington, *Letters on Agriculture from His Excellency, George Washington, President of the United States to Arthur Young, Esq. F.R.S. and Sir John Sinclair, Bart, M.P. with Statistical Tables and Remarks by Thomas Jefferson, Richard Peters, and Other Gentlemen on the Economy and Management of Farms in the United States,* ed. Franklin Knight (Washington, D.C.: Franklin Knight, 1847), 104. Peters is responding to Young's questions about whether American farmers could carry on without calculating profit by percent on capital.

10. George Washington, "Letter from George Washington to Arthur Young, Esq., from Philadelphia, June 18, 1792," in *Letters on Agriculture*, 65.

11. Thomas Jefferson, "Jefferson to President Washington, from Philadelphia, June 28, 1793," in *Washington, Jefferson, Lincoln and Agriculture*, ed. Everett E. Edwards (Washington, D.C.: Bureau of Agricultural Economics, US Department of Agriculture, 1937), 59; and Thomas Jefferson, "Jefferson to Jean Batiste Say, Monticello, March 2, 1815," in *Washington, Jefferson, Lincoln and Agriculture*, 69.

12. George Washington, "Letter from George Washington to Arthur Young, Esq. from Philadelphia, December 5, 1791," in *Letters on Agriculture*, 32.

13. George Washington, "Letter from George Washington to Arthur Young, Esq., from Philadelphia, June 18, 1792," in *Letters on Agriculture*, 63.

14. George Washington, "Washington to William Strickland, from Mount Vernon, July 15, 1797," in Edwards, *Washington, Jefferson*, 33; and George Washington, "Letter from George Washington to Arthur Young, Esq. from Philadelphia, December 5, 1791," in *Letters on Agriculture*, 32.

15. George Washington, "Letter from George Washington to Arthur Young, Esq., from Philadelphia, June 18, 1792," in *Letters on Agriculture*, 63; and George Washington, "Washington to William Strickland, from Mount Vernon, July 15, 1797," in Edwards, *Washington, Jefferson*, 32–33.

16. George Washington, "Letter from George Washington to Arthur Young, Esq. from Philadelphia, December 5, 1791," in *Letters on Agriculture*, 29, 31.

17. Charles Dickens, *A Tale of Two Cities* (Harmondsworth: Penguin, 1984), 399.

18. Thomas Jefferson, "Jefferson to [correspondent's name lost], from Philadelphia, March 23, 1798," in Edwards, *Washington, Jefferson*, 63.

19. Thomas Jefferson, "Mr. Jefferson to Washington, Philadelphia, June 28, 1793," in *Letters on Agriculture*, 103.

20. Thomas Jefferson, "Jefferson to John Jay, from Paris, August 23, 1785," in Edwards, *Washington, Jefferson*, 49.

21. Richard Peters, "Richard Peters's Observations and Criticisms on Mr. Young's Letter of January 15, 1793," in *Letters on Agriculture*, 108.

22. George Perkins Marsh, "Address Delivered before the Agricultural Society of Rutland County, September 30, 1847," Library of Congress, American Memory, http://memory.loc.gov/cgi-bin/query/r?ammem/consrv:@field(DOCID+@lit(amrvgvgo2div1)), 17–18.

23. George Perkins Marsh, *Man and Nature: Or, Physical Geography as Modified by Human Action* [1864], ed. and intro. David Lowenthal (1965; repr., Seattle: University of Washington Press, 2003), 1–8.

24. Marsh, "Address," 17–18.

25. Marsh, *Man and Nature*, 3.

26. Ibid., 36.

27. Ibid., 13.

28. H. Rubner, "Sustained-Yield Forestry in Europe and Its Crisis during the Era of Nazi Dictatorship," in *History of Sustained-Yield Forestry: A Symposium, Western Forestry Center, Portland, Oregon, October 18–19, 1983*, ed. Harold K. Steen (Santa Cruz, Calif.: Forest History Society, 1984), 171.

29. Julianne Newton [Warren], *Aldo Leopold's Odyssey* (Washington, D.C.: Shearwater Books / Island Press, 2006), 293–94.

30. For a fuller discussion of the concept of sustainability in relation to land health, see Julianne L. Newton [Warren] and Eric T. Freyfogle, "Sustainability: A Dissent," *Journal of Conservation Biology* 19, no. 1 (2005): 23–31.

31. P. A. Larkin, "An Epitaph for the Concept of Maximum Sustained Yield," *Transactions of the American Fisheries Society* 106, no. 1 (1977): 1–10.

32. Norman Borlaug, "The Green Revolution Revisited and the Road Ahead," Special 30th Anniversary Lecture, Norwegian Nobel Institute, Oslo, September 8, 2000, www.nobelprize.org/nobel_prizes/peace/laureates/1970/borlaug-lecture.pdf, 13, 17.

33. A. Barnosky et al., "Has the Earth's 6th Mass Extinction Already Arrived?," *Nature*, March 3, 2011, 51–57.

34. David Montgomery, "Is Agriculture Eroding Civilization's Foundation?," *GSA Today* 117, no. 10 (October 2007): 4–9.

35. According to David Montgomery, in "Is Agriculture Eroding Civilization's Foundation?," "A third of the total carbon dioxide buildup in the atmosphere since the industrial revolution has come from degradation of soil organic matter as hundreds of millions of acres of virgin land were plowed up in the late nineteenth and early twentieth centuries" (8). According to the Intergovernmental Panel on Climate Change (IPCC), forestry contributed about 17.4 percent and agriculture 13.5 percent of the 2004 global anthropogenic greenhouse gas emissions. Global carbon dioxide emissions are primarily from fossil fuel; methane emissions come predominantly from agriculture and fossil fuel use. N2o emissions are primarily due to agriculture. See Intergovernmental Panel on Climate Change, *Climate Change 2007: Synthesis Report*, contribution of Working Groups I, II and III to the Fourth Assessment Report of the Intergovernmental Panel on Climate Change, ed. Core Writing Team, R. K. Pachauri, and A. Reisinger (Geneva: IPCC, 2007), 36–37.

36. Royal Society, *Climate Change: A Summary of the Science* (London: Royal Society, September 2010), 6.

37. Ibid., 5, 9.

38. Elizabeth Kolbert, *Field Notes from a Catastrophe: Man, Nature, and Climate Change* (New York: Bloomsbury USA, 2006), 148, 159.

39. Julianne Warren, "Urgent: Dreams," *Journal of Environmental Studies and Sciences* 1, no. 3 (2011): 156–61.

40. Milan Kundera, *The Art of the Novel* (New York: Grove Press, 1986), 115–16.

41. Washington Irving, "The Devil and Tom Walker," in *The Complete Works of Washington Irving in One Volume* (Frankfurt: Sigismond Schmerber, 1835), 584.

42. Quotation from the late Jerry Falwell as cited in McKibben, *Eaarth*, 12.

43. Dickens, *Tale of Two Cities*, 207.

44. McKibben, *Eaarth*, 3.

45. Dickens, *Tale of Two Cities*, 141.

46. Edward Bellamy, *Looking Backward: 2000–1887* (1888; repr., New York: Penguin, 1982), 115.

47. Bill McKibben, *The End of Nature* (New York: Random House, 2006).

48. Lewis Mumford, *The Story of Utopias* (New York: Boni and Liveright, 1922), 167. Hayden White, "The Future of Utopia in History," *Historein: A Review of the Past and Other Stories* 7 (July 2007): 14, cites Benjamin: "The catastrophe would be if things stayed the same."

49. John Burroughs, "Hit-and-Miss Method of Nature," in *Summit of the Years* (New York: William H. Wise, 1924), 86.

50. Leopold, *Sand County Almanac*, 133.

51. Bellamy, *Looking Backward*, 198.

52. Mumford, *Story of Utopias*, 167.

53. Jörn Rüsen, "History and Utopia," *Historein: A Review of the Past and Other Stories* 7 (July 2007): 5–10; Frank Manuel and Fritzie Manuel, *Utopian Thought in the Western World* (Cambridge, Mass.: Harvard University Press, 1979).

54. Aldo Leopold, quoted in Julianne L. Warren, *Aldo Leopold's Odyssey* (Washington, D.C.: Island Press, 2006), 255.

55. Also see Milan Kundera, *Slowness* (New York: Harper Perennial, 1995).

56. Cormac McCarthy, *The Road* (New York: Alfred A. Knopf, 2006), 54.

57. Ibid., 286.

58. Kundera, *Slowness*, 3, 36.

59. Leopold, *Sand County Almanac*, 46.

60. McKibben, *End of Nature*, xv.

9 The Time of Living Dead Species

Extinction Debt and Futurity in Madagascar

Genese Marie Sodikoff

LIKE MUCH OF the science fiction of H. G. Wells, the short story "Aepyornis Island," set in Madagascar, plays with the mutability of time and the specter of extinction. It tells a tale of the fabled "Elephant Bird" of Madagascar, a species larger than the modern ostrich that was overhunted to extinction by humans by at least the seventeenth century. An English collector, named Butcher, travels to Madagascar to find rarities for a buyer at a museum in London. He is stranded by his Malagasy guides and forced to fend for himself. By luck he finds in a muddy swamp the bones and several eggs of an aepyornis. To his astonishment, the eggs appear to be freshly lain. Starving, he eats two, and sees that they contain developing embryos. He allows one to hatch, and an extinct species is brought back from oblivion, albeit briefly.[1]

"Aepyornis Island" offers an entrée into the themes of temporal dislocation, the terrible reckoning that happens when living beings are "out of time," and distortions in the evolutionist continuum between "primitive" and "civilized" in European imaginations. The story presciently captures the emergent sense of time forged by evolutionist thought and conservation practice and invoked by the contemporary biological concept of "extinction debt," defined as a lag time between habitat perturbation and the species deaths that inevitably result from it.[2]

Wells's story reveals Europeans' fascination with Madagascar as a biogeographical anachronism, an alternate evolutionary theater to mainland Africa.[3] In this essay, I contextualize Madagascar's historical, global identity within present-day anxieties about planetary degradation to understand how countries that are heavily indebted—both fiscally and biologically—serve as staging grounds for scientific efforts to secure the future of species. Through these efforts, I argue, human societies are re-visioning the future.

Since at least the eighteenth century, Madagascar has been depicted as a "land out of time," a "world apart," a "living Eden," a "living laboratory of evolution," and a "naturalist's paradise."[4] Literary and scientific descriptions of Madagascar as a "land out of time" allude to its accelerated rate of species death, biogeographical and cultural atavisms, and extinctions and resurrections. To these, I add an allusion to figurative and supernatural "undead" creatures—ones that should not be alive—in the scientific and eschatological imaginaries of westerners and Malagasy alike. In conservation biology, the term *living dead species* refers to species populations that have become critically small and therefore doomed to die out.

Madagascar, settled relatively late by human beings, is a "laboratory of evolution" where scientists can refine theoretical models of species' adaptation, migration, evolution, and extinction. The island's biotic assemblages shed light on evolutionary processes that apparently move at faster clip in the tropics.[5] Because most threatened species have small geographic ranges and because island species' ranges are smaller than those of continental ones, Madagascar affords a time-lapsed view of "inkblot" extinctions and remediation strategies.[6]

My focus on how conservation science and environmental degradation forge temporal perception in Madagascar reflects my broader interest in discerning how cultural and biological extinctions, habitat loss, and interventions into these processes are shaping twenty-first-century subjectivities. Conservation biology's "living dead" metaphor resonates with Malagasy beliefs in occult entities and more general conceptualizations of the future, including its directionality and geometrical shape, evolutionist ideas of social and biological difference, and predictions about the well-being of successive generations. (Will longevity mean increasing decrepitude or prolonged health, for example?) My larger aim is to scale up ethnographically to the plane of "species culture" and "species think" with respect to global change, concordant with scholarly analyses of the logics, modalities, and ethics of global capitalism, yet also transcending the limits of "mode of production" to explain the formation of historical subjectivities.[7]

Dipesh Chakrabarty argues that "species thinking," which has long been associated with "the enterprise of deep history" done by geologists and paleoanthropologists, can be helpful in navigating the future. Thought experiments about a world bereft of *Homo sapiens,* which essentially demand us to imagine the view from nowhere, precipitate "a sense of the present that disconnects the future from the past by putting such a future beyond the grasp of historical sensibility."[8] The accelerated rate of extinction and climate change provokes us to identify ourselves not only as devastating biological agents, as Alfred Crosby proved in his sweeping account *The Columbian Exchange: Biological and Cultural Consequences of 1492,* but also as geological agents, capable of disrupting geophysical processes on a planetary scale.[9]

While I do not claim that a singular futurity is taking shape, I believe that futurist visions that compete with the more cautionary or alarmist narratives of conservation and climate scientists—such as the optimistic, transhumanist view that the merging of mind and machine will immortalize us and resolve environmental crises—are in the minority.[10] Around the globe, narratives of existential risk construct the near future as increasingly unforeseeable or in decline.[11] The bleakest view of the future has been put summarily by Australian microbiologist Frank Fenner, who recently said that "homo sapiens will not be able to survive the population explosion and 'unbridled consumption,' and will become extinct, perhaps within a century, along with many other species."[12] Concerned that we have not even discovered all the extant species on Earth, scientists more urgently want to find unknown species and learn what they can about them before these too disappear.[13] Although such "cryptic" species may emerge from their eroded habitats as already living dead species, they have the potential to offer biochemical and physiological information that may enable us to evolve out of our current ecological predicaments.[14]

With respect to the political economy of temporal perception, a recent questionable though provocative study suggests that people in wealthier nations—a minority of the global population by far—have a keener interest in future trends than people in developing countries, at least judging by their terms in Google, which are more future oriented.[15] The global economic recession has exacerbated the pessimism insinuating itself into political and ecological discourses. For example, Fernando Coronil notes that in recent political rhetoric in Latin America, "the question of the future" proposes two visions. The future is presented either "as potentiality, a sense of possibility heightened in expansive historical periods, such as liminal phases, revolutions or even stable situations," or as "a future in doubt, in question, the future as a shrinking historical horizon, a temporality of decline, social anomie or historical depression."[16] This second future, the depressive one, is what interests me here because it subverts the idea of progressive history defining the modern era.

My ethnographic loci encompass discursive, physical, and creative sites/moments of apprehension induced by a sense of quickened species death and time "running out." I concentrate mainly on the ideas and practices of North American and European conservation representatives and of Malagasy people who live in biodiversity hot spots. Conservation biologists' adoption of the zombie metaphor with reference to species extinction, and the immense popularity of apocalyptic and zombie themes in US and European television and film, say something about the subjective experience of planetary change in the global North and the ways we are projecting the shape of things to come.[17] "This is our extinction event," says a character who works for the Centers for Disease Control in the AMC zombie series *The Walking Dead*.

This imagery is not unique to US and European societies but also pervades the imaginations of rural Malagasy people. The effects of the sixth mass extinction and global climate change, of which *Homo sapiens* are the perpetrators and will be the eventual victims, are especially hard on subsistence-based societies living in forest fragments and on islands and coastal areas around the world. Populations in these regions suffer the reduction of nutritious food sources and minerals, water pollution, flooding, and severe weather events, as well as the social responses to these transformations: specifically, the raft of state and foreign interventions designed to mitigate the damages. I suggest that the deepening of Madagascar's extinction debt by human actions guides the ways in which conservation scientists exploit the past and evaluate the social practices and ideas of Malagasy people; moreover, I believe that scientific and economic activities taking place in Madagascar offer foresight into global trends.

This essay centers on the following questions: (1) How have planetary changes and scientific data about these changes molded Western perceptions of the future (chronological time) and qualitative cultural difference (ethnological time)? (2) What makes Madagascar an exemplary place in which to examine the senses of time shaped by extinction debt and conservation practice? (3) By what means do dominant temporalities refract into the social contexts of biodiversity hot spots, such as Madagascar's east coast?

Resurrections and Revolutions in Time

Global conservation—a concerted effort to protect natural resources and ecosystems today to ensure the well-being of future generations—involves not only preserving habitats but also calling up the past in some form or another. Examples include diverse projects, such as dredging up native seeds buried in tracts of land that have been exhausted by strip mining, revitalizing obsolescent traditions deemed ecologically sustainable, maintaining "wild" biological traits of endemic species that get diluted through captive breeding, reanimating ancient genes via DNA synthesis, and preserving cultural or natural elements of "heritage" through the United Nations programs.[18]

I organize these disparate sites of activity around the concept of "resurrection" to understand how dominant formations of space-time are conceptualized in the twenty-first century. *Resurrection* invokes the metaphorical language of conservation biology, occult idioms in Madagascar, and popular culture in the United States and Europe, where zombies are all the rage (as opposed to the UFOs and aliens that preoccupied audiences of the 1950s and '60s). Resurrection projects differ from the salvage projects of early nineteenth-century anthropology and natural history in that they attempt to offset future damages rather than merely encase last survivors of species for scientific knowledge. Yet the offsets and the resurrections of past practice only pay interest on extinction debt. They often call up diminished versions of original forms: less robust, spectral, imperfect.

These revivifying practices, I argue, are revising a modernist ideology of technology-driven progress. Ursula Heise argues that "narratives of the decline of nature and the tragic and elegiac modes of storytelling are mobilized in the context of extinct and endangered species as a way of reflecting on particular histories of modernization, and in many cases of articulating resistance to the forms this modernization has taken."[19] Moreover, ideologies of cultural difference, intrinsic to modern philosophies of history that have condoned global social inequalities as inevitable and imperialist quests as "civilizing missions," are being disassembled, insofar as international agents of conservation and development are prone to valorizing elements of the evolutionary "past" deemed more biologically robust, environmentally sustainable, and data rich.

One might say that in place of an ideology of advancement that repudiates the past as "a strange and useless inheritance," denialism, or a refusal of accountability to the future, is redefining what it has meant to be modern.[20] In a deceptive reversal, markers of cultural and biological "primitiveness" are appreciating. Meanwhile, the tastes, technologies, and ontologies that have defined "the modern" appear maladaptive—leached of vitality and degenerate.

Currents of thought and practice suggest that we are in the midst of another "revolution in ethnological time," to borrow Thomas Trautmann's phrase, one that is linked to a perception of the future arcing backward.[21] The 1960s marks the onset of this process of temporal reimagining propelled by the revelations of popular scientific publications, particularly Rachel Carson's *Silent Spring* (1962), and a growing public awareness of human-induced climate change, biodiversity loss, and rising rates of cancer.[22]

According to Trautmann, the "revolution in ethnological time" occurred in the nineteenth century over a short duration (several decades) as scientists digested the significance of findings at Brixham Cave, in Devon, England, in 1819. Flint tools were found lying near the remains of long-extinct fauna, such as the tichorine rhinoceros, the cave bear, and the cave hyena. The implications of this coexistence in time of humans and ancient species triggered the relatively "sudden collapse, during the decade of Darwin, of the short chronology for human history based on the biblical narrative, a chronology in which the whole of human history had been crowded into the space of a few thousand years; . . . what replaced it was an ethnological time that extended human history indefinitely backward, for tens or hundreds of thousands of years, or more. Very suddenly the bottom dropped out of history and its beginnings disappeared into an abyss of time."[23] Trautmann elucidates how the deepening of human existence into an abyss of the past compelled European intellectuals to reassess their "us-them perspective," their explanatory framework for social difference that plotted societies along a continuum of savage to civilized. A new framework was needed because the biblical categories of "heathen, pagan, gentile" had become irrelevant.[24] The revolution in ethnological time, which predated but was firmly assimilated after the publication of Darwin's *The Origin of Species* in 1859, as Trautmann explains, was interknit with the change in chronological time launched by the discovery at Brixham Cave. The savage Other became the primitive or evolutionary ancestor of the European Self.

If the floor fell out from under us in the mid-nineteenth century, toward the end of the twentieth century the ceiling began falling down on us. Our exposure to information about, and our phenomenological experiences of, planetary change caused by the pollution of atmospheric, marine, freshwater, and soil systems are disrupting the dominant idea of time as linear and progressive in both the metropolitan centers of scientific research and the global economic peripheries. This is particularly so in bio-diversity hot spots, where the effects of degradation are acutely felt. As the space of the future contracts, we are compelled to search for survival resources contained in the natural historical and evolutionary past.

Most scientists concur that we must radically transform our modes of energy and commodity production to slow the pace of planetary degradation. The "survival of civilization may well hang on a cultural evolutionary sea change."[25] While acts of resurrecting ancient matter, landscapes, cultural practices, and dying languages may remediate present-day conditions, one gets the sense that these revivals will suffer a precarious existence. As Paul Alan Cox contends, the "indelible mark we now etch on the chronicle of time will not . . . so easily disappear, for we have chosen to destroy bio-logical species."[26] Having scarred the planet, human beings have become preoccupied with surviving, as anthropologists have noted. Marc Abélès declares that the matter of survival now lies at the "heart of political action."[27] Celia Lowe sees evolutionary sci-ence at the center of a "vital politics" in that its paramount concerns are to maintain the ability of life-forms to evolve and speciate, to maintain the still-existing store of resources that make the sustaining of life possible.[28]

This is not to say that subaltern *societies* are enjoying a moment of ascendancy in Western hierarchies of moral value; rather, select traits of indigenous culture—bits of indigenous knowledge and cognition, bits of biochemical and physiological data about endemic species, for example—are lighting the path forward. Conservation missions to "rewild" depleted habitats and reify heritage for tourism markets reflect deep mis-givings about the homogenization of nature, the taming of DNA, and the extinction of indigenous knowledge. Julie Cruikshank explains how "traditional ecological knowl-edge" (TEK) has routinely been appropriated by states and institutions planning for natural resource management: "Internationally, there has been an explosion of interest in indigenous knowledge or 'traditional ecological knowledge' during the 1990s. At the end of the 20th century, 'TEK' is a term ubiquitous in resource management plans concerning caribou, fisheries, and forestry management (the management having pri-marily to do with regulating human *use* of ungulates, fish, and forests)."[29] Cruikshank discusses how institutions selectively cull TEK for data that bolster resource manage-ment schemes, often giving the illusion of collective decision making between bureau-crats and indigenous peoples.[30]

At the same time, members of indigenous social movements find it advantageous to emphasize the utility of their cultural knowledge of local habitats and medicinal plants, as well as the intrinsic value of their unique cultural identities.[31] Indigenous social movements often seek to link up to conservation actors and institutions to increase their global visibility and political traction.[32] Advocates of indigenous lan-guage preservation, moreover, stress that the complex structures of indigenous languages contain a wealth of information about human cognition.[33] Through the rising valorization and exploitation of indigenous knowledge and ancient DNA, times are changing.

Advances in DNA recovery technology have begun to make *Jurassic Park* scenarios a reality. Serendipitously, as I was working on this chapter, I received an e-mail notice of an article by the science correspondent of the *Telegraph* of the United Kingdom. It reports that "the giant elephant bird of Madagascar could be resurrected after scientists discovered how to extract DNA from ancient egg shells. . . . The flightless elephant bird—related to ostriches and emus—is the largest bird ever to have lived. It had massive legs, taloned claws and a long, powerful neck. Its body was covered in bristling, hairlike feathers, like those of the emu, and its beak resembled a broadheaded spear. It evolved at a time when birds ruled the earth and probably existed on Madagascar for 60 million years until dying out in the 17th century."[34] In the present day, ancient DNA and indigenous knowledge do not merely tell the metropolitan something about deep time and his or her evolutionary past; they may also contain the sources of his or her salvation. The global politics of survival can be divisive, entailing a categorization of social groups in terms of how and to what degree they are seen to be existentially threatening. Yet it can also have unifying effects the more the interests of the species as a whole, rather than factions, become preeminent.

In what follows, I describe the natural historical and cultural attributes of Madagascar that have made it fertile ground for outsiders' reflections on mortality and time. The latter part of the essay offers two ethnographic examples of what I call resurrection projects: one focuses on conservationists' valorization of "indigenously conservationist" taboos in Madagascar that have long served to protect certain species from hunting; the other focuses on the captive breeding and reintroduction to Madagascar of endemic species, specifically lemurs. Ethnographic data derive from my ethnographic research in eastern Madagascar (1994–95, 1997, 1999, 2000–2002, for a total of two and a half years), interviews with conservation scientists at the Duke Lemur Center in 2007, and recent conversations with staff of the Bronx Zoo, which has institutional ties to the Makira National Park in northeast Madagascar.

The Distinctiveness of Madagascar

At this point, I will make a brief detour back to "Aepyornis Island" to plumb what the relationship among the past, present, and future in this fictional account portends for contemporary times. I left off where the stranded Englishman, Butcher, inexplicably isolated from human contact, nurtures the aepyornis chick and becomes very attached to his pet. When the bird matures to a height of fourteen feet, the friendship between man and bird begins to sour. Master becomes prey as the adult aepyornis begins to hunt the man, and Butcher's primal instincts spark to life. He must butcher his pet to save himself. He does so with much effort, since the bird is quite powerful. He is emotionally devastated by his act. Butcher, having become his name, has undergone a process of devolution in the wilds of Madagascar. Literary scholar Richard Pearson writes: "The egg/artefact, fossilized and extinct, returns the intellectual collector to a more primitive time; . . . we are continually reminded that the bird is 'an extinct animal' who should not be there."[35] A European man arriving in a primitive land, the rebirth of the aepyornis: these dislocations in time, as Wells imagined them in the late nineteenth century, demand a reckoning in the story. This happens through the degeneration of Butcher, rendering him coeval with the place, if not the animal. Reckoning also occurs through the slaughter of the bird, who was anyway "out of time," doomed to a second extinction. Wells's story portrays a landscape of doomed animals, scurrilous natives and foreigners, battles of survival, and an international market in exotic rarities. As I have suggested, these reversals of primitive and domesticated, savage and civilized, are implicated in contemporary conservation practices.

The aepyornis is what scientists today would call a "Lazarus species," a reference to Lazarus of Bethany who, in the Gospel of John, is restored to life four days after his death. The "Lazarus effect," a term invented by paleobiologist David Jablonski, refers to species that vanish from the fossil record, only to reappear in later geological strata.[36] In conservation biology, a Lazarus species may also be one thought extinct but then discovered alive, often in an unexpected location. One might say here that the aepyornis, a sole member of its species that, once hatched, reenters an ecology very different from that of its earlier existence, becomes a "living dead" species.

Living dead creatures animate the time delay of extinction debt: "The doomed species do not all die at once," explains Stuart Pimm, "but are spread over time as determined by the species survivorship curve."[37] Madagascar's extinction debt is large because island species are more vulnerable to environmental perturbations. Theorists of island biogeography hold that islands are spaces of concentrated, disproportionate extinctions relative to continents because of their limited geographical range and low population numbers.[38] Of all bird extinctions, for example, 90 percent have occurred on islands.[39] For decades, scientists believed that the species compositions of islands were a result of intersecting processes, a dynamic of species immigrations and extinctions achieving an equilibrium that was easily disrupted by human colonization. Today the prevailing view is that the species composition and diversity of islands result from more complex, nonequilibrial interactions, including, for example, climate change and tectonic activity, occurring at different temporal and spatial scales.[40] Beyond dispute, however, is the radical impact of human actions on the biodiversity and species population numbers on islands.

The island of Madagascar formed during the mid-Jurassic breakup of the supercontinent Gondwanaland approximately 160 million years ago, when a large chunk of land detached from the eastern edge of Gondwanaland and floated eastward, leaving its floral and faunal species, as well as species that migrated there later, to follow distinct evolutionary paths. According to new genetic evidence, Madagascar was colonized by voyagers from Indonesia approximately 1,200 years ago, although humans had probably visited the island before then.[41] The archaeological and fossil records reveal "wide-ranging and spectacular" megafaunal extinctions in Madagascar after the arrival of humans, including the extinction of "pygmy hippos, giant tortoises, elephant birds and giant lemurs up to gorilla size."[42] A prolonged extinction episode "eliminated all endemic species of Malagasy vertebrates larger than 10 kilograms in body mass."[43] Among the megafauna, only the crocodile endured.[44] In the late 1980s, scientists designated Madagascar a "biodiversity hot spot," as its forest biomes possess "exceptional concentrations of species with high levels of endemism" and an unusually high rate of depletion.[45]

Ethnologically, Madagascar also has a unique identity. It is renowned outside its borders for being a place where people revere the dead and ritually exhume and rebury ancestral bones. In the central highlands, for example, people occasionally remove the wrapped bones of deceased kin from the tomb in order to rewrap, dance with, and finally reinter them in a ritual called *famadiana*. Elsewhere, as in Mananara-Nord, a prefecture on the northeast coast where I conducted fourteen months of ethnographic research (2000–2002), northern Betsimisaraka people also exhume the remains of the dead. When the bodies are sufficiently decomposed, kin members transfer the skeletons into familial tombs, which may be either natural caves or holes dug into the ground and sealed with stones. In tombs, the corpses become ancestors, dead yet actively engaged in the lives of the living by ensuring health and harvest if their descendants pay them proper tribute.

Europeans' observations of these practices gave rise to descriptions of Madagascar as the "Island of Ghosts" and "Island of the Ancestors." From the Christian perspective, Madagascar has represented "the Earthly Paradise of the Fall."[46] Gillian Feeley-Harnik argues that images of the Fall allude to the "profligate childbearing" of the Malagasy people, which "is supposed to have driven their fellow creatures into extinction." One such creature, the nocturnal lemur, which "Linnaeus named after the Roman 'spirits of the dead,'" nevertheless seems "to haunt the land where they once lived."[47]

The social history of Madagascar begins with an extinction event: the extermination of one society by invaders. Of twenty different ethnic groups that make up a population of about twenty million today, the Merina of the central high plateau is the ethnic group that has dominated the central government. Based on Merina historical accounts, royal Merina ancestors arriving from Austronesian islands encountered a people, called the Vazimba, already living in the central plateau and proceeded to exterminate them. Writing in the *Geographical Journal* in 1940, Olive Murray Chapman writes: "Tradition states that the Hova [the name of the royal caste] on their arrival, at some uncertain date, conquered an aboriginal tribe then in Imerina; these people, the Vazimba, were of African origin and were said to be dwarfs, similar to the pre-Bantus of Central Africa. Later the Hova held these legendary folk in great reverence, worshipping their spirits from whom they claimed their kings were descended."[48]

Similar in plot and detail to the Vazimba legend is the recurrent and geographically dispersed tale of the *kalanoro,* supernatural humanoids who inhabit rural villages as spirit-servants to the living. I encountered talk of *kalanoro* spirits in Mananara-Nord, and these accounts closely match what Lesley Sharp heard in the northwest: *kalanoro* are "dwarfed and hirsute, with unkempt hair, long fingernails, eyes that glow red, and feet that face backwards on their short little legs. . . . If captured, a *kalanoro*'s human guardian can draw on this spirit's power to heal" or, in Mananara-Nord, to become clairvoyant.[49] The *kalanoro* were also victims of an extinction event, according to residents of the Mananara-Nord prefecture who told me that *kalanoro* had once inhabited the rain forest but had died out as the forest eroded.

Nonhuman animal extinctions also garnish the island's history. In the nineteenth century, European scholars of Madagascar were intrigued by discoveries of extinct megafaunal species. For example, excavations in the southern high plateau region by Norwegian missionaries who were building a bathhouse on natural hot springs uncovered the crania and tusks of extinct pygmy hippopotami, inspiring speculation on whether rumors of strange unidentified animals in parts of the island were possible last survivors of animals thought to have vanished.

The Reverend James Sibree Jr. writes in 1891 of these findings: "Perhaps the half-mythical stories of the Songomby, Tokandia, Lalomena, and other strange creatures current among the Malagasy are traditions of the period when these huge pachyderms were still to be seen in the lakes and streams and marshes of Madagascar."[50] A century later, in 1995, Malagasy archaeologist Ramilisonina and conservation biologist David Burney were still able to collect accounts of such mystery animals from living people, animals known locally as the *kilopilopitsofy, kidoky,* and *bokiboky,* which, they write, were "described in terms similar to creatures detailed in historical accounts and folklore recorded in Madagascar between the mid-1600s and the end of the nineteenth century."[51]

Descriptions by Malagasy people over three centuries of the form and behaviors of these animals have resembled those of the dwarf hippopotamus, a species of giant lemur, and several subspecies of elephant birds, known in Malagasy as *voron patra* or *voron patrana.* From radiocarbon dating of last known occurrences, these species have been inferred to have gone extinct early in the last millennium or perhaps a few centuries later.[52] The collection of oral histories about possible sole survivors not only informs the science of the process of extinction but also elevates inhabitants' experiential knowledge to the same plane as scientific knowledge, turning oral accounts that were once treated as "myth" into possible evidence and finally into data that inform scientific theories of island extinctions.[53]

Since the late twentieth century, the island has often been described as a "land bleeding into the sea" because of the streaming of its reddish soil into the Indian Ocean during heavy rains.[54] Along the densely biodiverse, forested east coast, the rate of species endangerment has steeply accelerated since the mid-twentieth century. Although rain forest depletion began with the first human colonization, it increased dramatically after France colonized the island in 1896.[55] Michael Williams writes: "Of the 58 million ha of the island, by 1920 about 20 percent was said to remain in primary forest. By 1949 it was 8.6 percent; 10.3 percent was in *savoka*, second-growth bracken fern with bamboos; and the rest was in grass and savanna."[56] In the past half century, roughly half of the forest cover has vanished.[57] Although rates of deforestation have been contested, satellite data of Madagascar from the late 1980s and early 1990s showed that 66 percent of the original primary forest of the eastern humid zone had been burned, mostly for the purpose of rice cultivation.[58] Mining, logging, and road and rail works have also contributed to the decline of the forest.

More recently, a coup d'état in March 2009 provoked the plunder of the island's protected areas on its east coast by Chinese and Malagasy timber exporters, who sent in teams of armed loggers to extract rosewood, ebony, and other hardwoods from the parks and convey it to the ports for shipment to China, Europe, and the United States. The "rosewood massacre" has derailed conservation efforts under way since the mid-1980s, when an era of neoliberal conservation policy was launched after a long hiatus of lax conservation enforcement.[59] Rosewood and ebony trees take hundreds of years to reach maturity and contribute to the unique ecology of rain forests. Logging has further endangered other plant and animal species, turning remnant rain forests, gene banks for survival, into troves of biological ephemera. News coverage of the logging, particularly images of piles of smoked lemur bodies which are consumed by the loggers in their forest encampments, has at times implied that Chinese imperialist practices in Africa, seemingly unconcerned about ecological ramifications of old-fashioned resource extraction, represent the new "primitive."[60]

I now turn to two applications of "resurrection" in Madagascar aimed at reducing the island's extinction debt. The first concerns the work of conservation biologists in the United States who breed Malagasy lemurs in captivity and in the late 1990s brought several animals "home" to Madagascar to restock depleted habitats. Although the effort has been put on hold since 2004, scientists at the Duke Lemur Center (DLC) are hoping to resume it. I call this a resurrection not only because it is "restorative," an attempt to restock a habitat with a depleted, endemic species, but also because the phylogenetic "primitiveness" of lemurs comes into play. The second case regards the efforts of conservation practitioners to revive "indigenously conservationist" Malagasy taboos, many of which are being abandoned by Malagasy people as wild protein sources diminish. Early anthropologists identified Malagasy people's animal taboos as relics of totemic thought. Contemporary anthropologists have refuted the idea that taboos are artifactual and have instead argued that taboos are dynamic practices, continually being abolished and established. Yet Malagasy people themselves note that taboos against hunting certain species that they have long upheld, at least in their own lifetimes, are increasingly being abandoned as protein sources die out.

Captive Breeding and Reintroduction

The Duke Lemur Center breeds endangered prosimians in captivity, including Malagasy lemurs, Asian lorises, and African galagos (bush babies), and it provides space for scientists to study them. Since 1966, the DLC has been the main provider of lemurs to the world's zoos and other captive breeding facilities. The study of prosimians such as lemurs sheds light on primate evolution.[61] Based on phylogenetic reconstructions of DNA sequence data, evidence suggests that "primates originated at around 90 [million years ago]. . . . Hence colonization of Madagascar by lemurs would have taken place at about 80 [million years ago]" in one or perhaps two separate migrations (how this happened is unknown).[62] Phylogenetic and paleocontinental evidence indicates that the "initial split between lorisiforms and lemuriforms would have occurred in Africa [and not in Asia, which has been a matter of debate], followed by an eastward migration of lemurs to Madagascar."[63] Once in Madagascar, the lemuriforms speciated and radiated out.

In 2007, I interviewed DLC scientists and representatives of the Madagascar Fauna Group in Durham, North Carolina. The Madagascar Fauna Group is a consortium of zoos and conservation organizations in the United States involved in the conservation of Madagascar's flagship endemic species and the reintroduction of lemurs to Malagasy soil. Beginning in 1997 and lasting until 2004, the Madagascar Fauna Group staff arranged the transport and release of the first five captive-bred, black and white ruffed lemurs in Madagascar. The effort was a dream come true for conservationists of the DLC.[64]

Yet as they knew, the likelihood that any of the individuals of the first group of "pioneers" to the homeland would survive to reproduce in the wild was at best uncertain. Captive-bred primates typically lose the behavioral competence to survive in the wild because inbreeding can result in genetic and phenotypic changes.[65] Elsbeth McPhee and Kathy Carlstead explain as follows:

> First, an individual can change its behavior to meet an immediate specific need, e.g., conforming to feeding schedules or conspecific groupings. Second, growing up in a captive environment that is more restrictive than the wild can alter how an animal learns and change how it responds to future events. These changes occur within an individual, but build as the animal develops. The third level of response comprises many individual changes, but is expressed across a population. Within a captive population, certain behaviors will confer greater survivorship on the individuals who express them, e.g. greater tolerance of loud noises. These behaviors will be passed on genetically from generation to generation, resulting in a distribution of traits within the captive population that is distinct from distributions observed in wild populations.[66]

But lemurs and other prosimians have some genetic advantages in that regard. Since they are more "primitive primates," lemurs retain their natural behaviors over generations of captive breeding better than higher-order primates, but these skills nevertheless deteriorate in captivity.[67] Captive-bred lemurs may be slightly more vulnerable to predators, and they generally fare better if they pair with a wild mate.[68]

At the DLC and in other captive-breeding facilities, scientists used to be able to maintain robust captive populations by bringing in wild-caught specimens to replenish the gene pool. Although the "older" DNA improves the longevity of species populations, wild-caught animals may be too old and not ideal breeders, so they come with risks. In the 1980s, however, "capture missions" of wild specimens for zoos and other breeding facilities fell out of favor, as animal rights activists objected to the practice, regulations about the transport of biological matter over state borders became more rigid, and international policy began to favor *in situ* conservation.

Because the offspring of wild captives become progressively more docile and risk lowering their chances for survival, their ancient species knowledge must be regularly exercised. Staff at the DLC must train captive animals in the ways of the wild ("natural behaviors") to increase survivorship should they be transported to Madagascar and liberated into the Betampona Reserve on the east coast. The DLC facility is designed to promote the species' health and longevity. It consists of three office buildings and a chain-link cage area that is covered with tarpaulin during the fall and winter. Most of the caged runs have indoor and outdoor access, and observations can be conducted on the animals year-round. Chain link separates species from one another. Each cage has climbing structures, tree trunks, and branches off which hang empty cardboard six-pack beverage containers. Caretakers place the animals' feed, called "monkey chow," in the beer and soda cartons rather than in bowls in order to hone the lemurs' foraging skills in anticipation of the day they might be returned to the wild. Buckets, children's plastic swings, and hammocks are also suspended from ropes to mimic forest vines. The facility is nestled in seventeen acres of fenced-in North Carolinian forest, subdivided into five Natural Habitat Enclosures (NHEs), where the animals live during the warm months.

Up until 2004, these NHEs served as "boot camps" for lemur individuals selected for reintroduction to Madagascar. The original species homeland, called "the wild," actually consists of a variety of habitats for lemurs. The wild for lemurs is not the same as the wild for other species, and the wild for black and white ruffed lemurs is not the same as that for, say, Coquerel's sifaka *(Propithecus verreauxi coquereli)*. Even more complicated, species within Madagascar are dispersed into different regional subpopulations, each possessing genetic adaptations to their specific environment. The interbreeding of individuals from different clades, or subpopulations, carries the risk of losing these adaptations to the unique "wild" they inhabit. For other species, the interbreeding of two captive-bred parents substantially reduces the success of offspring to survive outside captivity.

Between 1997 and 2004, a mere thirteen lemur pioneers were flown from North Carolina, held in acclimatization cages and fed tropical and native forest fruits, then released into the Betampona Reserve on the east coast of Madagascar. At the time of the first mission, news reports traced the lemurs' progress. The black and white ruffed lemurs had "begun an historic journey, the first of their species ever to be returned to the wild," read one 1997 report (ScienceDaily).[69] On the day of their release from cage into the wild, the Malagasy staff of the Betampona Reserve performed a ritual tribute to the ancestors. Such ceremonies (often called *fomba*) involve asking the dead ancestors of a locality to impart their blessings on the occasion. Malagasy park employees poured swigs of rum into folded green leaf cups and placed the offerings on stones at the base of the cage door. Everyone watched anxiously as the lemurs were freed into their native habitat, returning "home to a land they never knew."[70] In describing the reintroduction of endemic lemurs into the wild of Madagascar as beginning with a traditional ceremony to pay respect to the ancestors, newspaper reports implicitly connected Malagasy tradition and species endemism, distilling something of the essence of Madagascar's identity into the restoration process. The invocation of the ancestors and the request that they bless the lemur pioneers, although mediated by a foreign organization, represents an interesting moment in the history of Malagasy-animal relations, in which dead ancestors have for a long time mediated these relations through the institution of taboo.

At the time of the lemur reintroduction program, Malagasy officials had been enthusiastic about the effort. In the words of the DLC's conservation coordinator in October 2007, the Malagasy feel a "great sense of pride about lemurs; . . . it's something that's exclusively their national heritage." The association of nature and nation has a deep history, and since the onset of the neoliberal conservation effort in the late 1980s in Madagascar and elsewhere, endemic species, called "natural heritage," have been promoted as icons of national identity and worthy of protecting. At the time, however, Malagasy authorities also expressed displeasure that lemurs were being successfully bred in foreign nations. They wanted to launch similar breeding programs for lemurs and other species in Madagascar, as they have now done for the rare Malagasy pochard (awaiting introduction into the wild) and for several rare amphibians.[71]

In animal reintroduction efforts, ideas about species' origins and primary habitats periodize time in complicated ways. We know, for example, that lemurs are not autochthonous to Madagascar but migrated there millions of years after the land mass separated from the African continent. In the near past, however, lemur habitats that were millions of years old were decimated in the blink of an eye after humans arrived. Ecological restoration entails moving back the hands of the clock to the hour of presettlement. Conservation projects have advocated the utility of bolstering heritage preservation as a means of improving the survivorship of species. Heritage projects select high-value practices and species and specific configurations of nature-culture, such as the ritual invocation of ancestors, or obedience to taboos for the sake of species survival.

Conservationist Taboos and Totemic Thought

While wilderness is often imagined as original and static, antecedent to culture, putatively traditional forms of "culture" are also sometimes deployed to regenerate it.[72] My second example of resurrection concerns just such a process, the institution of *fady* (taboo) in Madagascar, specifically animal *fady*, which conservation representatives have studied with interest. The valorization of animal *fady* in the conservation sector of Madagascar again entails a mingling of ideas about cultural endogeny (or indigenous knowledge/practice) and species endemism. I have to qualify the term *indigenous,* for Madagascar's people are not typically described as such because of the island's relatively recent settlement. Malagasy people's obedience of animal *fady* until recent times implies their past resourcefulness or conservation-minded traditions.

Fady are observed by all ethnic populations in Madagascar and are integral to social life.[73] *Fady* are prohibitions established by dead ancestors who wield great power over the living and whose wishes are upheld by elders, the next in line to ancestorhood. They confer sacredness and danger on the proscribed object. European, North American, and Malagasy ethnographers have remarked on the pervasiveness of *fady* in Malagasy life, and some conservation scientists have treated *fady* as a golden key for sustainable conservation.[74]

Animal *fady* are only one category of taboo among many. *Fady* do not apply to all individuals of a village or larger community; they may apply only to an individual, a household, or an extended family. Animal *fady* proscribe the killing and consumption of the species, and sometimes animal *fady* require averting one's gaze before the animal, using euphemisms, or avoiding particular land features or resources tied to the animal.[75] In the northeast prefecture of Mananara-Nord, the Malagasy elders I knew often expressed apprehension about the rising incidence of taboo transgression among youth and migrants, many of whom had come to the region to try their hand at cultivating cloves and vanilla, very lucrative crops.

Conservation scientists argue that incidence of taboo abandonment by rural people is driven by people's need for new sources of wild protein. Where once residents of various localities avoided eating certain lemurs, sea turtles, and certain species of fish and fowl, now their preferred food sources are dying out as their habitats shrink.[76] Many reports, travel accounts, and scientific studies written by North American and European visitors to Madagascar over the past several decades comment on the abandonment of cultural taboos that have long protected certain lemur species and other endemic animals from extinction.

Early anthropologists of Madagascar considered animal taboos to be relics of totemic thought, a belief that human social groups descended from apical (often nonhuman) ancestors and that the descendants of these ancestors, such as indris (the largest Malagasy prosimian), sea turtles, crocodiles, and aye-ayes, were sacred.[77] Nineteenth-century anthropologists theorized totemism to be a form of primitive religion that shed light on the origins of the Europeans' "evolved" expressions of spirituality.

Since the 1990s, conservation scientists have articulated the potential of animal *fady* to complement conservation efforts. A number of conservation science studies promote efforts to study and ideally use *fady* toward conservation goals. For example, Joshua E. Cinner writes: "Although attempts have been made to integrate these taboos into contemporary marine conservation, these have met with limited success, particularly when the spiritual role of the taboo was not well understood by conservation agencies. Effectively integrating Malagasy taboos into the modern conservation context will require a thorough understanding of the history, spiritual role, spiritual leaders and rules associated with each location."[78] In another study, Jones et al. state that "few researchers have looked explicitly at the role *fady* play in governing interactions between local people and wild species, which makes it difficult for conservationists to make use of potential synergies between *fady* and conservation."[79] However, it is not always clear how one might use *fady* for conservation purposes, not only because they have never been fixed (one can never know exactly how long-standing a particular *fady* is), but also because people have resisted the appropriation of *fady* for conservation, an effort that Malagasy subsistence farmers have long decried because it recalls colonialist policies of land enclosure and compulsory labor.[80]

Conservation project staffs have at times sought to tap into the emotional potency of *fady* as a means of disciplining the actions of peasants who reside near protected areas. For example, Andrew Walsh writes that in Ankarana, northern Madagascar, an official sign at the boundary of a special reserve is marked "ALA FADY" (sacred/taboo forest) to deter trespassers.[81] *Ala fady* represents a widespread "habitat taboo" in Madagascar. It refers to the forest of familial tombs, and for Malagasy people it is customarily prohibited to burn such forest. To do so risks the vengeance of the ancestors. In my experience, the use of the institution of *fady* to benefit of the conservation program has been generally ineffective. Sometimes Malagasy people have pushed back by pressuring outsiders to conform to local *fady,* which introduces another problem for those who see conservationist potential in them. Not all animal *fady* refer to endangered species or even endemic species.

A case I have written about recently describes the problem of conservation representatives attempting to cherry-pick "good" animal *fady* from a socio-historical matrix.[82] The case concerns a local *fady* against killing the common rat in the Mananara-Nord Biosphere Reserve, my ethnographic research site between 2000 and 2002. The Biosphere Reserve encompasses rural villages of Betsimisaraka ethnic populations, a rain forest park, and a marine park that harbors a coral reef and three small islets. The largest of the islets, Nosy Antafaña, is infested with rats considered sacred by residents of Sahasoa, the village lying closest to the islet. A Malagasy employee of the Biosphere Reserve, Ali, maintained a small house on that islet, where he often stayed for several nights in a row. He was in charge of patrolling the activities of fishermen in the marine reserve and making sure their catches did not exceed allowed amounts or did not contain fish below the legal size.

The rats were *fady,* and since no one could kill or harm them, they fearlessly overran Ali's small house. Ali did not seem to mind; in fact he lived happily among them. Four other *fady* animals were specific to this islet: the skink (a type of large lizard), the tern, the zebu, and the wild boar. Of the five *fady* animals, only the first three, skinks, terns and rats, occurred there naturally, in the "wild." Not only was it prohibited to kill these animals while on the islet, but it was also *fady* to utter the real names (euphemisms were required) or to bring beef or pork to any of the islets. The rules of these *fady* had allegedly been established by dead ancestors who used to govern the area, three brothers named Rangontsy, whose bones were buried on one of the islets.

Fady transgression risks bodily injury or trouble of some kind. In a serious blow to the credibility of the conservation project managing the entire Biosphere Reserve, project representatives arranged a crop, rat, and non-native species eradication campaign for Nosy Antafaña in the late 1990s in order to restore its ecology to a presettled condition. Ali recounted to me in 2002 that administrators had ordered the manual conservation workers such as him to uproot the lemon and breadfruit trees, banana plants, and coconut palms. Then they hired a specialist to poison the rats, which outraged the residents of Sahasoa. Ali claimed that the Biosphere bosses had promised residents they would leave the rats alone, since killing them risked serious trouble. Residents believed transgression would make the sea choppy and unfishable; it could put fishermen at risk of capsizing or being stranded at sea with broken motors. As proof, the motor of the Biosphere project's canoe died for good after the rat eradication, Ali said, and the conservation project had to buy a new one.

By 2000, bad feelings had subsided, and the rat population had rebounded. The Biosphere Reserve's conservation project had desisted from further eradication plans in order to improve relations with the village. The animal *fady* in question here pertained not to an endemic, endangered species, which would have complemented conservation efforts, but instead to an invasive, alien rodent that has outcompeted endemic rodents in Madagascar. The common rat, symbolic of degeneration and decay (not only in urban sites of the North but also in Madagascar), diminished the extent to which Nosy Antafaña historical ecology could be resurrected; other non-native species were removed, but the abundance of the rats signified the foreshortened restoration potential of the islet as well as the potential pitfalls of championing animal *fady* as a conservation strategy.

The sense that time is running out for Madagascar's primordial-looking forests and species motivates attempts to resuscitate fragments of heritage. In Madagascar, conservation efforts have historically concentrated on the suppression of slash-and-burn horticulture *(tavy)*, a ritualized system that commemorates the ancestors and more recently includes the valorization of elements of cultural heritage.

This latter effort does not reflect a nostalgic romanticization of "savage" ecological nobility. Euro-Americans do not imagine rural Malagasy people to possess superior skills and acumen, especially with regard to environmental protection. Nevertheless, the valorization of select animal *fady* suggests that conservation scientists believe that ancestral practices of at least the near past may have indeed been more rational and that it serves the global public good to enlighten rural people to the virtues of certain moribund customs. By the same token, the atavistic creatures of Madagascar are cherished for their structural and genetic resources, which, like living time capsules, afford glimpses into an earlier, more vital ecology.

Anxious Times

I conclude with a reflection on affect and temporality, and on the significance of the living dead in contemporary, cross-cultural locations. It is reasonable today to be apprehensive about tomorrow, and dread, rather than "imperialist nostalgia," has become the prime mover of language and biodiversity salvage missions. The goal of conservation is less about eternalizing present-day fragments of habitat and heritage than about resetting the clock to cultivate the generative potential of these fragments for the sake of the future.

Longing for the past has inspired the encasement and immortalization of objects, and modernism has had a contradictory relationship to the past. Renato Rosaldo's concept of "imperialist nostalgia" captures the disingenuous yearning for cultures, environments, and ways of life that have been destroyed by the very people, projects and forces that mourn them: "'We' (who believe in progress) valorize innovation and then yearn for more stable worlds, whether these reside in our own past, in other cultures, or in the conflation of the two. . . . When the so-called civilizing process destabilizes forms of life, the agents of change experience transformations of other cultures as if they were personal losses."[83] In recent times, anxiety and dread—while they have surely always shaped the social worlds of colonized peoples—stimulate conservation missions to record and recover extinguishing life forms. Anxiety and dread are anticipatory sentiments, often of indeterminate origin, that lack the immediacy of fear yet make one take pause. One could make the case that rural Malagasy people have been suffering an intensification of dread over time, particularly in areas hard hit by ecological degradation and swelling population numbers, if the pronounced meddling of supernatural entities in the affairs of the living is any indication of historical change.

The condition of the material environment has made the present distinct from presents past in Madagascar. The lush forests that once lured Europeans to the island's shores have been decimated to patches. To many residents of the Mananara-Nord prefecture, the influx of outsiders, the scarcity of new land to cultivate, and the enclosure of relict rain forest by the national park service are threatening traditional livelihood practices that have given Malagasy people a sense of security and place. The act of zebu sacrifice, for example, so important to appeasing ancestors and therefore avoiding trouble, is growing more burdensome economically, as residents suffer dwindling harvests due to leached soils and a decreasing surface area of forest to cultivate. Anxieties often call up supernatural entities and events.[84]

Lesley Sharp's ethnographic work on possessing spirits (*tromba*) and zombies (*lolo angatra* and *lolo vokatra*) in northern Madagascar, in Sakalava territory, illustrates the panoply of living dead beings that haunt the postcolonial landscape of Madagascar and serve as emblems of "highly localized anxieties projected through a symbolic of difference."[85] She writes of people's fears and descriptions of migrant zombies of Tandroy ethnicity who wander Madagascar's northwest plantation region and "rob living Sakalava of their livelihood."[86]

The undead Tandroy resemble the zombie-laborers in the Northern Province of South Africa described by Jean and John Comaroff. Rumors circulate that the zombies are created and exploited by the newly rich, while living South Africans are left without jobs. South Africa healers mobilize public spectacles as they try to "liberate" zombies from their exploitative captors to "return them home," strangely echoing the news reports of the lemur reintroduction effort in Madagascar.[87]

With zombies, one confronts the risk of self-annihilation by Lazarus effect. It is probably a universal truth that zombies are associated with loss and decline. The living human being's encounter with a zombie, whether projected on the screen or the mind's eye, resembles gazing into a warped mirror in which the law of time is contorted and a dead self has risen. Zombies signify a bad death, a resurrection that perverts the moral order.

I have suggested that contemporary societies are cathecting their existential anxieties onto the image of the living dead and that this image materializes both in cultural formations and in scientific metaphor. In Madagascar, where extinction debt has given birth to numerous living dead creatures, conservation interventions are building a novel perception of the future. Because it is an island with unique temporal attributes and an accelerated tempo of evolution, Madagascar is an exceptional place in which to make predictive models.

Much ethnographic work remains to be done about Malagasy perceptions of *ho avy* ("the future"). The metaphors I supply here—a collapsing structure, an arcing line, resurrection—have been inspired by US- and Europe-based conservation science, which has had a strong influence on Malagasy lives and landscapes. The techno-scientific orientation toward the biocultural past in the present day demonstrates the ways in which history's lines are being redrawn. Progress depends increasingly on delving into the past, on investigating the structures, secrets, and wisdom contained in dying languages, indigenous cosmologies, and extinct DNA. These movements appear to offer the surest means of lessening extinction debt and straightening the arrow of time.

Notes

1. H. G. Wells, "Aepyornis Island," in *The Country of the Blind and Other Stories* (1894; repr., Fairfield, Ia.: 1st World Library, 2006), 67–80.

2. David Tilman et al., "Habitat Destruction and the Extinction Debt," *Nature* 371 (September 1994): 65–66.

3. Robert E. Dewar, "Does It Matter That Madagascar Is an Island?," *Human Ecology* 25, no. 3 (1997): 481–89.

4. Gillian Feeley-Harnik, "*Ravenala madagascariensis* Sonnerat: The Historical Ecology of 'Flagship Species' in Madagascar," *Ethnohistory* 48, nos. 1–2 (2001): 31–86.

5. Shane Wright and Jeanette Keeling, "The Road from Santa Rosalia: A Faster Tempo of Evolution in Tropical Climates," *Proceedings of the National Academy of Sciences of the United States* 103, no. 20 (2006): 7718–22.

6. Alison J. Stattersfield et al., *Endemic Bird Areas of the World: Priorities for Biodiversity Conservation* (Cambridge, Mass.: BirdLife International, 1998); Stuart L. Pimm, "The Dodo Went Extinct (and Other Ecological Myths)," *Annals of the Missouri Botanical Garden* 89, no. 2 (200): 190–98.

7. For scholarly analyses of global capitalism, see, for example, Arjun Appadurai, *Modernity at Large: Cultural Dimensions of Globalization* (Minneapolis: University of Minnesota Press, 1996) and *Fear of Small Numbers: An Essay on the Geography of Anger* (Durham, N.C.: Duke University Press, 2006); Kwame Anthony Appiah, *Cosmopolitanism: Ethics in a World of Strangers* (New York: W. W. Norton, 2007); David Harvey, *The Condition of Postmodernity: An Enquiry into the Origins of Cultural Change* (Cambridge, Mass.: Blackwell, 1990); and Aihwa Ong, *Neoliberalism as Exception: Mutations in Citizenship and Sovereignty* (Durham, N.C.: Duke University Press, 2006).

8. Dipesh Chakrabarty, "The Climate of History: Four Theses," *Critical Inquiry* 35 (2009): 213, 197.

9. Alfred Crosby, *The Columbian Exchange: Biological and Cultural Consequences of 1492* [1972], 30th Anniversary Edition (Westport, Conn.: Praeger, 2003); Chakrabarty, "Climate of History."

10. See, for example, Ray Kurzweil, *The Singularity Is Near: When Humans Transcend Biology* (New York: Penguin, 2006).

11. See, for example, Jane I. Guyer, "Prophecy and the Near Future: Thoughts on Macroeconomic, Evangelical, and Punctuated Time," *American Ethnologist* 34, no. 3 (2007): 409–21; and Ursula K. Heise, "Lost Dogs, Last Birds, and Listed Species: Cultures of Extinction," *Configurations* 18, no. 1–2 (2010): 49–73.

12. Quoted in Lin Edwards, "Humans Will Be Extinct in a 100 Years Says Eminent Scientist," Phys.org website, June 23, 2010, www.physorg.com/news196489543.html.

13. Q. D. Wheeler et al., "Mapping the Biosphere: Exploring Species to Understand the Origin, Organization and Sustainability of Biodiversity," *Systematics and Biodiversity* 10, no. 1 (2012): 1–20.

14. Ilkka Hanksi and Otso Ovaskainen, "Extinction Debt at Extinction Threshold," *Conservation Biology* 16, no. 3 (2002): 666–73.

15. Paul Marks, "Online Searches for Future Linked to Economic Success," NewScientist.com website, April 5, 2012, www.newscientist.com/article/dn21678-online-searches-for-future-linked-to-economic-success.html.

16. Fernando Coronil, "The Future in Question: History and Utopia in Latin America, 1989–2010," in *Business as Usual: The Roots of the Global Financial Meltdown*, ed. Craig Calhoun and Georgi Derluguian (New York: New York University Press, 2011), 231–66.

17. See Peter Y. Paik, "Zombies and Other Strangers: Thoughts on Robert Kirkman's *The Walking Dead*," University of Minnesota Press Blog, January 26, 2011, www.uminnpressblog.com/2011/01/zombies-and-other-strangers-thoughts-on.html.

18. See Joseph W. Thornton, "Resurrecting Ancient Genes: Experimental Analysis of Extinct Molecules," *Nature Reviews Genetics* 5, no. 5 (May 2004): 366–375, and John F. Collins, "Culture, Content, and the Enclosure of Human Being: UNESCO's 'Intangible' Heritage in the New Millennium," *Radical History Review* 109 (2011): 120–136. Regarding strip mining, a recent initiative concerns the conservation "offsets" of mining companies, like the British and Australian conglomerate Rio Tinto, such as the proposal to dredge up exhausted earth in Madagascar to reseed it "with key species the company found in the original forest" (Rowan Moore Gerety, "Mining and Biodiversity Offsets in Madagascar: Conservation or 'Conservation Opportunities?,'" WildMadagascar.org website, August 30, 2009, http://news.mongabay.com/2009/0830-rowan_rio_tinto_madagascar.html). Rio Tinto extracts ilmenite in southern Madagascar. Ilmenite is smelted and refined into titanium dioxide, a base pigment in paint, paper and plastics, most of which is sold to China. Jo Revill, "Madagascar's Unique Forest under Threat," *Observer* August 6, 2005, www.guardian.co.uk/science/2005/aug/07/

conservationandendangeredspecies.internationalnews. Rio Tinto representatives have drawn up plans to rehabilitate defunct mines by using "a floating dredge to pull up deposits of sand." The dredged-up deposits will provide the foundation for ecological restoration; the deposits will be reseeded "with key species the company found in the original forest" (WildMadagascar.org). Rio Tinto promotes its "Net Positive Impact" on biodiversity, boasts of its "Conservation Areas," "Conservation Committee," "Ecological Research Centre," and trials of "ecological ecosystem restoration." Yet Rio Tinto's subsidiary, QIT Madagascar Minerals, uses dredge mining to extract ilmenite and other minerals in southeast Madagascar, so it is unclear whether the dredging up of seeds represents a "biodiversity offset" or a positive spin on an extractive process already going on. Dredging up and reseeding dead earth at best suggests the possibility of a pale second life, an impoverished landscape.

19. Heise, "Lost Dogs," 68–69.

20. Shannon Dawdy, "Clockpunk Anthropology and the Ruins of Modernity," *Current Anthropology* 51, no. 6 (2010): 761–93; Bruno Latour, *We Have Never Been Modern* (Cambridge, Mass.: Harvard University Press, 1993).

21. Thomas R. Trautmann, "The Revolution in Ethnological Time," *Man*, n.s. 27, no. 2 (1992): 379–97.

22. Rachel Carson, *Silent Spring* [1962], 40th anniversary ed. (New York: First Mariner Books / Houghton Mifflin, 2002); Sandra Steingraber, *Living Downstream: An Ecologist's Personal Investigation of Cancer and the Environment* (Cambridge, Mass.: Da Capo Press, 2010).

23. Trautmann, "Revolution in Ethnological Time," 380.

24. Ibid., 385.

25. Gerardo Ceballos and Paul R. Ehrlich, "Discoveries of New Mammal Species and Their Implications for Conservation and Ecosystem Services," *Proceedings of the National Academy of Sciences of the United States* 106, no. 10 (2009): 3841–46.

26. Paul Alan Cox, "Indigenous Peoples and Conservation," in *Biodiversity and Human Health*, ed. Francesca Grifo and Joshua Rosenthal (Washington, D.C.: Island Press, 1997), 207.

27. Marc Abélès, *The Politics of Survival*, trans. Julie Kleinman (Durham, N.C.: Duke University Press, 2010), originally published as *Politique de la survie* (Paris: Éditions Flammarion, 2006), 15.

28. Celia Lowe, "Extinction Is Forever: Temporalities of Science, Nation, and State in Indonesia," in *Timely Assets: The Politics of Resources and Their Temporalities*, ed. Elizabeth Emma Ferry and Mandana E. Limbert (Santa Fe, N.M.: School for Advanced Research Press, 2008), 108.

29. Julie Cruikshank, "Glaciers and Climate Change: Perspectives from Oral Tradition," *Arctic* 54, no. 4 (2001): 377–93.

30. See Paul Nadasdy, "The Politics of TEK: Power and the 'Integration' of Knowledge," *Arctic Anthropology* 36, nos. 1–2 (1999): 1–18.

31. See, for example, J. Peter Brosius, "Endangered Forest, Endangered People: Environmentalist Representations of Indigenous Knowledge," *Human Ecology* 25, no. 1 (1997): 47–69.

32. Michael Hathaway, "Global Environmentalism and the Emergence of Indigeneity: The Politics of Cultural and Biological Diversity in China," in *The Anthropology of Extinction: Essays on Culture and Species Death*, ed. Genese Marie Sodikoff (Bloomington: Indiana University Press, 2012), 103–25.

33. K. David Harrison, *When Languages Die: The Extinction of the World's Languages and the Erosion of Human Knowledge* (New York: Oxford University Press, 2007).

34. Richard Alleyne, "Extinct Elephant Bird of Madagascar Could Live Again," *Telegraph*, March 10, 2010.

35. Richard Pearson, "Primitive Modernity: H. G. Wells and the Prehistoric Man of the 1890s," *Yearbook of English Studies* 37, no. 1 (2007): 66.

36. David Jablonski, "Keeping Time with Mass Extinctions," *Paleobiology* 10, no. 2 (Spring 1984): 139–45; Emmanuel Fara, "What Are Lazarus Taxa?," *Geological Journal* 36, nos. 3–4 (2001): 291–303.

37. Pimm, "Dodo Went Extinct," 195.

38. R. H. MacArthur and E. O. Wilson, *The Theory of Island Biogeography* (Princeton, N.J.: Princeton University Press, 1967); J. Terborgh, "Preservation of Natural Diversity: The Problem of Extinction Prone Species," *Bioscience* 24 (1974): 715–22, and "Island Biogeography and Conservation: Strategy and Limitations," *Science* 193 (1976): 1029–30; Jared Diamond, "Island Biogeography and Conservation: Strategy and Limitations," *Science* 193 (1976): 1027–29; and E .C. Pielou, *Biogeography* (New York: Wiley, 1979).

39. Larry D. Harris, *The Fragmented Forest: Island Biogeography Theory and the Preservation of Biotic Diversity* (Chicago: University of Chicago Press, 1984), 4.

40. James H. Brown and Mark V. Lomolino, "Concluding Remarks: Historical Perspective and the Future of Island Biogeography Theory," *Global Ecology and Biogeography* 9, no. 1 (2000): 87–92.

41. Murray P. Cox et al., "A Small Cohort of Island Southeast Asian Women Founded Madagascar," *Proceedings of the Royal Society B*, published online ahead of print, March 21, 2012, doi: 10.1098/rspb.2012.0012.

42. David A. Burney et al., "Environmental Change, Extinction and Human Activity: Evidence from Caves in NW Madagascar," *Biogeography* 24, no. 6 (1997): 755–67.

43. Laurie R. Godfrey and Emilienne Rasoazanabary, "Demise of the Bet Hedgers: A Case Study of Human Impacts on Past and Present Lemurs of Madagascar," in Sodikoff, *Anthropology of Extinction*, 167.

44. Burney et al., "Environmental Change," 755.

45. A biodiversity hot spot is furthermore defined as a region that contains at least 70 percent of its primary vegetation, of which at least 1,500 species of vascular plants are endemic. Norman Myers et al., "Biodiversity Hotspots for Conservation Priorities," *Nature* 403 (2000): 853–58. In Madagascar, scientists estimate the number of vascular plant species to be 8,500 and the total number of plant species to be 10,000 to 12,000. Laurence J. Dorr et al., "Madagascar," in *Floristic Inventory of Tropical Countries*, ed. David G. Campbell and H. David Hammond (New York: New York Botanical Garden, 1989), 238; Feeley-Harnik, "*Ravenala madagascariensis,*" 36.

46. Michel Tournier, "The Grey Matter of Madagascar," in *Madagascar: The Photographs of Gian Paolo Barbieri* (Cologne: Taschen, 1997), n.p. [viii], cited in Feeley-Harnik, "*Ravenala madagascariensis,*" 31.

47. Feeley-Harnik, "*Ravenala madagascariensis,*" 31.

48. Olive Murray Chapman, "Across Madagascar," *Geographical Journal* 96, no. 1 (1940): 14–25.

49. Lesley A. Sharp, "Wayward Pastoral Ghosts and Regional Xenophobia in a Northern Madagascar Town," *Africa* 71, no. 1 (2001): 56.

50. James Sibree, "The Volcanic Lake of Tritrìva, Central Madagascar," *Proceedings of the Royal Geographical Society and Monthly Record of Geography*, n.s. 13, no. 8 (1891): 478–79.

51. David A. Burney and Ramilisonina, "The Kilopilopitsofy, Kidoky, and Bokyboky: Accounts of Strange Animals from Belo-Sur-Mer, Madagascar, and the Megafaunal 'Extinction Window,'" *American Anthropologist* 100, no. 4 (1998): 957.

52. Ross D. E. MacPhee and David A. Burney, "Dating of Modified Femora of Extinct Dwarf Hippopotamus from Southern Madagascar: Implications for Constraining Human Colonization and Vertebrate Extinction Events," *Journal of Archaeological Science* 18 (1991): 695–706.

53. See Cruikshank, "Glaciers and Climate Change."

54. M. R. Helfert and C. A. Wood, "Shuttle Photos Show Madagascar Erosion," *Geotimes* 31 (1986): 4–5.

55. Pierre Boiteau, *Contribution à l'histoire de la nation Malgache* (Paris: Éditions Sociales, 1958), 225.

56. Michael Williams, *Deforesting the Earth: From Prehistory to Global Crisis* (Chicago: University of Chicago Press, 2003), 343.

57. Ilkka Hanski et al., "Deforestation and Apparent Extinctions of Endemic Forest Beetles in Madagascar," *Biology Letters* 3, no. 3 (June 22, 2007), 344.

58. Christian Kull, *Isle of Fire: The Political Ecology of Landscape Burning in Madagascar* (Chicago: University of Chicago Press, 2004); Glen M. Green and Robert W. Sussman, "Deforestation History of the Eastern Rain Forests of Madagascar from Satellite Images," *Science* 248 (1990): 212–15.

59. Barry Bearak, "Tottering Rule in Madagascar Can't Save Falling Rosewoods," *New York Times*, May 25, 2010.

60. Jody Bourton, "Lemurs Butchered in Madagascar," *BBC Earth News*, August 20, 2009, http://news.bbc.co.uk/earth/hi/earth_news/newsid_8210000/8210355.stm.

61. See Matt Cartmill, "New Views on Primate Origins," *Evolutionary Anthropology* 1, no. 2 (1992): 105–11.

62. Robin D. Martin, "Origins, Diversity, and Relationships of Lemurs," *International Journal of Primatology* 21, no. 6 (2000): 1022.

63. Anne D. Yoder et al., "Ancient Single Origin for Malagasy Primates," *Proceedings of the National Academy of Sciences* 93 (1996): 5124–25.

64. Natalie Angier, "Lemurs Bred in Captivity May One Day Return to Repopulate Madagascar," *New York Times*, May 19, 1992, C1.

65. Adam Britt, "Encouraging Natural Feeding Behavior in Captive-Bred Black and White Ruffed Lemurs (*Varecia variegata variegata*)," *Zoo Biology* 17, no. 5 (1998): 379.

66. M. Elsbeth McPhee and Kathy Carlstead, "The Importance of Maintaining Natural Behaviors in Captive Mammals," in *Wild Mammals in Captivity: Principles and Techniques for Zoo Management*, ed. D. G. Kleiman, K. V. Thompson, and C. K. Baer (Chicago: University of Chicago Press, 2010), 303.

67. Patricia Wright, "Considering Climate Change Effects in Lemur Ecology and Conservation," in *Lemurs: Ecology and Adaptation*, ed. Lisa Gould and Michelle L. Sauther (New York: Springer Science + Business Media, 2006), 385.

68. Karen Freeman, "Science Watch: Survival Roulette," *New York Times*, March 24, 1998.

69. ScienceDaily, "Duke Lemurs Arrive Safely In Madagascar after Arduous Journey," *ScienceDaily* website, October 29, 1997, www.sciencedaily.com/releases/1997/10/971029055534.htm.

70. "Endangered Mammals Go Home to a Land They Never Knew," *New York Times*, December 2, 1997.

71. Katie Kindelan, "Madagascar Pochard Ducklings Born, Could Save 'World's Rarest Bird,'" *ABC News*, April 6, 2012, http://abcnews.go.com/blogs/headlines/2012/04/madagascar-pochard-ducklings-born-could-save-worlds-rarest-bird/; Nirhy Rabibisoa, "New Amphibian Captive Breeding Center Opens in Madagascar," *Conservation International*, January 13, 2012, http://blog.conservation.org/2012/01/new-amphibian-captive-breeding-center-opens-in-madagascar/.

72. Marianne E. Lien, "'King of Fish' or 'Feral Peril': Tasmanian Atlantic Salmon and the Politics of Belonging," *Environment and Planning D: Society and Space* 23 (2005): 659–71; Franklin Ginn, "Extension, Subversion, Containment: Eco-Nationalism and (Post)colonial Nature in Aotearoa New Zealand," *Transactions of the Institute of British Geographers* 33 (2008): 335–53.

73. Arnold Van Gennep, *Tabou et totémisme à Madagascar: Étude descriptive et théoretique* (Paris: Leroux, 1904); James George Frazer, *The Golden Bough: A Study in Magic and Religion*, vol. 3, pt. 2, "Taboo and the Perils of the Soul" (London: Macmillan, 1922); Jorgen Ruud, *Taboo: A Study of Malagasy Customs and Beliefs* (Oslo: Oslo University Press, 1959).

74. See Julia P. G. Jones et al., "The Importance of Taboos and Social Norms to Conservation in Madagascar," *Conservation Biology* 22, no. 4 (2008): 976–86. For a critique of Jones's view, see Eva Keller, "The Danger of Misunderstanding 'Culture,'" *Madagascar Conservation and Development* 4, no. 2 (2009): 82–85.

75. Oe Bodin et al., "The Value of Small Size: Loss of Forest Patches and Ecological Thresholds in Southern Madagascar," *Ecological Applications* 16, no. 2 (2006): 440–51.

76. Jones et al., "Importance of Taboos," and Jeanneney Rabearivony et al., "Taboos and Social Contracts: Tools for Ecosystem Management—Lessons from the Manambolomaty Lakes RAMSAR site, Western Madagascar," *Madagascar Conservation and Development* 3, no. 1 (2008): 7–16.

77. G. A. Shaw, "The Aye-Aye," *Antananarivo Annual and Madagascar Magazine* 2 (1896); Van Gennep, *Tabou et totémisme*.

78. Joshua E. Cinner, "The Role of Taboos in Conserving Coastal Resources in Madagascar," *SPC Traditional Marine Resource Management and Knowledge Information Bulletin* 22 (December 2007): 22.

79. Jones et al., "Importance of Taboos," 977.

80. Genese Marie Sodikoff, "Forced and Forest Labor Regimes in Colonial Madagascar, 1926–1936," *Ethnohistory* 52, no. 2 (2005): 407–35.

81. Andrew Walsh, "The Obvious Aspects of Ecological Underprivilege in Ankarana, Northern Madagascar," *American Anthropologist* 107, no. 4 (2005): 654–65.

82. Genese Marie Sodikoff, "Totem and Taboo Reconsidered: Endangered Species and Moral Practice in Madagascar," in Sodikoff, *Anthropology of Extinction*, 67–87.

83. Renato Rosaldo, "Imperialist Nostalgia," *Representations* 26 (1989): 108.

84. Jennifer Cole, "Sacrifice, Narratives and Experience in East Madagascar," *Journal of Religion in Africa* 27, no. 4 (1997): 401–25.

85. Lesley A. Sharp, *The Possessed and the Dispossessed: Spirits, Identity, and Power in a Madagascar Migrant Town* (Berkeley: University of California Press, 1993); Lesley A. Sharp, "Wayward Pastoral Ghosts and Regional Xenophobia in a Northern Madagascar Town," *Africa* 71, no. 1 (2001): 39.

86. Sharp, "Wayward Pastoral Ghosts," 40.

87. Jean Comaroff and John Comaroff, "Alien-Nation: Zombies, Immigrants, and Millennial Capitalism," *South Atlantic Quarterly* 101, no. 4 (2002): 789.

10 Unintended Consequences and the Epistemology of Fraud in Dickens and Hayek

Eleanor Courtemanche

ONE SURPRISING AND unnerving result of the 2007–8 financial crisis has been the reactivation of the long-dormant Victorian debate about the difference between "investment"—a term that connotes fiscal soundness, prudence, and morality—and irrational, emotional "speculation," which shades into "gambling" and which might be thinly disguised "fraud."[1] Given the increasing democratization of finance culture on both sides of the Atlantic, and the widespread vestment of prestigious pension funds and university endowments in growth equities, the thought of avoiding the stock market because of moral hesitations about gambling would, up until the late unpleasantness, have seemed positively medieval. It is easy to find places in Victorian literature where this distinction is represented crudely as one of personal character, with scam artists distinguishable by their Jewish or otherwise foreign mannerisms while the "gentlemen" cling to outmoded standards of philanthropy that may or may not actually make them money.[2] In many of these novels you can detect who is moral and who is not simply by looking at their flashy clothing or noting their untrustworthy slang. One of the most frustrating elements of the recent crash, however, was the discovery not only that many investments made with perfect confidence were in fact deeply unsound in retrospect (something true of most scandals) but that as a result of inaccurate ratings by the credit ratings agencies it had become at a certain point impossible to tell the difference between sound and unsound investment. Contrary to previous crashes, the victims of the crash included not just the foolish individual investors who are the usual victims of financial scams but the investment banks themselves, which despite multiple safeguards seemed not to be aware that they remained liable for so many bad equities. As journalist Michael Lewis reports in *The Big Short,* "The big Wall Street firms, seemingly so shrewd and self-interested, had somehow become the dumb money. The people who ran them did not understand their own businesses, and their regulators obviously knew even less."[3] Anna Quindlen expressed this widespread unease in a 2009 column noting that "the great unspoken issue behind the tanking of the market, the mess in subprime mortgages and the bailout bill is that Americans don't understand the basics of the economy."[4] Because no one seemed to understand the complexity of the bad investments, government regulators had no choice but to turn over the cleanup to those who had made the bad investments in the first place.

Thus the recent crisis was not just one of insolvency but one of financial epistemology. If there had been fraud, who had committed it? Was the difference between sound and fraudulent investment discernible either at the time or after the crash? Did any of the many interest groups that created the crisis understand what they had done? It might be seen as an advance over the Victorian era that no particular ethnic group was routinely scapegoated, except for those who blamed the entire mortgage securities crisis on minorities who, despite their total disenfranchisement in every other way, were supposed to have gamed the entire banking system into extending them cheap housing loans.[5] The search for scapegoats mostly came up empty, since the perpetrators had all conveniently vanished or gone out of business, with the exception of Goldman Sachs. There were several kinds of political response to this atmosphere of paralyzing universal distrust, one of which was to return to the Keynesian politics of stimulus, deficit spending, and regulatory restraint that had arisen in response to the Great Depression but had been gradually eliminated during the post-Reagan era of financial deregulation. Both parties participated in the politics of stimulus and new regulatory probity, but there was also a return among conservatives to issuing warnings about the "unintended consequences" of government action (warnings that had been strangely silent during the previous administration). David Brooks, for example, in his *New York Times* op-ed of April 22, 2010, claimed that what he called "progressive conservatism" was something that "starts with the wisdom of Edmund Burke—the belief that the world is much more complex than we can know and [therefore] we should be skeptical of handing too much power to government planners."[6] Though one might see the financial collapse as a massively unintended consequence of the creative repackaging of home mortgage repayment risk and the perverse incentives that rewarded short-term speculative greed, in this particular moderate-conservative reading the unintended consequences were the bad results not of market action but of government *intervention* into an otherwise autonomous and self-cleansing market. Invoking respect for the "unintended consequences" of human action in this context might seem sensible in its reflection of the widespread fear created by the crisis—but also tragically belated, as well as totally disingenuous in its recommendation to restrain the new mood of regulatory severity instead of the financial markets whose fraudulent innovations precipitated the crisis.

The concept of "unintended consequences" is in fact the basis for modern neoclassical economics, and so it seems natural for political groups allied with big business to extend the concept into a warning against Great Society–style government meddling. But the concept is too useful a way of representing social complexity and opacity to be considered merely an axiom of free market fundamentalism; consider, for example, its relevance to the discourses of foreign policy (where it appears as "blowback"), ecological disaster, and technological innovation. I begin here by briefly tracing the history of the idea of "unintended consequences" as it leads from Smith to Hayek, as a way of framing the difference between economic and literary ways of representing how knowledge spreads through society. One of the most interesting aspects of Hayekian price-system epistemology is the historical link between Hayek's insistence on the spontaneous order produced by dispersed individuals and certain aspects of cybernetic theory and distributed information processing.[7] Hayek's influential theory of social epistemology has a weakness, however, which is that he makes no allowances for the possibility of fraud—on the part of either individuals or large corporations. In Hayek, as in much of neoclassical economics, self-interest translates with only minor difficulties into larger social benefits.[8] But Hayek renounces any understanding of how that happens, asserting that society is simply too complicated to do anything other than gauge aggregate outcomes of wealth production. In this realm, the epistemological structure of any long Victorian novel—and here I'll be focusing on Dickens's *Little Dorrit* and *Bleak House*, though I could have discussed *Vanity Fair* or *Middlemarch*—is more morally nuanced, specific, and complex than Hayek's vision.[9] In its apparent embrace of spontaneity and chance, Hayek's epistemology would appear to have a certain amount of overlap with a narratological organization that combines an omniscient but helpless narrator with active but limited characters. But if you are looking for a way of explaining the relation either between hardworking individuals and massive schemes of fraudulent delusion, or between sneakily selfish individuals and larger structures of institutional constraint, a Dickensian paradigm will be much more helpful than Hayek's morally limited understanding of how information spreads through a complex society.

The concept of unintended consequences, though it can be traced all the way back to ideas of fate and providence, is first theorized economically in Bernard de Mandeville's satirical 1714 poem "The Fable of the Bees." In this poem Mandeville makes the self-consciously scandalous argument that individual vices like luxury and ambition are at the root of what seem to be virtuous commercial arrangements.[10] When Adam Smith came to explain what kept a free market from being a moral disaster, he kept Mandeville's Enlightenment secularism (that is, Smith's idea of providence is noninterventionist, if it exists at all) but distanced himself from Mandeville's description of commercial activity as "vice." In Smith's 1776 *The Wealth of Nations* the idea of the "invisible hand" is invoked to smooth over the disparity between selfish individual actions and the nation's general welfare. This hand, though, is more an effect than a cause; it does not intervene to make people act in a way that will unwittingly benefit others but relies on a relatively simple and universal principle of human behavior: the propensity to "truck, barter, and exchange" common to all economic agents. For a figure that has come to stand in for almost all of moral theory in neoclassical economics, the metaphor of the invisible hand is actually fairly fragile and limited. In context, it describes only the tendencies of a merchant to keep "some part of his capital always under his own view and command," what today is known as "home bias."[11]

Some kind of synthesis between Smith's idea of the free market and Burke's caution about radical social change is often considered to be the basis of modern conservative thought, post Reagan and Thatcher. But for Smith, unintended consequences always have a positive, even comic outcome: selfish actions are surprisingly reversed into social benefits. For Burke, in contrast, unintended consequences are the negative effects you risk creating when you mistakenly attack established institutions. Smith was drawing from the work of the French physiocrats in his argument that the mercantile establishment should be reformed along the more rational principles of laissez-faire. Burke's *Reflections on the Revolution in France,* however, demonstrates a very different response to French radicalism, concluding from the example of the Terror that organic political traditions, including monarchy and all the messy inheritance of British constitutionalism, had better be kept as they are or reformed with incremental slowness.[12] In terms of economics, Burke may have been suspicious of Smith's francophilic radicalism at first, but (in a story told by Emma Rothschild in her book *Economic Sentiments*) he gradually became convinced that one could be a partisan of economic liberty without necessarily endorsing political liberty.[13] In *Riches and Poverty,* Donald Winch also traces several fault lines between Smith and Burke, pointing out ways that Smith was closer to Thomas Paine's cosmopolitanism or even the sermons of Richard Price, the radical cleric attacked in Burke's *Reflections.* Winch argues that Burke is closer to Mandeville in accepting that public morality is based on an "ignoble lie," concluding "that public morality requires an element not only of mystery, but of mystification."[14] We see here two different responses to the problem of our inability to track the moral benefits of every single selfish action: Smith couches his hypothesis in general terms, suggesting that these benefits "generally" or "in many . . . cases" follow from selfish actions, while Burke takes a more mystical, organicist approach to the totality of human relations, suggesting limits to rational understanding in contrast to Smith's Enlightenment rationalism.[15]

To jump ahead to the mid-twentieth century, Hayek may be said to combine Smith's optimism about the unintended consequences of selfish economic action, Burke's quasi-mystical respect for the spontaneous orders created by human society, and one other element: a more thoroughgoing reliance on organicist metaphors derived from Darwinist theories of evolution. Hayek first emerged on the American scene when his 1944 antisocialist polemic *The Road to Serfdom,* originally directed against the British welfare state, was abridged and serialized the following year by *Reader's*

Digest, where it was received with great joy in the context of American business resistance against the New Deal.[16] Hayek turned the idea of unintended consequences into a model of limited economic knowledge in response to what was known at the time as the "socialist calculation debate."[17] In *The Road to Serfdom,* Hayek articulates a vision of complex modern society as spontaneous and yet ordered in a way that he describes as fundamentally "liberal," hence revealing his European heritage by identifying liberalism as a mode of individualism. He identifies this liberalism as "the fundamental principle that in the ordering of our affairs we should make as much use as possible of the spontaneous forces of society, and resort as little as possible to coercion."[18] Somewhat paradoxically, however, he resists what he calls the "wooden insistence of some liberals on certain rough rules of thumb, above all the principle of laissez-faire. . . . The [proper] attitude of the liberal toward society is like that of the gardener who tends a plant, and in order to create the conditions most favorable to its growth, must know as much as possible about its structure and the way it functions" (71). Though he eschews the planning function of his socialist and Keynesian adversaries, Hayek here admits that the role of the gardener/theorist might be to help understand and even adjust the proper conditions for economic flourishing. Hence Hayek admits the need for regulations in capitalist societies against "deforestation," "poisonous substances," and so on (87), which is more than some of his followers would admit.

Hayek's principal polemic is against the idea of central economic planning: he describes it as doomed to fail because of its distortion of the price system, which is the only way of really knowing the true relations of producers and consumers to each other—so that if you intervene in the economy to correct an injustice, you cut yourself off from the very knowledge that would enable you, the planner, to organize that economy efficiently. Writing in a time of increasing government regulation of the economy in both East and West, Hayek laments that "the question is no longer how we can make the best use of the spontaneous forces found in a free society. We have in effect undertaken to dispense with the forces which produced unforeseen results and to replace the impersonal and anonymous mechanism of the market by collective and 'conscious' direction of all social forces to deliberately chosen goals" (73). In reaction against what he describes as "the horror inspired by the idea of everything being directed from a single center" (89), Hayek argues that distributing financial decisions as widely as possible is not only more just but more accurate. The multiple factors that influence every part of a complex modern economy, he says,

> have . . . become so numerous that it is impossible to gain a synoptic view of them . . . and because all the details of the changes constantly affecting the conditions of demand and supply of the different commodities can never be fully known, or quickly enough be collected and disseminated, by any one center, what is required is some apparatus of registration which automatically records all the relevant effects of individual actions and whose indications are at the same time the resultant of, and the guide for, all the individual decisions.

> This is precisely what the price system does under competition, and which no other system even promises to accomplish. It enables entrepreneurs, by watching the movement of comparatively few prices, as an engineer watches the hands of a few dials, to adjust their activities to those of their fellows. (95)

Hayek thus poses the objective measurements produced by "engineers" of the price system with the clumsy and biased tyranny of government planners. The whole government-versus-the market dichotomy, of course, is a response to twentieth-century history and so doesn't quite fit with Smith's warnings against businessmen colluding to keep prices high: a point brought up by Christina Petsoulas in her book *Hayek's Liberalism and Its Origins,* which argues that Hayek is wrong to see Smith, Mandeville, and Hume as sharing his ideas that liberal society is based on spontaneous order and the gradual cultural evolution of rules and laws. Petsoulas points out that while Hayek always defends mercantile activities from a predatory state, Smith acknowledged that "however beneficial they may otherwise be, the activities of the mercantile order have to be contained by appropriate institutions which, by preventing economic interests from colonising the state, guarantee the benefits gained from free trade."[19] Edna Ullmann-Margalit in her article "The Invisible Hand and the Cunning of Reason" also critiques Hayek's use of the invisible hand, on the grounds that Smith's view of the invisible hand is a cornerstone of secular rationalism while Hayek's stress is on accepting the limitations of human reason. She points to a confusion in Hayek's views between biological evolution, in which organic features can be assumed to serve some beneficial function, and cultural evolution, in which inherited structures may or may not actually be optimal or even useful.[20] It is true that while Hayek on the one hand claims not to be a mystical or traditional conservative, he argues later, in his 1964 essay "The Theory of Complex Phenomena," that "while the assumption of a sufficient knowledge of the concrete facts generally produces a sort of intellectual *hubris* which deludes itself that reason can judge all values, the insight into the impossibility of such full knowledge induces an attitude of humility and reverence toward that experience of mankind as a whole which has been precipitated in the values and institutions of existing society."[21] This invocation of society as created by a kind of sedimentary wisdom sounds closer to Burke than Smith, and it's surprisingly insensitive to the possibilities of radical change, even in terms of what Schumpeter would call the "creative destruction" of capitalism or the really visionary entrepreneur, much less anything like a large-scale movement toward social justice.[22]

But the more significant blindness of Hayek's theory is—as I mentioned before—his inability to theorize the possibility of fraud. His idea of prices is one constructed from a combination of the limited horizons of individual economic agents, and their specific situational knowledge of their own self-interest that cannot be added up or tabulated from a distance but that emerges with ineffable subjectivity in the moment of competition. It does not usually *achieve* equilibrium, yet tends to approach it: "The combination of fragments of knowledge existing in different minds bring[s] about results which, if they were to be brought about deliberately, would require a knowledge on the part of the directing mind which no single person can possess."[23] Yet in Hayek's model the self-interest of the economic individual is always based on trying to reflect as nearly as possible some kind of real or natural relation between the supply and demand of a given commodity. So there is no incentive to lie about a price. The idea that people might speculate to drive prices up and down in ways that are damaging to the rest of the economy—or might even *wreck* the economy so that major companies would need to be bailed out by the government, in conformity with their genuine if short-term self-interest—seems to be beyond his imaginative powers. He thinks of economic agents as "engineers," creating an image of carefully calibrated structures built to last, while ignoring the idea that a trader might *lie* to achieve some competitive advantage, or that many traders together might create a bubble in which prices come completely untethered from what Marx called "use-value."[24]

Though the appeal of Hayek's theory is clear—it makes explicit the analogy between economics and biology, arguing that capitalist activity can be as miraculously self-sustaining and spontaneous as the growth of a plant—the recent financial crash provides a sad illustration of its limits. For the problem was not that the government was impairing proper transmission of price-signals to all parts of the economic organism but that no one in any part of the economy really knew what was going on. As Lewis reports, "The closer you were to the market [in the mid-2000s], the harder it was to perceive its folly."[25] So the engineers' dials were wrong—or if they were correct, there were too many incentives to not respond to them. So many people were so wrong about the crisis that Lewis's narrative is built around the disproportion between the tiny number of people who suspected the system was fraudulent and were willing to bet on it and the vast number who went along for the temporary ride.

Dickens's depiction of how economic knowledge flows through social systems is more subtle than Hayek's because it combines Hayek's obsession with the relation between local knowledge and mass ignorance with an awareness that an entire economic system can delude itself into mushroom growth based on lies and fraud. Thus I differ from the approach of Paul Cantor and Stephen Cox in their book *Literature and the Economics of Liberty,* which claims to be written in Hayek's spirit of defending capitalism against collective thought. Although I agree with the editors that Hayek's work on spontaneous order is interesting from a narratological point of view, they also proceed from a weirdly dogmatic assumption that capitalism has been "prove[n]" to work, thus sharing Hayek's blindness about the way that not every spontaneous order is either virtuous or sustainable.[26] There are two ways Dickens incorporates not just ignorance—which is central to Hayekian epistemology—but outright fraud into the structure of his complex narratives about unintended consequences: one we might call thematic, and the other epistemic or narratological. In terms of thematic incorporation, he shared the general Victorian suspicion of speculative economic activity and usually contrasted speculators sentimentally with the humble hardworking people bankrupted by great financiers, as Clennam and Doyce are undone by the fall of Merdle in *Little Dorrit*.[27] In that novel Merdle is merely the most prominent and dramatic example of a lying businessman: after he commits suicide it becomes known that he was "the greatest Forger and the greatest Thief that ever cheated the gallows" (449). In terms of narrative incorporation, Dickens's depiction of how the news of the suicide spreads around the city—a scene that Hayek might have interpreted as merely a new fact that would readjust prices—dramatizes the means by which self-delusion is painfully enlightened as to the essential inadequacy of its ability to evaluate others, and then passes again into comfortable and deluded self-confidence. First, the Physician who sought a physical source for Merdle's "complaint" realizes that he completely misdiagnosed Merdle, who in fact has died of financial ruin and shame; then everyone in London hears that Merdle is dead of some obscure "Pressure" (448) on the brain; next they are forced to revalue their previous overestimation of his worth when doubts arise as to his solvency; and finally they lash him with "every form of execration" (449) not only because he has ruined them but because they want to disguise their own collusion in having been fooled.[28]

Economic knowledge is depicted repeatedly in this novel as a kind of contagious disease that wreaks destruction as it spreads through the body politic. What makes the debt collector Pancks peculiarly susceptible to contagion is his sense of superiority to the poor debtors he squeezes: "These people don't understand the subject" of "figures," but he feels perfectly secure in his own "calculations" about the "safe and genuine" nature of his investments with Merdle (366). The narrator opines that the most poisonous element of this scene is Pancks's false sense of knowledge: "In these moments, Mr Pancks began to give out the dangerous infection with which he was laden. It is the manner of communicating these diseases, it is the subtle way they go about. . . . Of whom Mr Pancks had taken the prevalent disease, he could no more have told than if he had unconsciously taken a fever. Bred at first, as many physical diseases are, in the wickedness of men, and then disseminated in their ignorance, these epidemics after a period, get communicated to many sufferers who are neither ignorant nor wicked" (366–67). The origin of the illusion cannot be traced with any precision, except in the general human tendency to "wickedness" and false representation. Where Hayek depicts a social system in which true information about prices ultimately vanquishes ignorance (in the absence of distorting pressure from the state), Dickens expresses doubt that such true information can ever survive in an epistemological environment so given to "fevers" of delusional overvaluation. Note also the implications of the reliance of both Hayek and Dickens on organic metaphors for knowledge shared among a group of people: Hayek assumes that the system is self-correcting and healthy, while Dickens sees the organic body as weak and vulnerable to infection. Dickens also shares Hayek's sense of the universal dispersal of knowledge among a vast multitude of individuals, and the relative egalitarianism of that knowledge—but with the proviso that for him the poor can be as delusional about their own valuations of their environment as the rich. Merdle's is the most cataclysmic fraud, but almost all Dickens characters suffer from some characteristic blindness if they are not actively out to cheat or exploit each other. Poor Mr. Dorrit, for example, begins the novel thoroughly humbled by his years in the debtor's prison of the Marshalsea but becomes just as delusional and misguided as any of the rich.

So where the economic models of complex social behavior are dogmatically comic—they assert that the only outcome of unintended consequences in economic exchange is optimistic, therefore untouchable in a mystic or sacred way—Dickens's novels (along with many other realist novels) play with multiple moral outcomes that might result from the unintended consequences of interactions between characters. Some of these results are indeed restorative of comic equilibrium in a Smithian way, but they can equally be tragic or destructive. Dickensian sentimentality cannot always fully disguise the moral anarchy of these unintended outcomes.

The epistemological part of my argument has to do with the relations in these two authors between ignorance and subject position. Hayek's understanding of the infinite complexity of social life is in fact rather novelistic, though his assertion of the inevitable failure of human imagination is articulated in the very unliterary modes of philosophical objectivity or polemical assertion. As in a realist novel, there is in Hayek's work an omniscient knower—Hayek himself—who makes sense of the chaos of individual life. He uses his insight into his own ignorance not, as Dickens does, to moralize about the sorrowful state of modern life, but both to celebrate his own inability to understand any individual decision made by the sensitive "engineers" and to attack the position of the socialist planner, whose false assertion of omniscience would allow him to meddle in economic life via some form of price-fixing. The planner's attempt to adjust economic life to create justice would also destroy the economy's nerve system of prices through which information is discovered and transmitted. In Hayek, the omniscient knower—the theorist—has the task of guarding the multiple limited perspectives of economic agents from any outside force that wants to impose distorted knowledge on them in the name of social justice.

The main difference between Dickensian and Hayekian models of knowing is, obviously, that a novel is a fiction created by an author, while an economic system is not. As a result, each form of knowing offers a different form of confidence. Hayek is very confident about the general policy prescriptions drawn from his assertions about the inevitably subjective nature of knowledge, though he has to trust the "engineers" to report accurately from their subject positions. Dickens's narrators, meanwhile, can only make indirect political recommendations based on the selective limit case of the imaginary events of any one novel—though Dickens's narrators are not shy about how they think readers should respond to the events narrated. Merdle is a fraud, but Dickens does not say that all speculation is fraudulent—just that it *may* be. Dickens the *author,* on the other hand, has a kind of omniscient power that exists nowhere in Hayek's system: as an author, he both has theoretically omniscient knowledge of the world of the novel and can plan accurately how the novel's plot will proceed. The realism of the novel depends on the degree to which the characters appear to be free agents, though of course they are all ultimately determined by the author's choices and wear their disguises of freedom more or less convincingly.

It is a bit of a paradox, then, that fiction, the form of knowing based on disguising the characters' lack of freedom, is better at modeling fraudulent systems than Hayek's model, in which individuals are not only perfectly free and perfectly selfish but entirely reliant on their subjective perceptions to judge the world around them. Though Dickens the author really does have total power over his fictional world, the relations between narrators and characters are much more self-contradictory and interactive than in Hayek's model of spontaneous economic order. In Dickens's *Bleak House*, for example, the work of knowing is split between two clashing narrators, much as in Hayek's unbridgeable gulf between bad planner and knowing economic agent—but in Dickens their relation is much more symbiotic, and though they never actually trade information they do serve as epistemological supplements to each other.[29] Half of *Bleak House* is narrated by the usual enraged Dickensian omniscient narrator, who, in the novel's opening set piece, is the only figure in the whole city of London who can describe the fog of ignorance that spreads up and down the Thames and can see not only that the Londoners are each enwrapped in their own particular kind of fog but that the heart of the physical and metaphorical fog is the Court of Chancery, whose failure to adjudicate allows blight to radiate out in all directions, destroying lives and neighborhoods. The other half of the story is narrated by self-effacing but dutiful Esther Summerson, who actually does act much as one would expect a Hayekian individual to act, that is, deliberately limiting her actions to what she can see, know, and care about—though with the big difference that while Hayek's individual is an engineer able to judge shifting prices through a kind of neural network, Esther is determined to do good rather than merely selfish acts. I think the splitting of the narratorial function here is kind of like the economic model of helpless planner and limited agent, as if Dickens were admitting that the "combination of fragments of knowledge existing in different minds" is a necessary supplement to narratorial omniscience. Though she finds true love at the end, Esther's program of doing good is derailed when she contracts a case of smallpox she surely doesn't deserve, as a result of inhabiting an environment so dense with unforeseen connections that she catches it from a street urchin who (unbeknownst to her) contracted the illness from the putrid burying ground that is the site of her own father's grave. (Despite Dickens's sentimentality, he depicts a world in which virtue has to struggle to make any impact, while the effects of evil intent or bad accident rapidly infect the innocent.) For all the good work Esther does in this book, it is much easier to identify with the omniscient narrator—and in fact we would not be able to understand the system at all if we did not have some kind of view from the center. In the novel, Esther does the work of reform, but in the real world inhabited by author and reader it is the omniscient narrator who does that work, providing us with a meaningful context in which to interpret the moral and epistemic experience of chaos.

So to conclude, Dickens's novels are just one way of imagining the problem of unintended consequences that is both epistemically and morally more satisfying than the line of economic reasoning that stretches from Smith to Burke, Hayek, and David Brooks. Without a concept of fraud or tragedy, the idea of liberal society as structured only by unintended consequences is far too narrow to serve as a base for useful policy conclusions. Rather than accepting a model of unintended consequences that combines only the good possible outcomes of economic activity with only the bad possible outcomes of government initiative, we should reclaim this concept as a more general cautionary trope for human fragility and blindness.

Notes

1. See, for example, Martin Daunton's discussion of these distinctions in his afterword to *Victorian Investments: New Perspectives on Finance and Culture*, ed. Nancy Henry and Cannon Schmitt (Bloomington: Indiana University Press, 2009), 202–19. Daunton points out that it was not just writers like Trollope and Ruskin who were anxious to police the divide between "investment" and "speculation" but also Victorian businessmen and political economists (205). In the twentieth century, Labour policy was to discourage the speculation associated with the stock market by turning investment decisions over to managers who could make "long-sighted decisions" (204).

2. Dickens's *Our Mutual Friend* abounds in examples, such as the associates of Mr. Lammle, who are "too gaudy, too slangey, too odorous of cigars, and too much given to horseflesh . . . friends who seemed to be always coming and going across the Channel, on errands about the Bourse, and Greek and Spanish and India and Mexican, and par and premium and discount and three quarters and seven eighths. . . . They were all feverish and boastful and indefinably loose." Charles Dickens, *Our Mutual Friend* (Harmondsworth: Penguin, 1997), 259–60. See also Audrey Jaffe, "Trollope in the Stock Market: Irrational Exuberance and *The Prime Minister*," in Henry and Schmitt, *Victorian Investments*, 143–60.

3. Michael Lewis, *The Big Short: Inside the Doomsday Machine* (New York: Norton, 2010), 244. Lewis's story benefits from the omniscient point of view made possible only in hindsight, contrasting sharply with the almost infinite amount of ignorance of the web of liability extending far beyond Wall Street ("One trillion dollars in losses had been created by American financiers, out of whole cloth, and embedded in the American financial system" [225]). When the crash comes, its narrative power is increased not only by the combination of near-universal ignorance with the hindsight certainty of collapse but by the marginal status of the protagonists, a small number of investors who wager their careers on the likelihood of total systemic collapse. Characteristically, even these protagonists, the only investors to be vindicated by events, were tortured by doubt about the soundness of the financial system as a whole: "They had stumbled either upon a serious flaw in modern financial markets or into a great gambling run . . . [and] were not sure which it was" (115). Lewis's story ends, like *Bleak House* and *Little Dorrit*, with the sunshine of truth finally revealing a long-hidden and ultimately unsustainable fraud, and Lewis's hope that the age of "deeply dysfunctional" (262) financial culture is finally coming to an end, although he notes that he was wrong when he thought the system would finally reform itself after the excesses of the 1980s that he chronicled in *Liar's Poker: Rising through the Wreckage on Wall Street* (New York: Penguin, 1989).

4. She continues, "Faced with financial instruments increasingly arcane and complex and financial institutions increasingly faceless and vast, most outsourced knowledge and responsibility

to those they assumed were ethical and responsible. . . . Most of us didn't know enough to suspect the emperor had no clothes." Anna Quindlen, "Dollars and Sense," *Newsweek*, March 21, 2009.

5. In Lewis's *The Big Short* these ethnic minorities are represented as the "Jamaican baby nurse or Mexican strawberry picker with an income of $14,000 seeking to borrow three-quarters of a million dollars" (100) for home mortgages, though the book clearly places blame elsewhere for the systemic problems that led to the crash. See Daniel Gross's critique of the political narrative blaming the crash on lending to minorities in "Subprime Suspects," *Slate*, October 7, 2008, www.slate.com/id.2201641. The excessive availability of credit to socially marginal borrowers with good (because untested) credit scores complicates one element of Theodore Burczak's critique of Hayek in his *Socialism after Hayek* (Ann Arbor: University of Michigan Press, 2006), released just before the crash. Burczak argues that since the socially marginal cannot access the credit available to wealthier entrepreneurs, the market is not as just or as open to innovation as Hayek claims (58–59, 66–77); in fact, once brokers created "innovative" ways of disguising and selling the risky mortgages, credit flooded into the subprime market.

6. David Brooks, "The Government War," *New York Times*, April 22, 2010.

7. See Mark C. Taylor, *Confidence Games: Money and Markets in a World without Redemption* (Chicago: University of Chicago Press, 2004), 46, 77, 88. Hayek actually credited Adam Smith with being "the originator of cybernetics" because of his "breakthrough . . . evolutionary approach." Friedrich Hayek, *The Fatal Conceit: The Errors of Socialism*, ed. W. W. Bartley III (Chicago: University of Chicago Press, 1989), 146, quoted in Taylor, *Confidence Games*, 46.

8. I include Hayek among the neoclassicists here for his policy recommendations, even though Burczak suggests that Hayek's hermeneutical rather than mechanistic understanding of human agency makes him closer to postmodernism than to the neoclassicists (*Socialism after Hayek*, 17–18).

9. See my chapter on Thackeray in *The "Invisible Hand" and British Fiction, 1818–1860: Adam Smith, Political Economy, and the Genre of Realism* (Houndmills: Palgrave Macmillan, 2011), which links "ripple effects" in *Vanity Fair* to, among other things, Hayekian models of social complexity.

10. Bernard Mandeville, *Fable of the Bees: or, Private Vices, Publick Benefits*, ed. Phillip Harth (Harmondsworth: Penguin, 1970).

11. Adam Smith, *An Inquiry into the Nature and Causes of the Wealth of Nations*, eds. R. H. Campbell and A. S. Skinner, 2 vols. (1976; repr., Indianapolis, Ind.: Liberty Fund, 1981; reprinted from Oxford edition 1976, 1:454–55.

12. Edmund Burke, *Reflections on the Revolution in France*, in *Two Classics of the French Revolution: Reflections on the Revolution in France and The Rights of Man* (New York: Anchor, 1989).

13. Emma Rothschild, *Economic Sentiments: Adam Smith, Condorcet, and the Enlightenment* (Cambridge, Mass.: Harvard University Press, 2001).

14. Donald Winch, *Riches and Poverty: An Intellectual History of Political Economy in Britain, 1750–1834* (Cambridge: Cambridge University Press, 1996), 180.

15. Smith, *Wealth of Nations*, 1:456.

16. Bruce Caldwell, introduction to *The Road to Serfdom. Text and Documents: The Definitive Edition*, by Friedrich A. Hayek, in *The Collected Works of F. A. Hayek*, vol. 2, ed. Bruce Caldwell (Chicago: University of Chicago Press, 2007), 19.

17. Caldwell illuminates the intellectual backstory to both the German-language and English-language socialist calculation debates in *Hayek's Challenge: An Intellectual Biography of F. A. Hayek* (Chicago: University of Chicago Press, 2004), 116–19, 199, 214–20.

18. Hayek, *Road to Serfdom*, 71. All further citations to this work are given parenthetically in the text.

19. Christina Petsoulas, *Hayek's Liberalism and Its Origins: His Idea of Spontaneous Order and the Scottish Enlightenment* (London: Routledge, 2001), 189.

20. Edna Ullmann-Margalit, "The Invisible Hand and the Cunning of Reason," *Social Research* 64 no. 2 (1997), 181–98.

21. Friedrich Hayek, "The Theory of Complex Phenomena," in *Critical Approaches to Science and Philosophy*, ed. Mario Bunge (New Brunswick, N.J.: Transaction, 1999), 332–49, 348.

22. Joseph A. Schumpeter, *Capitalism, Socialism, and Democracy* (New York: Harper and Row, 1976), 83.

23. Friedrich Hayek, *Individualism and Economic Order* (Chicago: University of Chicago Press, 1948), 54.

24. For Marx, of course, most of the capitalist economy consists of a series of insanely productive frauds, starting with the decoupling of exchange-value from use-value that leads ultimately to commodity fetishism. *Capital: Volume One*, trans. Ben Fowkes (New York: Vintage, 1977), 125–77.

25. Lewis, *Big Short*, 91.

26. Paul Cantor, "The Poetics of Spontaneous Order: Austrian Economics and Literary Criticism," in *Literature and the Economics of Liberty: Spontaneous Order in Culture*, ed. Paul Cantor and Stephen Cox, (Auburn, Ala.: Ludwig von Mises Institute, 2009), 24. Cantor's work is full of baffling generalizations such as the idea that "many authors have been predisposed to socialism [because] they are used to planning in their own line of work and have a hard time conceiving how any form of order can be produced without it" (25).

27. Charles Dickens, *Little Dorrit* (Ann Arbor: Scholarly Publishing Office, University of Michigan Library, 2005). Subsequent citations are to this edition and are given parenthetically in the text.

28. When the BBC television production *Little Dorrit* was released in 2008, it reawakened interest in Dickens's insightful treatment of financial crashes in all his novels; see, for example, Robert Douglas-Fairhurst, "Financial Crisis: We Should Turn to Charles Dickens in Hard Times Not Just Little Dorrit," *Daily Telegraph*, October 21, 2008, www.telegraph.co.uk/culture/books/3562382/Financial-crisis-We-should-turn-to-Charles-Dickens-in-hard-times-not-just-Little-Dorrit.html.

29. Charles Dickens, *Bleak House*, ed. George Ford and Sylvère Monod (New York: Norton, 1977).

11   The Resurrection of an Economic God

Keynes Becomes Postmodern

Michael Tratner

THE BUSH AND Obama stimulus packages have inspired numerous claims that John Maynard Keynes is back from the dead. But the resurrected figure is strangely different, rather literally a ghost of his former self, because what is most decidedly left out is the relationship of Keynes's economics to the human body. In the 1930s Keynes proposed economic stimuli in order to release "pent-up demand," a concept quite close to the Freudian language of "pent-up desire." The similarity derives from a common underlying notion of physiology, that human action starts with instinctual drives found in the body. One reason Keynesian economics went out of fashion is that neoclassical theory claimed that human action can be rational, so economists could ignore bodily drives. The recent crash has caused numerous economists to say that we need to restore a Keynesian notion of irrationality.

But something has happened to the very notion of irrationality in the new versions of Keynes: it is no longer a result of bodily influence on the mind but rather a result of discursive structures, of "conventions" and "stories" that people fall into believing. This shift in the nature of irrationality has broad ramifications: for one thing, it mirrors a change in biology itself, in which it has come to seem that patterns of information are primary, while fleshy or chemical structures are secondary. Probably the most familiar version of this shift is the role of DNA and the genome in biological theories, which imply that our fleshy bodies are essentially constructed from DNA patterns. In a peculiar way, this theory says that each human body is actually a representation, a copy, of an original that is stored simply as a symbolic pattern. Biologists such as Paul Grobstein have recently begun extending this notion so completely that some argue that the way animal and human bodies develop—their "morphogenesis"—is not simply a process of the "unfolding" of chemical and material processes but rather an "information-gathering process . . . [in which] each part of a developing organism acquires information about other parts; many, in addition, gather information from the external environment."[1] Every organ inside our bodies is now considered a mini-computer connecting to other minicomputers.

In many other fields a similar shift has occurred, often called the "postmodern turn": as a recent collection of essays puts it, data have replaced flesh as the basis of everything.[2] We can see this postmodern turn in a uniquely clear way in the transformation of Keynes's ideas as they are supposedly resurrected after the recent crisis. I am going to focus on two books: first, *The Return of the Master: Why Sixty Years after His Death, John Maynard Keynes Is the Most Important Economic Thinker for America*, by Robert Skidelsky, historian and biographer; and second, *Animal Spirits: How Human Psychology Drives the Economy, and Why It Matters for Global Capitalism*, by George A. Akerlof and Robert J. Shiller, economists.[3] I start my discussion with Akerlof and Shiller because they title their book with a phrase from Keynes that seems to allude directly to the bodily or instinctual part of human motivation. *Animal spirits* is a term Keynes uses to describe what causes irrational choices, and these irrational choices lead to crashes but also keep good economies running smoothly. Akerlof and Shiller argue that the very concept has been lost in the economics of rational expectations. But there is a crucial difference between their view of "animal spirits" and what Keynes himself said back in the 1930s: Akerlof and Shiller ignore the allusion to animality. Instead, they trace the phrase back to the Latin *animalis spiritus,* in which *animalis* means, they write, "of the mind" or "animating."[4] Drawing on that Latin source, Akerlof and Shiller define "animal spirits" as discursive phenomena, with essentially no relation to anything animalistic at all. They give five categories of animal spirits: "confidence, fairness, corruption and antisocial behavior [that is one category], money illusion, and stories."[5] That last category ends up being kind of a catchall because what their explanations show is that all the others are basically various kinds of stories. Confidence, for example, shapes behavior when people circulate stories of good events about to happen, and "corruption and antisocial behavior" take over when stories circulate of corrupt people running the economy.

Let me go back to Keynes in the 1930s to show that when he spoke of "animal spirits" he was alluding to something animalistic and instinctual. He cites the term in his *General Theory* as "a spontaneous urge to action rather than inaction," or "our innate urge to activity which makes the wheels go round," and he explains what this means: "In estimating the prospects of investment, we must have regard, therefore, to the nerves and hysteria and even the digestion and reactions to the weather of those upon whose spontaneous activity it largely depends."[6] Spontaneous urges do not derive from stories but are innate and related to things like nerves and digestion. This is the language of bodily sources of human motivation.

It is not just an oddity of Akerlof and Shiller's views that they have changed Keynes's notion of the source of irrationality from the body to a set of stories. Skidelsky does much the same thing. Here is Skidelsky's account of what he thinks Keynes said about what makes people irrational: "Keynes argues that, faced with varying degrees of uncertainty, [we] fall back on conventions, stories, rules of thumb, habits, traditions in forming our expectations and deciding how to act."[7] Skidelsky settles on the term *conventions* as his catchall, saying that Keynes's theory is one of "conventional expectations" in contrast to recent theories of "rational expectations."

All three authors also admit that they are drawing on recent psychological theories to explain what Keynes was getting at. Skidelsky writes that "Keynes was anticipating something which has been subsequently developed by behavioural psychologists: that our tendency to follow the crowd may be 'hard-wired.'"[8] *Hard-wired* might seem to suggest a bodily source of the human tendency to follow conventions, to follow the crowd, but the term rather suggests that brain circuitry is responsible for this behavior, not some part of the body outside the brain that influences it. In such psychological theories, humans are simply computers throughout, not divided into body and brain.

Similarly, Akerlof and Shiller turn to a contemporary psychologist to support their view that human irrationality is due to our following stories. The treatise they turn to could even be said to be a direct rejection of Freud, because it directly transforms sexuality from something instinctual into something social, even something socially constructed. This treatise is entitled *Love Is a Story: A New Theory of Relationships,* by Robert Sternberg.[9] Akerlof and Shiller summarize what they see in this book in terms that make it sound as if love affairs operate exactly the way, in their theory, economic systems operate. They write that according to Sternberg "Couples create a shared story" so that "ultimately the success of [a] marriage [or any other relationship] depends on the partners' confidence in each other and on how that confidence is symbolically reinforced by repeating the stories."[10] *Confidence* is a key term in Akerlof and Shiller's analysis of what makes economic systems successful or unsuccessful, so their portrayal of this psychological theory suggests that marriages operate just as economies do: through the endless repetition of stories that either generate or destroy confidence.

"Confidence" is also central to Keynes's original theory, but what confidence leads to in Keynes in the 1930s is "effective demand," and lack of confidence leads to "pent-up demand." If we translate this back into a theory of marriage, we could say that 1930s Keynes would say confidence is tied to good sex among marriage partners, not just to good stories. And comparing these two theories, we might ask, Do marriages depend on the bodies of the marriage partners being satisfied, or just on their minds being filled with the right stories? That would be one way to describe the shift from Keynes in 1930, with his emphasis on restoring consumption, on unleashing pent-up demand, to the new Keynes in 2010, with an emphasis on everyone telling the right stories to each other, or, we might say, having the right conventions and symbols through which people interpret their lives and their wealth.

It may seem that I am pressing rather hard to turn "pent-up demand" into a bodily state akin to Freudian repression. Let me then give a more detailed comparison of one of the "conventions" or "stories" that Akerlof, Shiller, and Skidelsky all examine, namely the notion of "money illusion." This is the mistaken belief that the amount of money one has determines how rich one is. This can be an illusion when inflation or deflation occurs: for example, under inflation people may get more money in income and so feel richer but may actually be poorer if prices rise more than their income does. Akerlof, Shiller, and Skidelsky call this illusion a prime example of mistaken thinking, based on letting the conventional representation of wealth—in other words money— tell the story of what is going on, rather than looking for the real story told by what money can buy.

Keynes in the 1930s agrees that people mistake money for real wealth, but he goes on to theorize why money ends up replacing real objects, and it is not just due to stories and conventions—it is due to instincts. The problem, according to Keynes, is that money becomes an object of love. In an essay entitled "Economic Possibilities for Our Grandchildren," written in 1930, Keynes says that "the love of money as a possession— as distinguished from the love of money as a means to the enjoyments and realities of life . . . is one of those semi-criminal, semi-pathological propensities which one hands over with a shudder to the specialists in mental disease."[11] Furthermore, he writes, "we have been expressly evolved by nature—with all our impulses and deepest instincts— for the purpose of solving the economic problem" and that evolution has developed our current form of "love of money." He wonders in the essay what would happen if the "accumulation of wealth [were] no longer of high social importance"—if the love of money were no longer needed, and he concludes, "I think with dread of the readjustments of the habits and instincts of the ordinary man, bred into him for countless generations, which he may be asked to discard. . . . To use the language of today, must we not expect a general 'nervous breakdown'?"[12]

It seems clear that Keynes is invoking instincts and bodily reactions in explaining why money ends up becoming a symbol that is believed more than what that money can actually buy. Keynes's concern about the ways that money alters our thinking goes far beyond merely saying that it leads to some miscalculations: the money illusion distorts the entire human personality, and to escape the illusion of what money appears to be would be tantamount to having a nervous breakdown. When discussing the related fixation on the gold standard as a key to creating the value of money, he directly invokes Freud, writing in his essay "A Treatise on Money": "Dr. Freud relates that there are peculiar reasons deep in our subconsciousness why gold in particular should satisfy strong instincts and serve as a symbol."[13] Here we see in Keynes something that is utterly left out of the new accounts of Keynes, and that is a theory of why some "conventions" or "stories" or "symbols" come to be believed and others do not: the reason Keynes gives is that these stories and conventions "satisfy strong instincts."

In other words, Keynes believed that human bodies, full of strong instincts developed over centuries, are the source of irrational behavior. Akerlof, Shiller, and

Skidelsky believe that humans operate entirely as hard-wired machines following social conventions or stories. That makes the current proposed solutions to the economic problems caused by irrationality quite different from those proposed by Keynes in 1930, even though all these economic writers say that what are needed are "stimuli." For Keynes in 1930 the word *stimulus* carries its biological meaning, and not merely as an analogy. When a society falls into "pent-up demand" it is because the "propensity to consume" of the average person drops. "Propensity to consume" means tendency to spend money, but it also means willingness to take actions to satisfy the body, to consume things. To alter this propensity, Keynes needs to activate bodily drives.

There is even a rather strange way in which Keynes ends up suggesting that stimuli need to be applied to the "body" of the nation itself and not to its mind. Keynes writes that "measures for the redistribution of incomes in a way likely to raise the propensity to consume" may be necessary to solve an economic depression.[14] Wealth needs to be in the hands of the working class during a depression because the working class has a much higher propensity to consume when given money. The richer classes have already satiated their bodies, and they will respond to the stimulus of extra money by simply putting more in the bank. Keynes was not the first to note this problem; as early as 1878, a writer in the *Atlantic Monthly* argued that the roots of a developing economic crisis "lay in the unwillingness of the rich to consume more extensively and in their quixotic and self-destructive habit of excessive saving and investment."[15] Keynes's theory of pent-up demand is not just an economic one; it also blurs together other theories of what is wrong with the modern world—and that is why he ended up speaking of "nerves and hysteria" in that earlier quotation. Nerves and hysteria are problems of the rich, problems of people no longer knowing how to use their bodies, problems of *overcivilization,* as it was called—or, as economists called it, *underconsumption.* Underconsumption is underutilization of the body as well as not spending enough money. Note that in the title of Keynes's main treatise he doesn't use the word *wealth;* rather, he speaks of a general theory of "employment, interest, and money." The book so titled starts with a definition of economic success in terms of bodily activity—the need for employment—and it ends with the symbol that has absorbed so much of our instinctual energy, money. Keynes's entire treatise is about how to maintain the national body, to maintain full employment. His economic theory was entwined with a whole array of other theories about the need to restore the actual human bodies of nations and about the weakness and inability of upper-class bodies to provide this restoration because upper-class bodies have weak desires, weak consumption: they have a low propensity to consume. The cure for national ills lies in strong, desire-filled, working-class bodies.

That all this notion of the bodily involvement in economic crises has disappeared from recent invocations of Keynes may be, not simply a misinterpretation of Keynes, but a result of the fact that the current economic crisis is simply not the same as the one Keynes wrote about. Akerlof and Shiller argue quite directly that though they want to bring back some of Keynes's ideas his overall theory just doesn't apply any more: "This recession is different. It is not just due to low demand. The overwhelming threat to the current economy is the credit crunch. . . . It is fairly easy now to project the fiscal and monetary stimulus necessary for aggregate demand to be at full employment—*if* financial markets are freely flowing."[16] Note that they distinguish two different kinds of government intervention: first, the stimulus needed to increase "aggregate demand" to produce full employment—that is the kind of stimulus Keynes focused upon, and they say it is apparently easy to provide; but they see a second kind of intervention, a second kind of stimulus, needed to solve the problem of the "credit crunch" and the lack of "freely flowing financial markets." The focus on what needs to be cured has shifted: it is not a bodily state—low demand, low propensity to consume—that is causing the crisis; it is the credit crunch. In other words, this crisis is not about demand but about financial systems, the systems that we might say produce and manipulate the stories and symbols that shape people's behavior. And so employment has *not* been the main goal of either the Bush or the Obama stimulus; restoration of the financial system has been the goal. In this conception, the financial system is essentially the brain of the economic system, and the problem is that the brain has short-circuited, so the stimulus that is being applied is an electrical jolt to get it up and running. That is different from Keynes's view that stimuli are ways to unleash inhibited bodily drives. So it is actually fairly logical that we have the result of what seems to be an economic recovery while employment goes down: in other words, we have separated our definitions of what the economy is into two parts, one a discursive system involving the creation and manipulation of symbols (such as credit default swaps and derivatives) and the other a bodily system measured in terms of numbers of bodies employed. Recently, there have been calls for the old kind of stimuli, for stimuli designed to increase employment, but these calls seem to be oddly weak in the face of what seems to be a recovery of the financial system without a recovery of employment. This leads me to ask whether economics is about to become fully postmodern by attempting to discard the body entirely in favor of information and representations of wealth. Is the restoration of banks while employment continues to drop a way of moving toward eliminating bodies entirely from the economy, so that money can circulate without people doing anything?

Of course I am being a bit facetious here, but no more facetious than what seems to be becoming a major part of our recent fantasy life. Works such as *Neuromancer* and *The Matrix* suggest that it may be possible for people to leave their bodies behind and live entirely in virtual worlds. Most such works have tended to have rather dark overtones. But we now have a movie presenting such a possibility as utterly wonderful. I refer to what has already become the most popular movie of all time, *Avatar*. This movie masquerades as a return to nature, an escape from the mechanized and artificial modern world, but it is based on a vision of biology in which the essence of a person is entirely mental or at least immaterial and so transferable from one body to another via systems that do not even require physical contact between the two bodies.

A personality can be beamed across space into another body. The movie alludes to the recent developments in biology: an "avatar," a new body that a person can inhabit, is built on the "genome" of that person. Jake Sully, the main character, is able to have an avatar only because his genome matches that of his twin brother, for whom an avatar was constructed. The movie traces Jake's learning to prefer this avatar to his "real" body, and so we could say he learns to recognize his genome as more essential than the flesh and organs of his human body.

Oddly, in this movie, it is modern technology that seems to be equated with having bodies, while going back to nature is equated to seeing one's essence as immaterial, as something that can even be stored after death in a tree that looks like a giant fiber optic network. I may seem to have strayed from the topic of economics, but I want to suggest that the movie *Avatar* is also about economics, and indeed about the move in economic theory away from the body and material labor as the ultimate source of wealth. The bad guys in the movie use huge machines to dig up rocks that are supposedly incredibly valuable, and this desire to have big machines and collect rocks has destroyed Earth. In other words, the bad guys in this movie are the materialists who rely on bodies and labor for their wealth. But this system is failing economically, and in particular because it uses up bodies. The story begins with Jake Sully paralyzed in a VA hospital, saying that he could get his legs back through a spinal operation but that government "benefits" are not sufficient, "especially in this economy." So the movie starts with what seem quite direct allusions to current issues in the news: an economic crisis and a government that is not providing good enough health care even for the soldiers returning from some distant war. On Pandora, in contrast, nobody has a defective body at all (before they are attacked by the forces from Earth), and it seems that this derives from their living so much in harmony with nature, leaving the rocks in the ground and getting instead intangible wonderful things from nature's use of those magical rocks, such as the ability to communicate with animals.

But here is the kicker: I suggest that the tree at the center of Pandora is in a very direct way a bank, and what is stored in this bank is essentially information that is downloaded into bodies or transmitted to living creatures and plants through a vast network of information channels. Everything people live on results from their accepting and following the electrical signals flowing from that tree: in other words, everything of value on this world starts from the tree, is used by people for a while, and then is returned to the tree. As Natiri, the Pandoran who teaches Jake, summarizes the way the planet works, "A network of energy connects everything together. All that we have is borrowed and someday must be returned." Pandora is explicitly a world run on credit, on borrowing from a central bank. And that fits with the fact that there seems to be no need for employment at all. For Keynes in 1930, employment was the origin of wealth: you start with bodies that labor to build things, thereby increasing wealth. On Pandora, there really isn't any labor at all—nobody builds anything; all they do is teach each other how to plug into the central bank, and the better they plug in, the more they will be given by the world around them. Pandorans are essentially computer modules inside disposable bodies, borrowing energy from a giant network that is already fully constructed.

The movie is a lovely image of the financial system replacing the labor force as the driver of the economy, and so mirrors, I suggest, the postmodern version of Keynes. It is a vision of a central bank as the source of all wealth, even, it seems, personalities, which apparently are loaned out to bodies and returned to the tree bank when those bodies die. If the notion that banks ought to distribute our personalities along with our incomes seems rather horrifying, then maybe we ought to reconsider how much we are moving toward believing that information is the source of all that is valuable in a person. Academics, in particular, tend to believe that their brains contain everything that matters, everything that makes them who they are. But to escape becoming subsidiaries of a central bank, we may need to begin seeing value in our individual physical bodies in all their distinctiveness and recognizing that our personalities are products not just of our ideas but also of our flesh.

Notes

1. Paul Grobstein, "From the Head to the Heart: Some Thoughts on Similarities between Brain Function and Morphogenesis, and on Their Significance for Research Methodology and Biological Theory," *Experientia* 44 (1988): 960–71, http://serendip.brynmawr.edu/complexity/hth.html.

2. Robert Mitchell and Philip Thurtle, eds., *Data Made Flesh: Embodying Information* (New York: Routledge, 2003). See also N. Katherine Hayles, *How We Became Posthuman: Virtual Bodies in Cybernetics, Literature and Informatics* (Chicago: University of Chicago Press, 1999).

3. Robert Skidelsky, *The Return of the Master: Why Sixty Years after His Death, John Maynard Keynes Is the Most Important Economic Thinker for America* (New York: Public Affairs, 2009); George A. Akerlof and Robert J. Shiller, *Animal Spirits: How Human Psychology Drives the Economy, and Why It Matters for Global Capitalism* (Princeton: Princeton University Press, 2009).

4. Akerlof and Shiller, *Animal Spirits*. 3–4.

5. Ibid., 5.

6. John Maynard Keynes, *The General Theory of Employment, Interest and Money* (London: Macmillan, 1936), 162–63.

7. Skidelsky, *Return of the Master*, 87.

8. Ibid., 94.

9. Robert J. Sternberg, *Love Is a Story: A New Theory of Relationships* (Oxford: Oxford University Press, 1999).

10. Akerlof and Shiller, *Animal Spirits*, 52.

11. John Maynard Keynes, "Economic Possibilities for Our Grandchildren," *Nation and Athenaeum* 48 (October 11 and 18, 1930): 321. For a more complete treatment of Keynes's indebtedness to Freud's view of money, see Gilles Dostaler, "Keynes and the Love of Money: The Freudian Connection," paper presented at the 36th Annual Conference of the History of Economics Society, 2009, www.scribd.com/doc/87564183/Keynes-and-the-Love-of-Money-the-Freudian-Connection-1.

12. Keynes, "Economic Possibilities," 321.

13. John Maynard Keynes, *A Treatise on Money*, vol. 1 (London: Macmillan, 1930), 258.

14. Keynes, *General Theory*, 373.

15. Uriel H. Crocker, "Saving versus Spending," *Atlantic Monthly* 42 (1878): 696.

16. Akerlof and Shiller, *Animal Spirits*, 86–89.

12 China and the United States

The Bonds of Debt

Donald D. Hester

IN THE PAST twenty-five years the United States has had a growing balance of trade deficit with the People's Republic of China (PRC). Beginning with the 1971 reestablishment of diplomatic relations between the two countries, international trade between them expanded, first slowly and then rapidly. In 1985, US imports of goods from and exports of goods to China were modest and relatively equal, while in 2009 the trade deficit in goods was more than $226 billion.[1] This essay examines the distinctive features of this trade imbalance and proposes a crude game-theoretic discussion of what each country might gain and lose from their large growing financial entanglement in the short and long run. It also analyzes how US debts to and Chinese claims on other countries affect the relation between the PRC and the United States, and it concludes with a discussion of the paradox of a poor and rapidly growing authoritarian country financing an undisciplined and relatively declining democratic superpower.

The trade deficit began to grow rapidly after decisions taken by the Twelfth Central Committee of the Chinese Communist Party on October 20, 1984, radically reformed the economy.[2] The reforms effectively transformed state enterprises so that they began to function somewhat like private enterprises in capitalist countries and encouraged the development of privately owned firms and foreign trade. China had been growing fairly rapidly over the period from 1952 through 1985; starting from a very low level its index of total production had grown 14.4 times, but quite unevenly in the last years of Chairman Mao.[3]

Deng Xiaoping took control in 1978, and total production roughly doubled in the next seven years as he experimented with changes that would be incorporated in the 1984 reforms. One of the experiments was the establishment of Special Enterprise Zones where foreign firms could establish manufacturing facilities that employed inexpensive Chinese labor, as in Shenzhen in 1979. The zones allowed Chinese workers and managers to become familiar with foreign technologies and organizational techniques that would pay high dividends in future years. This experiment eventually led to a large number of international manufacturing firms operating in China, either alone or in joint ventures with Chinese collaborators; together they accounted for about 75 percent of Chinese international trade in 2005.[4] In 1978, the sum of Chinese imports and exports was about 7 percent of its national output; it rose to 25 percent of GDP in 1987, 37 percent in 1998, and about 43 percent in 2008.[5] China's policies under Deng were adapted from a highly successful export-oriented strategy employed by Japan in the years after World War II, which the Asian tigers—Hong Kong, Singapore, Taiwan, and South Korea—had also adopted. The economies of these five countries were expanding at a time when there was growing global demand for the goods they exported.

Between 1980 and 1995, Japan's—and, to a lesser extent, South Korea's—exports had reached levels where they were substantially adversely affecting some US industries. German and other European country exports to the United States were also very high in the early 1980s. In part, the problem was caused by an appreciating US dollar resulting from expansionary fiscal policy associated with large Reagan administration tax cuts and a restrictive monetary policy imposed by the Federal Reserve. A basic result in Keynesian economics is that this mix of policies causes real interest rates to rise, which in turn causes a country's currency to appreciate against those of other countries. As a result, the prices of goods imported by the United States fell and the prices of US exports rose, with detrimental consequences for the US balance of trade. An international agreement to reduce the value of the dollar at the Plaza Hotel in 1985 and a recession in 1991 reduced the US trade deficit. The overall trade deficit, however, increased again during the Clinton presidency, and by 2005 the combined Japanese and Chinese bilateral trade surplus with the United States was about twice as large a percentage of US GDP as it had been in 1995—more than three-quarters of it was Chinese.[6] While the recent recession has reduced the trade deficit, it is likely to widen again in coming years.

In 2008, the World Trade Organization (WTO) reported China's global merchandise exports were $1,428 billion and merchandise imports were $1,132 billion. Thus US trade was a relatively small fraction of China's world trade but a very large fraction of its balance of trade surplus, $296 billion in that year. Some of China's trade was with other countries that sent raw materials and components to China, where they were assembled and exported, largely to the United States. (China joined the WTO in December 2001.) By way of comparison, the Federal Reserve reported that overall US exports and imports of goods and services were respectively $1,827 and $2,523 billion and that the US trade balance deficit was $696 billion. China trade accounted for about 43 percent of the US trade deficit.

The exchange rate between the Chinese yuan and the US dollar is believed to be an important contributor to the growing trade deficit of the United States with China. The yuan and the dollar were officially inconvertible until 1994, but a multiplicity of rates existed that were negotiated between the Chinese government and different entities that, among other things, allowed firms in enterprise zones to import and export commodities and withdraw profits from activities in Special Enterprise Zones. In 1987 these rates were about 3.73 yuan to the dollar, and by 1993 they had climbed to 5.80 yuan to the dollar.[7] Reforms in 1994 established a uniform exchange rate of 8.70 yuan to the dollar, which was roughly equal to an average of swap rates. There was a high rate of inflation in China between 1993 and 1995, and Ronald McKinnon and Gunther Schnabl argue that the sharp change in the nominal exchange rate from 5.80 yuan to the dollar in 1993 to 8.33 yuan to the dollar in 1995 roughly allowed the real exchange rate between 1993 and 1995 to be constant.[8]

From the end of 1995 until the fourth quarter of 2005, the yuan was pegged at 8.3 yuan to the dollar by the Chinese government. This peg was widely assailed as being responsible for the surging US trade deficit with China: the claim was that the yuan was undervalued. It was argued that if the yuan had been allowed to appreciate, the trade deficit would have been smaller, Chinese economic growth would have been slower, the rate of loss of US jobs in competing industries would have been slower, and US consumers would have faced higher prices. In this view the Chinese exchange rate policy was an attack on the foundations of the US economy.

McKinnon and Schnabl have proposed a very different interpretation.[9] They argued that when China opened its economy in 1994 and allowed relatively free trade, the People's Bank of China, the nation's central bank, was operating in a highly uncertain environment where inflation was uncontrolled. A strategy for coping with domestic inflation was to fix its exchange rate to another currency that had little domestic inflation. Other countries have pegged their currencies to the dollar for similar reasons. McKinnon and Schnabl reported that the difference between Chinese and US CPI inflation rates was negligible between January 1997 and January 2007, so that the price stabilization policy appears to have worked. An interpretation of China's growing international trade surpluses then would be that reallocations of resources within China led to changes in relative costs that gave it substantial advantages in world markets—initially in basic commodities. Introducing large quantities of relatively inexpensive labor together with modern technology in world markets was bound to create disequilibria that would only gradually converge to a new balance. Global adjustment costs would be large.

The McKinnon and Schnabl argument is appealing as a short-run tactic for establishing a new exchange rate. Through 2000 the major nominal and real exchange rates of the United States were rising, and so the yuan was actually appreciating against most other countries.[10] It is not, however, a defensible policy for a large country that has the ability to have discretionary monetary policy. The United States experienced a minor recession in 2001, and US imports from China were stagnant. In response to the recession, the Federal Reserve aggressively cut short-term interest rates, which led to decreases in major US dollar nominal exchange rates. As a result of the yuan being pegged to the falling dollar, it also fell in value against most other currencies, beginning in 2002 in the case of major currencies. As Paul Krugman recently explained, this led to a massive further trade imbalance with other countries and to soaring international reserves in China.[11] A Chinese policy of allowing the yuan to float or be pegged to an average of a number of foreign currencies would have helped to contain imbalances that now threaten global stability.

China did begin to allow the yuan to appreciate against the dollar in the summer of 2005. It rose by about 21 percent between the summers of 2005 and 2008, after which it was again pegged to the dollar at a rate of about 6.83 yuan to the dollar. The second peg again occurred at a time when the dollar was falling sharply against other major currencies—especially the Japanese yen and the euro. One effect of removing the peg in 2005 may have been to slow down the rate of growth of the bilateral trade deficit. Unreported monthly trade data, however, are very erratic, and the recession that began in the United States in December 2007 makes any strong conclusion about the effects of removing the peg dubious.

The trade imbalance has meant that China holds large amounts of foreign exchange reserves. Changes in foreign exchange reserves are the sum of a country's current account balances with other countries, net private capital movements into the country, and net government capital movements into the country. The current account balance is equal to the sum of the trade balance on goods and services, investment income, net government international transfers, net private transfers, and remittances into the country. Private foreign direct investment utilized in China has risen from $48.8 billion a year in 2001 to $92.4 billion in 2008.[12] China's official year-end levels of foreign exchange reserves, net of gold, were US$20.6 billion in 1992, $212 billion in 2001, and $2.4 trillion in 2009.[13] The levels are expressed in dollars but consist of a number of foreign currencies. The currency composition of Chinese reserves is not available, but it has been reported that China held $1.2 trillion of US securities at the end of June 2008.[14]

International accounts are notoriously difficult to interpret and typically have large discrepancies. In this discussion such measurement problems are being ignored. What is clear beyond any accounting niceties is that China's foreign exchange reserves increased more than tenfold in the most recent eight years.

It is important to recognize that foreign exchange reserves of all nations have risen markedly in the current decade. The International Monetary Fund (IMF) reports that total foreign exchange holdings have risen from $1.4 trillion in 1995 to $2.0 trillion in 2001 and to $7.3 trillion in 2008. The amounts of reserves held in dollar-denominated assets may also have risen irregularly, but the evidence is unclear. Of the amounts that were allocated to currencies by the IMF, 59 percent were in dollars in 1995, 72 percent were in dollars in 2001, and 64 percent were in dollars in 2008. The percentage of total exchange holdings, however, that were not allocated to currencies has risen from 26 percent in 1995 to 43 percent in 2008. In 2009, the IMF reported world foreign exchange reserves to be $8.2 trillion. China's $2.4 trillion in 2009 was more than one-quarter of world foreign exchange reserves.

An Interpretation of the Growing Interdependence of China and the United States

Game theory provides one way to analyze the economic imbalances between China and the United States. One can set the two countries in a bilateral game in which the actions of all other countries are ignored. The players are the two governments, consumers in each country, and multinational firms. The principal assumptions in this section are: (1) Labor costs for equally productive workers are lower in China, (2) trade is not subject to tariffs or other barriers, (3) capital is mobile between the countries, and 4) the exchange rate is set administratively by the Chinese government. The first assumption implies that the administered exchange rate of yuan for dollars is high, as is commonly believed to be the case.

Under these conditions consumers in the United States prefer to purchase goods made in China to those made in the United States, if they are of similar quality, and multinational firms choose to locate manufacturing facilities in China. China has a balance of trade surplus and in the absence of capital flows has rising dollar exchange reserves. Because of the continuing relatively low wage rates in China, multinational firms desire to invest in new facilities there, so private direct capital flows to China also result in rising dollar exchange reserves. Dollar reserves in China will continue to rise until something changes. This is a caricature of the current disequilibrium situation, but it has obvious similarities.

As Chinese workers continue to take market share from the United States, American workers suffer increasing job losses and decreasing wage rates. An endogenous limit on the trade imbalance is that multinational firms may eventually be unable to market goods to US consumers. In this simple example, China's growing balance of trade surplus and corresponding accumulation of dollars must be invested in asset-backed securities that finance US consumers' purchases of goods. At some point China is unlikely to tolerate excessive US consumer indebtedness because of the growing risk of default. Multinational firms would need to find other markets or trade would atrophy.

In what other ways can the disequilibrium in the model be resolved so that balance is restored? Clearly, allowing the yuan to appreciate is one answer. Why doesn't that happen? Large segments of the Chinese population are extremely impoverished and experience large increases in income when multinational firms or other Chinese exporters hire them. With a pegged yuan, per capita Chinese income is rising, even though workers are being underpaid relative to US workers. Thus the pegging policy could be defended as part of a program to increase average income of all Chinese workers. The Chinese government, however, may eventually allow the yuan to appreciate after the reserve army of its impoverished population has been substantially depleted. A higher-valued yuan could allow its workers to enjoy benefits from trade, as Ricardo argued in his discussion of comparative advantage. In this hypothetical two-nation world, China is now temporarily trading off losses from holding low-yielding dollar assets with gains from more effectively allocating human capital.

Another way to restore balance would be to penalize multinational firms that are investing in China. The United States does not tax corporate profits that are earned overseas until they are repatriated. China collects taxes from foreign enterprises, but at rates that are lower than would be paid on repatriated profits. If corporate profits were taxed when they were earned anywhere, there would be less of an incentive to locate facilities in China. The importance of this tax advantage is unclear, but it does provide incentives to produce in China.

A third way to restore balance would be for the United States to threaten to increase its money stock rapidly through inflationary monetary policy. Irresponsibly large US fiscal deficits would have a similar effect if investors perceived that interest obligations on a surging federal deficit could not be met without turning to the printing press. Thus the United States could make the trade-off mentioned above too expensive. Such irresponsible monetary or fiscal policies would, of course, have dire consequences for the United States.

Finally, the two countries could try diplomacy. This is where a game strategy comes to the fore. The United States could argue that while it appreciates and approves of the gains in average Chinese income, they have become intolerable for US citizens; the transfer of gains from good jobs in the United States to China has been excessively severe. The bargaining chips of hyperinflation or default on debt are too heavy-handed, but other threats are available. Although assumed away at the outset of this section, tariffs and other controls could be mentioned. Both countries are already posturing in a limited way with these tools of economic warfare, for example, with tariffs on tires, steel pipe, automobiles, and chicken feet. Obviously and unfortunately, both countries are also investing heavily in their military establishments. The United States has rebuffed China when it sought to buy an American oil company (Unocal), banks, and other properties. The island nation of Taiwan seems always to be in play when tensions arise between the United States and China. All of these and other moves could be represented in a matrix summarizing a nonconstant-sum dynamic game between these two countries. Assigning parameters to cells of the matrix and proposing its dynamic (intertemporal) structure is no small task, but it is almost surely being done in both countries. Whether a stable and mutually acceptable solution between them exists in this game is an open question that cannot be answered in this short essay.

Domestic policies could also address the imbalance, but they are awkward for politicians and difficult to put into effect. I have already mentioned increasing taxes on offshore corporate profits. In China the personal saving rate is believed to be very high because of the need for precautionary funds to cover education, medical emergencies, and retirement. Consumption there can be stimulated by improving social infrastructure for example, by introducing a public retirement program and increasing subsidies for education and health. Expanding access to consumer credit in China would also help. In principle, these initiatives could be funded by its foreign exchange reserves. In the United States consumption could be discouraged by (1) limiting the deductibility of interest on home equity lines of credit and otherwise deterring equity extraction by house owners, (2) introducing a national sales tax, (3) penalizing early withdrawals from retirement accounts further, and (4) encouraging saving by automatically signing up workers to retirement accounts, as has been recommended by some behavioral economists.

With no elaborate gaming by the countries, the simple trade imbalance is likely to be eliminated eventually, when the reserve army of the impoverished is depleted. Convergence may not be monotonic, and the reserve army might even appear in the second country. But it is in the interest of both countries to end the imbalance in a minimally disruptive way. In a two-country game there is no choice of other currencies in which to hold foreign exchange reserves. However, in a multicountry game it is not clear that eliminating a trade imbalance would be in everyone's interest, and there are portfolio choices to be made in the currency composition of foreign exchange reserves.

Curbing Bilateral Imbalances in a Multicountry World

In the real world, as opposed to a game, China trades with the rest of the world as well as the United States, and US trade imbalances involve other countries along with China. The US trade deficit with China in 2008 was nearly 90 percent of China's reported trade surplus with the rest of the world but only about 43 percent of the overall US trade deficit. In 2002 the United States had the largest value of summed exports and imports in the world, followed by Germany and then China; the estimated ranking in 2008 was unchanged, with Germany being the largest exporter and the United States the largest importer.[15] (It has recently been reported that China has become the largest exporter in 2009.) In 2005, however, the sum of exported and imported goods of China was 64 percent of its GDP, about three times the share of other major countries.[16]

The continued peg of the yuan to the falling value of the dollar has resulted in a depreciation of the yuan against currencies of China's other main trading partners of 7.6 percent between March and the end of October 2009, although its current account surplus was expected to fall by 50 percent in 2009 because of the global recession and strong Chinese growth.[17] The yuan had depreciated 11.9 percent against the euro, based on monthly averages, between March and October 2009. The US balance of trade in goods and services deficit has fallen more than 50 percent between the second quarter of 2008 and the second quarter of 2009. The future course of Chinese imbalances with the United States and other countries in this volatile environment is very difficult to predict, but certain principal strategies are being used or are likely to be used in the coming years to address this situation. These strategies involve China's trade with the rest of the world, and US trade with the rest of the world, for the game involves far more than two players.

First to China's trade with the rest of the world. When China opened Special Enterprise Zones, it located them on the coast in part to facilitate importing technical components so that it might assemble products to export. Significant amounts were also exported to Hong Kong for re-export to other countries in the 1980s, which partly accounts for the discrepancy between US and Chinese trade balance accounts, because the United States views such exports as Chinese when they reach the United States, whereas China records them as exports to Hong Kong. There is a large volume of trade between China and other East Asian countries, and measuring the intercountry trade balances is very difficult. For example, using their own systems of accounts, both China and Japan claim to have trade deficits with one another.[18] Similar but less severe reported inconsistencies exist for balances between China and Hong Kong, Taiwan, South Korea, and Singapore.

Table 12.1 reports recent national product accounts for Mainland China. There are several remarkable features of these accounts. First, since 2003 China is probably unique among all the countries of the world in having fixed investment that exceeds consumption. Second, the Chinese economy was achieving spectacular growth. Third, China's fixed and inventory investment and net exports (exports less imports) have been growing much more rapidly than its gross domestic product; the growth in its net exports in 2007 accounted for 14.4 percent of the growth in its GDP. In the recession year of 2008, however, the growth in its net exports accounted for only 1.7 percent of GDP growth. Fourth, inflation as measured by the rate of change in the GDP deflator was not excessive but rose a bit more rapidly in 2007 and 2008.

The goals of the Chinese government in the multicountry game are not entirely clear, but I assume its primary goal is to maximize China's rate of growth. A second major goal is to secure access to scarce raw materials, such as petroleum, some metallic ores, and, before long, agricultural products.[19] The last reflects likely future shortages of water as global warming depletes Himalayan glaciers, population continues to grow, and increasing desertification occurs in much of northern China. A third goal is to expand China's ability to defend itself against possible hostile international rivals as it becomes more dependent on foreign resources. This third goal is a change from the days of Chairman Mao, when China struggled to be self-sufficient and thus not dependent on foreign trade.

Finally, as one of the world's most rapidly expanding markets, China appears to be attempting to structure access to its markets for consumption goods and labor so as to maximize some arbitrary welfare function that its leaders have chosen. The high level of investment evident in table 12.1 implies that its citizens today are making large sacrifices so that their heirs can live better. This emphasis on growth may or may not reflect

Table 12.1 National Product Accounts for Mainland PRC: 2002–8 (billions of yuan)

	2002	2003	2004	2005	2006	2007	2008
Consumption	5257	5683	6383	7122	8048	9360	10839
Government	1912	2062	2320	2661	3012	3519	4072
Fixed investment	4363	5349	6512	7731	9015	10544	12621
Inventory change	193	247	405	334	425	548	740
Net exports	309	299	408	1022	1665	2338	2414
GDP	12033	13582	15988	18322	21192	25731	30067
GDP price deflator	87.9	90.1	96.4	100.0	103.6	111.3	119.3

Source: International Monetary Fund, *International Financial Statistics*, December 2009, 340.

preferences of its consumers today, which is an acknowledgment that China is not a democracy and has not adopted a free enterprise, laissez-faire ideology.[20] It is possible to commit too many resources to investment.[21] While the situation is murky, recent press reports suggest that the government is also actively working to concentrate some manufacturing and service activities in state enterprises and to use its power to control mergers by large multinational firms.[22] As in the cases of the European Union and the United States, regulatory authorities in China must approve mergers among large firms if the resulting new firm is to have access to Chinese markets.

The goals of the United States and other countries are also unclear and differ among countries. Unlike the United States, most developed countries have relatively old and rapidly aging populations. (China, as a result of its "one child" policy, will also soon face an aging population.) As a consequence, they generally need to make income-earning investments that can support these populations. They are unlikely to welcome trade deficits that leave surplus countries with funds to invest that will compete with the needs of these populations. On the other hand, poor and developing countries need capital and tend to welcome funds, even if they are a consequence of trade deficits. Economists appreciate the virtues of Ricardo's theory of comparative advantage and countries' desire to acquire goods and services through trade from low-cost suppliers, but the theory assumes the presence of competitive markets. No country seems to be willing to open up its borders to free competition, even if it respects and loosely complies with rules established by the WTO. Politicians everywhere are sensitive to pleas about trade-related unemployment, and many are open to the temptations of graft and political contributions.

Why does China desire to amass exchange reserves in this multicountry game? First, it is likely to desire liquidity in a perceived potentially hostile world. While international currencies and sovereign debt of more developed countries are risky in terms of future value, they are likely to be readily accepted by many countries in payment for goods and services. China's currency, the yuan, may not be as convenient for making contracts in the next few years.[23] As it seeks to develop foreign sources of raw materials in the coming years, China's large international exchange hoard implies that it can afford to make long-term credible commitments to diverse suppliers. There is, however, some evidence that China has recently been shifting the composition of its reserves away from the US dollar.[24] As noted earlier, the currency composition of its exchange reserves is not known—it's a state secret.

Second, the low international value of the yuan may have strategic advantages for China because independent firms in other countries may not have adequate resources to survive a price war effected through devaluation. Chinese firms can borrow from state banks that can be funded by exchange reserves. The low yuan is inflicting enormous damage on international suppliers of goods that compete with Chinese exports.[25] Its low and falling value has prompted extensive criticism on the grounds that it perpetuates imbalances that threaten world trade.[26] Indeed, some critics view its low value as effectively serving to impose a tariff barrier on imports from other countries, much in the tradition of the Smoot-Hawley US tariff and related tariffs put on by other countries during the 1930s, which worsened the Great Depression. One writer has even argued that the United States should respond to this policy of mercantilism by imposing a 10 percent tariff on imports from China.[27] Others, however, have claimed that recent surges in Chinese imports imply that the yuan is not especially undervalued.[28]

A different interpretation of China's low-valued yuan policy is that to prevent domestic political unrest from rising unemployment and falling per capita income the government feels it must maintain a high rate of growth. Irrespective of its motives, there is little doubt that the government itself is declining to use imported goods; it has not yet signed a WTO agreement in which government institutions are obliged not to favor domestic suppliers.[29] Of course, all countries in a serious recession are subject to the threat of political unrest, so this interpretation is fundamentally indefensible. Further, the argument fails to acknowledge that China's economy is clearly growing much more rapidly in 2009 than economies of other large nations.[30]

Third, China's state banks have been rapidly expanding loans to its state enterprises and to its provinces, municipalities, and counties during the current recession. The latter include nonrecourse loans to urban development investment corporations (UDICs).[31] The banks are reported to require about $73 billion in new capital in 2010 to cover expected future losses from recent lending.[32] In the past, China has used exchange reserves to absorb losses the banks have sustained.[33] The low value of the yuan together with this recent policy of increased lending appears to have raised the rate of inflation. The Chinese domestic money supply has recently been rising at a rate of about 30 percent per annum.[34] In addition to increased lending, part of this increase in money is a consequence of its policy of pegging the yuan to the dollar; when the dollar threatens to fall, China buys dollars and pays for them with its own currency. At some point, rising inflation may force China to increase the value of the yuan relative to the dollar, which would tend to exacerbate loan losses. The condition of banks is not transparent but is likely to be important for setting the future value of the yuan.

Fourth, a major reason for China's desire to accumulate reserves may be the high rate of investment evident in table 12.1. Roughly 88 percent of China's GDP growth in the first half of 2009 was investment.[35] Such a rapid increase in capacity is likely to yield low rates of return and produce gluts of commodities that cannot be sold profitably, or the new capital will lie idle as excess capacity.[36] It is not clear who is investing in plants and equipment, but among the candidates are firms from abroad that make foreign direct investments, Chinese state firms, UDICs, and private individuals and firms in China. In 2005 the greatest amount of foreign direct investment came collectively from Hong Kong, Taiwan, Macao, and tax havens in the Caribbean and elsewhere.[37] The second largest group had about 40 percent as much; it included Japan, the United States, and the European Union. The actual nationalities of foreign investors are unknown and their activities are not conveniently available, but they are likely to be engaged in exporting and in relocating production facilities from high-cost, offshore locations to China. Foreign direct investment was only about 3 percent of China's GDP in 2005 and was not more than 5 percent in the preceding decade; it seems unlikely to account for much of the recent surge shown in table 12.1.[38] Data about recent investment by private firms in China are not available. Given the large increase in lending to state enterprises and UDICs, it seems likely that they are mostly responsible for the surge in investment. China's per capita consumption has been growing rapidly, but less rapidly than GDP; its own consumers are not likely to be able to absorb a large increase in output resulting from the investment surge. Foreign consumers are also unlikely to increase purchases of consumer goods dramatically unless prices fall further, which may partly explain why the yuan has remained stubbornly pegged to the dollar. Reserves can smooth shocks to an economy.

Some investment, of course, is not intended to result in increased export capacity. For example, the massive waterworks infrastructure projects involving transporting water from the Yangtze River basin to the Yellow River basin are addressing severe ecological problems and shortages. The Three Gorges dam and China's reported increased defense spending on equipment are other examples. To support such massive undertakings, China may need to import food and other materials in the future; such imports will require funds. If a series of additional large infrastructure projects such as introducing high-speed trains and highway expansion describes the future, even with the undervalued yuan the Chinese positive trade balance could shrink substantially in the coming years. Indeed, further devaluations of the Chinese currency might be needed.

We turn from China's trade with the rest of the world to US trade with the rest of the world, the second aspect of this more complex game. The United States has large merchandise trade imbalances with other countries besides China. Its largest trading partner is Canada, with which it had a trade deficit of $112 billion in 2008.

After China and Canada it had large 2008 trade deficits of $85 billion with Mexico, $78 billion with Japan, $46 billion with Germany, $42 billion with Saudi Arabia, $38 billion with Venezuela, and $34 billion with Nigeria. Canada and Mexico have tariff advantages because of being signatories of the North American Free Trade Agreement (NAFTA), Japan and Germany are high-technology countries that supply both US consumers and manufacturing firms, and the last three are oil exporters and members of the Organization of Petroleum Exporting Countries (OPEC). Indeed, thirty-six of the top fifty US trading partners, measured by summed imports from and exports to the United States, had surpluses with it.[39] The point of this enumeration is that while China's $270 billion trade surplus with the United States was the largest, it was not alone; collectively Canada, Mexico, and Japan's was larger.

Why does the United States have such large trade deficits with so many countries? The answer can be found in a simple national income accounting identity. Specifically, a country's saving equals the sum of its domestic investment, government deficit, and trade surplus. The personal saving rate and net private saving as a percentage of GDP in the United States have fallen dramatically over the past thirty years, and especially in the decade ending in 2007. Gross private domestic investment and the federal government deficit as a percentage of GDP have trended up over these periods. The only way the accounting identity can be satisfied is for the United States to have a large and growing aggregate balance of trade deficit. A lack of federal fiscal discipline, beginning with the tax cuts by the Reagan administration in 1981, is the root of the problem. The federal debt as a percentage of GDP has risen from 33 percent in 1980 to 66 percent in 2007, and a further increase is in progress.

The deficits with China and Mexico are partly the consequence of decisions made by large multinational firms that choose to export components made in the United States to these countries where final products are assembled and then sold back to the United States. Maquiladoras, an example of this practice, are facilities owned and managed by US firms that are located just over the Mexican border; there are no duties or tariffs paid on their imports or exports to the United States. To an unknown extent, similar activities exist in China's Special Enterprise Zones and elsewhere in China. These practices suggest that an analysis of US/China or other trade imbalances is seriously incomplete if it restricts attention only to governments. In a world where independent capitalist entities thrive, there are forces beyond governments in the world—markets and firms struggling to escape rules and regulations. US corporations with overseas subsidiaries, for example, have little interest in repatriating their profits earned abroad, because, as noted above, they are subject to US corporate income taxes only when profits are returned to the United States.

Foreign direct investment in the United States is another part of the story. Firms based in Canada, Japan, and western Europe make about 75 percent of all foreign direct investment in the United States, which amounted to $237 billion in 2007 and $325 billion in 2008.[40] Foreign direct investment allows countries with large trade surpluses to avoid accumulating large amounts of dollar-denominated financial assets. Instead they acquire productive physical assets in the United States. Foreign direct investment from China in 2008 was only about $373 million. The US government has discouraged or prevented a number of Chinese attempts to buy banks, oil companies, and other firms in the United States. The US government's actions are sometimes defended on national security grounds. Without this channel for disposing of its trade surpluses, China has little choice but to accumulate foreign exchange balances or to let the yuan appreciate against the dollar. Its recent efforts to purchase Volvo from Ford show another route by which China can avoid holding dollars.

The recent growth in Chinese foreign exchange reserves is mostly a consequence of the large continuing balance of trade surplus that China has had with the United States. There are several interdependent reasons for the surplus. The saving rate in the United States has been very low, and the saving rate in China has been high. Other things being equal, a low saving rate will tend to be associated with a trade deficit and vice versa.

The low value of the yuan relative to the dollar has made Chinese goods relatively inexpensive for US consumers. If exchange rates were flexible and set in markets, a glut of dollars would drive the value of the dollar down relative to the yuan. Except for a brief period between the end of 2005 and the middle of 2008, the Chinese government has pegged the yuan/dollar exchange rate. Between 2005 and 2008, however, the yuan was allowed to appreciate about 21 percent against the dollar.

China, of course, is a totalitarian state, and its ruling communist party makes decisions that are designed to achieve the party's goals. From the investment data in table 12.1 it is clear that the party has a very ambitious set of goals. China's very high and rising domestic investment and trade surplus imply that it has had a large government budget surplus and/or a high personal saving rate. (The distinction between public and private saving is somewhat blurry in a socialist economy.) Domestic investment inevitably involves sacrifices by the present generation so that future generations can live better. The continuing high rate of investment is designed to maintain an almost unprecedented high rate of growth of the Chinese economy, but it exacts a high price in foregone current consumption. To be sure, per capita consumption is rising, but at a much slower rate than might be expected. One could interpret high investment as providing for a soon-to-be-aging Chinese population.

By way of contrast, in the United States the federal surplus and private saving have been very low after 1980, and especially so after 2000. This democratic society has adopted an impatient, hedonistic attitude, much in the tradition of the late Roman Empire. The GDP growth rate was reasonably stable between 1980 and 2000 because households and the federal government were funding their spending by increased borrowing. GDP growth in the most recent decade has been anemic, in part because of the United States' rising trade deficit with the rest of the world. Further, the government has underfunded its social programs like Medicare and has greatly expanded its overseas military activities, without accounting for future financial burdens that these activities will entail. The federal government has borrowed large amounts from the Social Security Trust Funds, which it must begin to pay back in the near future—perhaps starting in 2017. Private borrowing, a form of dis-saving, has been abetted by a lack of government regulation of US financial institutions and, in the last decade, by low lending interest rates that were caused by Federal Reserve policies. Consumption as a percentage of GDP was close to 63 percent in the years between 1959 and 1980, after which it rather steadily trended up to about 70 percent in the years 2005–7.

These diverse trends in China and the United States have set the stage for the growing dispute about whether the yuan should continue to be pegged to the dollar. Both countries have contributed to the problem, and no one knows at this point how the dispute will be resolved. China's premier, Wen Jiabao, has recently said: "We will not yield to any pressure of any form forcing us to appreciate. As I have told my foreign friends: on the one hand, you are asking for the renminbi to appreciate; and on the other hand you are taking all kinds of protectionist measures."[41] American politicians and a host of economists have argued that the yuan must be allowed to resume its appreciation against the dollar. Both countries have undertaken vigorous monetary and fiscal policy actions to combat the "great recession," but both continue to experience disruptions. The actions appear to be working in both countries; China's GDP rose at a rate of 8.7 percent in 2009 because of its very large investments in infrastructure, and the US GDP grew at an annualized rate of 2.2 percent in the third quarter of 2009 and about 5.9 percent in the fourth quarter.

While it is too early to draw confident conclusions, there are some indications that the imbalance between China and the United States is beginning to weaken. China's 2009 exports to the United States appear to be much lower than in previous years, which may partly explain its hesitancy to allow the yuan to appreciate at this time. If its trade surplus is actually shrinking, it will accumulate reserves more slowly. China's inflation rate is apparently beginning to accelerate, which may prompt it to let the value of the yuan rise.[42] There is some evidence that labor shortages are developing in China, so the reserve army of impoverished employable workers may be shrinking.[43] Further, there are reports that China is using its reserves at an increasing rate to arrange mergers with foreign firms, a form of foreign direct investment. The estimated amounts of outgoing funds were $9.6 billion in 2005, $25.4 billion in 2007, $50 billion in 2008, and $46 billion in 2009.[44] In the United States the personal saving rate has begun to rise, which is partly a consequence of diminished access to credit at banks and a welcome reaction to excessive spending by households in the past decade. China is beginning to export more to other countries, especially countries in the Association of Southeast Asian Nations (ASEAN).

These modest adjustments, however, may not be enough to deter countries from raising tariff barriers against Chinese exports. The IMF predicts large continuing imbalances through 2014.[45] It would be a tragic development if trade imbalances were resolved through tariff increases, as occurred in the 1930s, but it cannot be ruled out.[46] All countries would suffer from disrupted supplies of goods, and global productivity would be seriously diminished. One can only hope that cooler heads will prevail and that both China and the United States can make adjustments to avoid such a calamity.

Notes

1. Source: U.S. Census Bureau Foreign Trade Statistics, table entitled "Trade in Goods (Imports, Exports and Trade Balance) with China," August 17, 2009, www.census.gov/foreign-trade/balance/c5700.html. Chinese government data on the trade balance are very different. For example, Chinese data show that China had a trade deficit with the United States from 1984 through 1992 and that its surplus with the United States was only $114 billion in 2005. For a discussion of the reasons for these differences, see Thomas Lum and Dick K. Nanto, *China's Trade with the United States and the World* (Washington, D.C.: Congressional Research Service, January 2007), 6–8.

2. Gregory C. Chow, *China's Economic Transformation*, 2nd ed. (Malden, Mass.: Blackwell, 2007).

3. People's Republic of China State Statistical Bureau, *Statistical Yearbook of China* (Beijing: National Bureau of Statistics, 1986), 25.

4. Ma Guonan and Zhou Haiwen, *China's Evolving External Wealth and Rising Creditor Position*, BIS Working Paper No. 286 (Basel: Bank for International Settlements, July 2009), 2.

5. Chow, *China's Economic Transformation*, 54.

6. Ronald McKinnon and Gunther Schnabl, *China's Financial Conundrum and Global Imbalances*, BIS Working Paper No. 277 (Basel: Bank for International Settlements, March 2009), 25.

7. Federal Reserve Board, "Foreign Exchange Rates," Statistical Release H.10, www.federalreserve.gov/releases/h10/hist/.

8. McKinnon and Schnabl, *China's Financial Conundrum*, 2–3.

9. Ibid., 3–4.

10. Board of Governors of the Federal Reserve System, *Statistical Digest: 1996–2000* (Washington, D.C.: Board of Governors of the Federal Reserve System, March 2002), 233–37.

11. Paul Krugman, "The Chinese Disconnect," *New York Times*, October 23, 2009.

12. Ken Davies, "FDI Inflows into China 1984–2009," n.d., *Chinability* blog, www.chinability.com/FDI.htm, accessed April 17, 2012. There is a distinction between Chinese foreign direct investment that is "contracted" and investment that is "utilized." The latter is relevant in this paper.

13. China has been acquiring gold reserves recently, but they are less than 10 percent of its total reserves. See Chris Flood, "Bank Moves Spur the Gold Rush," *Financial Times*, November 7–8, 2009.

14. Wayne M. Morrison and Marc Labonte, *China's Holdings of U.S. Securities: Implications for the U.S. Economy* (Washington, D.C.: Congressional Research Service, July 30, 2009), 5. Focusing on securities with a maturity of more than one year, these authors reported that China held $568 billion of Treasury securities, $527 billion of government agency securities, $26 billion of corporate bonds, and $100 billion of equities at the end of June 2008. They also reported China held $30 billion of US short-term debt on that date.

15. Chow, *China's Economic Transformation*, 301.

16. Barry Naughton, *The Chinese Economy: Transitions and Growth* (Cambridge, Mass.: MIT Press, 2007), 377.

17. Geoff Dyer, "China's External Surplus Set to Halve," *Financial Times*, November 5, 2009.

18. Lum and Nanto, *China's Trade*, 42.

19. Javier Blas, "China Oil and Iron Ore Imports Surge," *Financial Times*, August 12, 2009; Carola Hoyos, "Burning Ambition," *Financial Times*, November 4, 2009.

20. It is a gross simplification to suggest that China has a well-defined social welfare function. For an illuminating discussion of China's and the Chinese bureaucracy's goals, see Chow, *China's Economic Transformation*, ch. 18, which discusses the challenges of making foreign investments in China.

21. Edmund S. Phelps, "The Golden Rule of Accumulation: A Fable for Growth Men," *American Economic Review* 51 (September 1961): 638–43.

22. Sundeep Tucker and Patti Waldmeir, "The People's Police," *Financial Times*, November 30, 2009; David Pilling, "The State's Dead Hand Returns to Haunt China," *Financial Times*, October 15, 2009.

23. China, however, may be attempting to increase the acceptability of its currency in foreign trade. See Peter Garnham, "Beijing Seeks an Escape from the Dollar Trap," *Financial Times*, July 31, 2009.

24. See Floyd Norris, "Debt Burden Now Rests More on U.S. Shoulders," *New York Times*, January 23, 2010; Robert Cookson and Michael Mackenzie, "Beijing's Rebalancing Raises Fears for Treasuries," *Financial Times*, February 19, 2010.

25. See Michael Wines, "China's Growing Economic Power Is Unsettling the Neighbors," *New York Times*, December 12, 2009; Kevin Brown and Geoff Dyer, "Neighbours Learn to Live with Faltering Renminbi," *Financial Times*, October 16, 2009.

26. See Martin Wolf, "Grim Truths Obama Should Have Told Hu in Beijing," *Financial Times*, November 18, 2009; Geoff Dyer and Andrew Ward, "China Warned on Trade Backlash Threat," *Financial Times*, November 29, 2009; Michael Pettis, "Protectionism Is Gaining Currency," *Financial Times*, December 2, 2009.

27. Robert Aliber, "Tariffs Can Persuade Beijing to Free the Renminbi," *Financial Times*, December 8, 2009.

28. Rebecca Wilder, "I Have to Side with China on This One," *News N Economics* blog, February 6, 2010, www.newsneconomics.com/2010/02/i-have-to-side-with-china-on-this-one.html.

29. Keith Bradsher, "As China Stirs Economy, Some See Protectionism," *New York Times*, June 24, 2009.

30. Bettina Wassener, "China Is Thriving, Its Economic Data Shows," *New York Times*, December 12, 2009.

31. Jonathan Bell, "Infrastructure Loans a Possible Achilles Heel to Chinese Banks," *Financial Times*, February 23, 2010.

32. Geoff Dyer and Jamil Anderlini, "Chinese Banks Aim to Boost Capital," *Financial Times*, December 22, 2009.

33. Eswar Prasad and Shang-Jin Wei, *The Chinese Approach to Capital Inflows: Patterns and Possible Explanations*, NBER Working Paper 11306 (Cambridge, Mass.: National Bureau of Economic Research, April 2005), www.nber.org/papers/w11306.

34. Geoff Dyer, "Chinese Stimulus Measures Spark Inflation Risk as Production Rises," *Financial Times*, December 11–12, 2009.

35. Stephen Roach, "I've Been an Optimist on China. But I'm Starting to Worry," *Financial Times*, July 29, 2009.

36. Michael Pettis, "China's September Data Suggest that the Long-Term Overcapacity Problem Is Only Intensifying," *Economonitor*, A Roubini Global Economics project, October 2009, www.economonitor.com/blog/2009/10/chinas-september-data-suggest-that-the-long-term-overcapacity-problem-is-only-intensifying/; Geoff Dyer, "No One Home," *Financial Times*, February 22, 2010.

37. Naughton, *Chinese Economy*, 403.

38. Ibid., 422.

39. US International Trade Commission, "U.S. Trade Balance, by Partner Country 2011, in Descending Order of Trade Turnover (Imports plus Exports)," http://dataweb.usitc.gov/scripts/cy_m3_run.asp.

40. Organization for International Investment, *Foreign Direct Investment in the United States*, March 18, 2009 (Washington, D.C.: Organization for International Investment, 2009), www.ofii.org/docs/FDI_2009.pdf.

41. Geoff Dyer, "China Dismisses Currency Pressure," *Financial Times*, December 28, 2009.

42. Tom Mitchell and Geoff Dyer, "China Inflation Spurs Wage Rise Fears," *Financial Times*, February 10, 2010; Bettina Wassener, "China to Slow Lending to Fight Inflation," *New York Times*, January 21, 2010.

43. Keith Bradsher, "Chinese Plants Starting to Feel Labor Shortage," *New York Times*, February 22, 2010.

44. Sundeep Tucker, "China's Hunger for Mergers Outweighs Fears over Crisis," *Financial Times*, December 31, 2009.

45. Olivier Blanchard and Gian Maria Milesi-Ferretti, *Global Imbalances: In Midstream?*, IMF Staff Position Note SPN/09/29 (n.p.: International Monetary Fund, December 22, 2009).

46. Michael Pettis, "Why a Trade War Is Likely to Break Out This Year," *Financial Times*, January 27, 2010.

13 Debt's Moral

Kennan Ferguson

ACCORDING TO HEGEL, a quarrel about law arose between two ancient Roman jurists: Favorinus of Arelata and Sextus Caecilius. In response to Favorinus's contention that laws needed to be based on real situations, Caecilius showed that while law had to make sense, it did not actually have to go into effect.[1] He gave the Roman law on debt as an example. If a debtor was unable to repay his loan, the creditor had the right to his body, that is, to kill him or to sell him into slavery. In fact, if a debtor owed several creditors, they could cut up his body and divide it among them. The very horror of the legal result, Caecilius argued, made the trust and credit system so secure that the legal particulars could exist without ever being carried out.

This particular debate can underlie a number of positions. For Caecilius it showed the nature of purely positive law; for Hegel it showed the need to synthesize the historical nature of law with its form; for the contemporary mind, it likely evokes a horror of such uncivilized practices. But for those of us attempting to better understand the dynamics and meaning of debt in their theoretical and historical contexts, this debate helps bring the extremities of debt, and of the burdens of debt, into focus.

The intensity of this punishment, its symbolically charged meaning, remains germane today. The question here is less "How can debt be made less violent and gruesome?" than it is "Why is debt so potentially violent and gruesome in the first place?" The stakes of debt have always been high: highly politicized, highly policed, and highly moralized. Not only was it ever thus, but it cannot be otherwise. Contrary to those who hope to eventually tame debt, to make it serve its proper masters (value, for example, or growth, or stability, or even "the people"), I argue that it cannot be otherwise.

Balance Sheets

Two major contemporary attitudes toward debt currently exist, which could be termed, in turn, "accountancy" and "accountability." The first poses itself as morally neutral and takes as its exemplary vision a model of economics as purely technical in nature. Laws of supply and demand must be obeyed; profit serves as a neutral arbiter in the marketplace; rationality and foresightedness serve as the only major frameworks. In this reading, evaluation and value exist in separate spheres, and the confusion of the two is a category mistake.

The second, the "accountability" model, seems to reject the accountancy presumptions entirely. Rather than seeing debt as neutral, it claims that debtors (and creditors) must be held accountable for the consequences of debts. This position sees debt as being left unchecked in the contemporary financial universe, running amok through some people's lives for other people's profit. In place of contemporary corporate capitalism, proponents of this position argue that we need to make debt serve people rather than allow it to feast on them. Debt and credit, while useful, must be brought to heel so that they may serve human (and humane) values.

But both these outlooks, while putatively opposed, ultimately resemble one another, and both are wrong in the same ways. Both rely on a particular accountant's fiction, one practiced as early as the thirteenth century: that of "double-entry bookkeeping." As codified by Luca Padcioli (an assistant to Leonardo da Vinci) in the fifteenth century in the *Summa de Arithmetica*, double-entry bookkeeping uses a "balance sheet" to summarize the state of a business through two parallel columns of "Assets" and "Liabilities."[2] By introducing the concept of "equity" to the liability column, balance sheets manage to *balance*: that is, both sides equal the same amount.[3] While this fiction works astonishingly well to track and maximize cash flow and obligation, it also falsely intimates that debts always balance out, that equivalence to any debt always exists.[4]

Thus, in assuming that debt and credit have a proper balance, those who conceptualize debt often look for the moral balance, the proprietary interrelationship between credits and debits. In their fictionalization of debt and credit, they imply a false equivalency, a mythically balanced relationship. But this takes divergent forms. In the bookkeeping model, debt and credit cancel out one another; the weight of the world must be morally neutral, and human beings mistakenly read these transactions through ethical lenses. Thus those who claim that debts incur a moral relationship must be wrong; in fact, the moral neutrality is guaranteed by the doubling of entries. To assume that an ethics of debt exists makes as little sense, in this model, as does the moralization of natural laws or of mathematics.

Those who do moralize debt, on the other hand, make a similar mistake. In the social justice model, debt and credit are out of balance in the contemporary world, and only through radical interventions (political rather than economic) can they be cancelled. Lenders have corrupted the equivalences that make up the proper functioning of economies, drawing profit from nonproductive sources. Such loans, whether of capital, housing, or necessities, eat away at the ability of humans to produce their own conditions of existence; they must therefore be unnatural and parasitic, according to this model. It is the role of political actors, preeminently the nation-state, to rebalance this relationship to be both productive and correct. Each model in its own way presumes that balance sheets determine debt, that a proper relationship exists between them, that equivalence is possible.

Most importantly, both also insist on a division between value and values: the value of money and the values of human morality. They presume a vast gap between the markets we engage in daily and the ethical engagements we have. One side wants to defend this gap against the moralizers and the other wants to overcome it to reinstate the natural balance, but this distinction proves less important than their shared analytic emphasizing the distance between the two. It is what the two approaches assume in common, that debt could be properly managed and correctly apportioned, that gives them their moral force. But the attempt to thereby locate responsibility is a political response, one that attempts to displace an unavoidable truth: that we are all, already and always, indebted.

Antitheology

In our contemporary economic and political climate, debt's moral component is fraught: a conversation about the relative responsibility of banks, mortgage brokers, and home owners, for example, quickly breaks down along lines of justice, responsibility, or guilt. So why does indebtedness have such a moralistic cast? Why does the temporal repayment of capital bring out the ethical judge in us?

It does so precisely because debt inextricably links us to other people. Our pre-existing debts are legion: to parents who created us, to societies that educated us, to governments that protect us, to food that provisions us, even to an inhuman and prehuman world that makes our very recognition of it possible. We can never be free of these debts, of course, not only because we can never repay them but because they are unpayable.[5] We are born indebted, we live indebted, we die indebted.

And yet the modern desire to be free, to be unencumbered individuals, leads us to see the state of debt as a fallen state. In the contemporary imaginary, a failure to be independent is a failure of self. Liberal individuals must be responsible to themselves above all; to be unable to support one's lifestyle, justify one's opinions, and determine one's course of life means the failure of the liberal project of one's own self. In the larger political sense, this outlook slides imperceptibly into the attempt to affix blame. If capitalism, for example, necessitates debt as a process of worker disempowerment, as some critics argue, then the financial system must bear the moral burden of debt. Conversely, if individuals have failed in their personal obligation to understand and manage their debt, as free market economists claim, then their failure to repay their loans is a personal failure. In either case, debt is necessarily inculpatory, while the ideal of a world free from debt is intimated.

One intellectual and conceptual tradition seems best prepared to analyze and acknowledge the ever-presence of indebtedness: that of theology, especially in its Western formulations. The most important dynamics of debt—responsibility, gratitude, repayment, and interconnectedness—are already central to individuals' relationships with God. In a theological register, God serves as a focus of debt and gratitude: the being who both gave everything (including other givers) and has the true power to overcome and forgive debt. Thus theological debt and its various iterations (interest, jubilee, money-changing, usury) comprise important components of Western religious traditions, showing that the distrust of debt is not a modern liberal invention.

Philip Goodchild, the preeminent theorist of theological economics, defines contemporary worldly existence as one of perpetual deferral and continuous debt. Money, he notes, exists solely as "a promise of value." As the abstraction of, and consequent multiplication of, the promise of repayment, money both allows the perpetual deferral of debt and encourages debt's infinitely generative properties.[6] Money allows debts to transcend lenders and borrowers, making relationships impersonal, making material reality fungible, and making time a component of economy. Thus money has replaced value in the contemporary human experience, leaving an expanding hierarchy of debt that can never be repaid or forgiven: the precise opposite of God's promises.

Theology has long been suspicious of monetary debt, noting its threat to godliness. Often in monotheism, debt is overtly proscribed. Jesus famously chases the money-changers from the Temple (Mark 11:15). In Luke 6:35, Jesus announces that one must "lend, hoping for nothing again"; in Matthew 6:12, he announces that all debts are to be forgiven. Being concerned with money, Jesus makes very clear, causes one to serve Mammon instead of God, and any structural or motivating forces in the world that lead one to focus on money are therefore theologically suspect. The Old Testament is even stronger in prohibiting usury.[7] Both the Pentateuch and the Psalms overtly proscribe lending at interest, especially to one's "brothers."[8] Islam's prohibitions on interest, while no less ambiguous than those in Christianity or Judaism, still remain in partial force in the contemporary world (even more so than in early Islamic society).[9] Thomas Aquinas, following Aristotle, declared debt a sin against both nature and justice: it is "unjust in itself for something is sold which does not exist."[10]

Yet this attack on debt also remains deeply problematic, because theological renditions attempt to extinguish the monetary form of debt. Goodchild, for example, aims for a "new mode of representation, a new political body—one capable of redemption from debt at the same time that it constitutes the texture of an entirely different social order."[11] Those who preached against debt, Mohammed and Jesus among them, distrusted it precisely because it replaced a more important and deeper theology of indebtedness. To analyze monetary debt against divinity certainly teaches something about monetary debt, but replacing one form with the other remains a poor solution.

Nietzsche famously calls theological debt "bad conscience," defining it as the historical practices of internalizing aggression and will, turning them into fantasies of "irredeemable penance" and "eternal punishment."[12] The emergence of Christianity, Nietzsche thus holds, "was therefore accompanied by the maximum feeling of guilty indebtedness on earth."[13] Denying the moral component of monetary debt too easily slides into a celebration of divine debt.

The myth that underlies the moralization of debt is that of the individual, a myth that serves as the building block of both contemporary liberal society and monotheistic theology. Individuals must be responsible, this mythology holds; each person can be ontologically determined through his or her intents, acts of will, behaviors, and consequences. Above all else, you are responsible for you—the moralization of theology remains very close to the moralization of the contemporary economic world.

This mythology of personal independence necessitates morality. More importantly, it also necessitates the moralization of debt. Because debt is the dependence upon, and obligation to, others, it cannot be conceived of except in moral codings. As such, it can be neither avoided nor regularized: it is both ubiquitous and excessive. We are always indebted, and we always will be: those debts can never be paid. Debts never cancel out; neither does morality.

Love and Debt

If debt cannot be escaped, its moralization becomes both more understandable and less a problem to be solved than a state of being to be understood. Debt as an ontological precondition of humanity can be recast as a form of morality: How, ultimately, do we value, recognize, and recapitulate our imbrications of self and others? If debts cannot be repaid, how can they be lived? One answer to these questions arises from a originary form of debt: that of our own beings to our parents.

What does the parent ask of the child? A multitude of things, of course, depending on cultural presuppositions, legal expectations, and particularities of circumstance. One way to summarize this host of expectations and responsibilities is to name it: the parent wishes to be loved. To be cared for, to be valued, even to be left behind when appropriate: each of these shows a child who can negotiate the competing demands of gratitude and responsibility.

Few, however, have properly written of the connection between debt and love. One social scientific tradition that has touched glancingly on it has been that of anthropology, which has tried since Marcel Mauss to make sense of how the relationships between communities and leaders are shaped by the practices of the gift.[14] Gifts, these theorists have held, serve to connect communities to one another through complex social chains of debt and obligation. They thus embody and replicate group connection as material economies.

And the most powerful gifts are not those between differing social circles, but those that mean to symbolize the intimacies of closeness and family. A ring, a child's painting, a bouquet, a dowry, a dinner: these are the gifts of intimate connection, and between those to whom we owe our greatest debts. As emblems of love, these gifts allow for the most intimate of exchanges, as well as the most likely misunderstandings and resentments.

One of the most famous and yet least understood explorations of debt must certainly be Shakespeare's *The Merchant of Venice,* correctly seen both as an eloquent humanization of Shylock the Jew and as an anti-Semitic treatise against moneylending. As an analysis of the relationships between hatred and love, debt and gift, and the incommensurability of social life with individual experience, it remains unequaled in the modern canon.

For all the academic analysis of *The Merchant of Venice* (which has been extensive), few readers have noted the profound resemblance of the play's two parts. For both of the two stories told—that of the mutual debt of Antonio and Shylock and that of the mutual love of Portia and Bassanio—tell of created linkages between individuals, connections of law, of emotion, and of necessity. Scholars are understandably drawn to only half the play, namely the story of the "pound of flesh," where Shylock proves one of the most troubling and productive antiheroes in the modern world. In doing so, they generally leave out the tropes that give the play its form: a doubled romance, a protofeminist celebration of women's legal wisdom, and a triumphal comedy of marriage.

That Shylock's hatred of Antonio (justified in no small part by Antonio's habit of spitting upon Shylock and kicking him in passing [1.3.112–14]) mirrors Bassanio's love of Portia is lost upon those who reduce the play to one of its two parts.[15] Even those who recognize the interrelated nature of the plots tend to justify the less memorable romantic comedy in terms of the Shylockian tragedy. George Lyman Kittredge, for example, argues that "the nature of true love" serves as "the true theme of the play" and that Shylock stands as an example of a pre-Christian inability to love.[16] In doing so, he (like other commentators) attempts to subsume one half of the play to the other.

But neither are these disconnected halves. Both stories focus on obligations legal and moral; the clash of the tragic and the comic makes this one of Shakespeare's most intriguing works. In one a pound of flesh is the horrific symbolization of the economic bonds between Shylock and Antonio; in the other a ring is the comic symbolization of Bassanio's commitment (both to his friend and to his love). Both are materializations of commitments to others, of debts that prove impossible to repay. Their legal consequentialism proves necessary as well. When the judge in Shylock's failed case against Antonio demands the ring off Bassanio's hand, Bassanio fails to recognize the judge as a disguised Portia, who gave him the ring in the first place (4.1.432–62). Thus he is put in the impossible situation of a double debt: both to his wife, to whom he promised never to surrender the ring, and to the judge, who has saved the life Antonio risked for him. Only through the Shakespearean trope of double identity—having both debts merge into one beloved—can the biformity be resolved.

Like love, debt is a relationship, not a status. One is never purely "in debt"; one is always "in debt to someone else." And that creditor remains as tied to the relationship thus created as does the debtor; borrowers and lenders exist only in relationship to one another. That Jessica, Shylock's daughter, herself steals from him a ring that was given to him by his wife (presumably Jessica's mother) speaks to the unending cycle of debt that can never be broken. And it is one that can never be upended either: one of the most affecting moments of the play is Shylock's heartbreak over hearing that Jessica has traded the ring for a monkey (that is, that she has trivialized its worth to him and that she does not recognize her debt to her own parents [3.1.118–23]). Shylock reminds us that we are born indebted to those who raise us, we remain indebted to those who love us, and we will die indebted to those who remember us.

The Plight of Debt

Debt cannot escape morality. The fiction that each of us has a self that can be unencumbered, relieved of obligation to others, to the world, underlies debt's moral. It reflects, in fact, the foundations of modern secular theology: that independence can be achieved, that actions can be wholly good, that people can be free. Thus are the ethics of religious traditions the same as the morality of the marketplace: a search for a fundament of responsibility upon which we can lay the dynamics of interdependence. A conquest of debt promises a conquest of the burdens and responsibilities we have to the world outside ourselves.[17]

But such a state would be an impoverished, abject, bereft state. The only way to conquer debt would be through pure and inhuman aloneness. Such an identity proves not only undesirable (Who, after all, truly wishes to be cut off from other people, from books, from the world?) but also impossible. An unindebted human being could never exist, for our whole experience, our existence within language, and our very creation depend on an outside from which we emerge.

In other words, the end of debt would also be an end to politics, to community, to family, to everything outside the self (or, in the case of the theologically minded, the ineffable). Debt is never-ending, never complete, never paid nor payable. Gifts serve to mitigate and to recognize debt, but they can never overcome it. To deny debt is to deny politics, to deny connection, and to deny love. To recognize debt, that is, to moralize it while also embracing it, means to reject both radical individuality and theological transcendence. Only through living *in debt*, recognizing its permanence and inescapability, can we live as engaged, ethical, and responsible human beings.

Notes

1. Georg Wilhelm Friedrich Hegel, *Philosophy of Right*, trans. T. M. Knox (Oxford: Oxford University Press, 1967), § 3.

2. John Lancaster, *I.O.U.: Why Everyone Owes Everyone and No One Can Pay* (London: Simon and Schuster, 2010), 26–28.

3. For the development of double-entry bookkeeping as a technology of commerce, see Sandra Sherman, *Finance and Fictionality in the Early Eighteenth Century: Accounting for Defoe* (Cambridge:

Cambridge University Press, 1996); Mary Poovey, *A History of the Modern Fact: Problems of Knowledges in the Sciences of Wealth and Society* (Chicago: University of Chicago Press, 1998).

4. This fiction underlies many of the common misunderstandings not only about debt but about economies. It is difficult, under the sway of this conception, to comprehend how an economy can grow: it seems that for every credit to one person there must exist a debit to someone else. No less insightful analysts of economics as Smith, Marx, and Simmel have fallen prey to this misconception.

5. See Jacques Derrida, "The Right to Philosophy from the Cosmopolitical Point of View," *Ethics, Institutions, and the Right to Philosophy*, trans. Peter Pericles Trifonas (Lanham, Md.: Rowman and Littlefield, 2002), 2–19.

6. Philip Goodchild, *Theology of Money* (Durham, N.C.: Duke University Press, 2009), 155.

7. The hermeneutics of the Talmudic scholars interpreted these to mean that lending to Jews was forbidden but it was allowed to those who were not brethren—*viz.*, Christians. The Christians used the same logic to lend to followers of Islam.

8. Mervyn K. Lewis, "Comparing Islamic and Christian Attitudes toward Usury," in *Handbook of Islamic Banking*, ed. M. Kabir Hassan and Mervyn K. Lewis (Northampton, Mass.: Edward Elgar, 2004), 65.

9. Timur Kuran, "Why the Middle East Is Economically Underdeveloped: Historical Mechanisms of Institutional Stagnation," *Journal of Economic Perspectives* 18, no. 3 (2004): 73.

10. Thomas Aquinas, *Summa of Theology*, query 78, in *St. Thomas Aquinas on Politics and Ethics*, ed. Paul E. Sigmund (New York: W. W. Norton, 1988), 74.

11. Goodchild, *Theology of Money*, 68–69.

12. Friedrich Nietzsche, *On the Genealogy of Morals and Ecce Homo*, trans. Walter Kaufmann (New York: Vintage, 1967), 84–93.

13. Ibid., 90.

14. Marcel Mauss, *The Gift: The Form and Reason for Exchange in Archaic Societies*, trans. W. D. Halls (New York: Norton, 2000), first published in French as *Essai sur le don: Forme et raison de l'échange dans les sociétés archaïques* in 1924. See also Marilyn Strathern, *The Gender of the Gift: Problems with Women and Problems with Society in Melanesia* (Berkeley: University of California Press, 1990); and Kennan Ferguson, "The Gift of Freedom," *Social Text* 25, no. 2 (Summer 2007): 39–52.

15. William Shakespeare, *The Merchant of Venice*, ed. George Lyman Kittredge (Waltham, Mass.: Blaisdell, 1966).

16. George Lyman Kittredge, introduction to *The Merchant of Venice*, by William Shakespeare, ed. George Lyman Kittredge (Waltham, Mass.: Blaisdell, 1966), xiv.

17. Neil Hertz points out the similar impossibility of scholarship without indebtedness, arguing that teachers' pathological hatred of plagiarism arises from their inability to be truly and totally original. See "Two Extravagant Teachings" in his *The End of the Line: Essays on Psychoanalysis and the Sublime* (New York: Columbia University Press, 1985), 144–59.

14 Debt, Theft, Permaculture

Justice and Ecological Scale

Gerry Canavan

If, as Fredric Jameson once wrote, it has become easier to imagine "the thorough-going deterioration of the Earth and of nature" than the end of capitalism, this is in part because we are increasingly aware that the two phrases describe in fact the same event.[1] But the imagined extinction of alternatives to capitalism associated with Francis Fukuyama's "end of history" that so concerns Jameson carries with it a type of ideological shadow: if capitalism is, as K. William Kapp once put it, "an economy of unpaid costs," then our increasing recognition that the bill is finally coming due must be recognized as a kind of nascent revolutionary consciousness.[2] Bruno Latour, who in his most well-known book famously declared, "We have never been modern," recently wrote that "it has now almost become common sense that we were able to *think* we were modern only as long as the various ecological crises could be denied or delayed."[3]

Though Latour and I part ways on many questions about ecology, on this he is surely correct: we cannot believe anymore that we are modern, that is, we cannot believe anymore that we have made some final break with the material realities of soil, air, and water that sustain us and on which everything depends. This essay seeks to make a preliminary accounting of the circuits of dependence that characterize capitalism's relationship with the environment through the assertion of an *ecological debt* that has long been in arrears, though the bearers of this mortgage may be distant in both space and time.

The Second Contradiction of Capitalism

When approaching ecology as the "second contradiction" of capitalism, commenters often begin with a passage on soil ecology from *Capital,* volume 1, chapter 15: "All progress in capitalistic agriculture is a progress in the art, not only of robbing the labourer, but of robbing the soil; all progress in increasing the fertility of the soil for a given time is a progress towards ruining the lasting sources of that fertility."[4] John Bellamy Foster has traced Marx's interest in (and horror at) this "metabolic rift" to its origins in the work of Justus von Liebig, whose recognition of the breakdown in the cycle of soil replenishment led to the development of a process to replenish fields artificially through the use of chemical fertilizers—which led to a colonial project of importing guano and other materials from places as far off as Peru and the South Pacific, and which itself ultimately leads to an unbalancing of the nitrogen cycle and further ecological degradation of soil, water, and the climate.[5] *Nature* magazine recently published an article identifying the nitrogen cycle as one of three ecological boundaries whose crisis thresholds we have already far overshot; with 35 million annual tons projected as the "safe" annual limit, we currently convert over 120 million tons of nitrogen per year.[6] Scientific management of the soil has, in this way, only made the problem worse.

In the soil cycle we find a first mode for imagining ecological debt. Here we have ecological debt at a kind of zero-level: when you grow food and ship that food far away—when, that is, you strip necessary minerals from the soil and ship them out of the local ecosystem—you destroy the long-term sustainability of your own agricultural practices. In a sense here the "debt" is owed to oneself, or at least to one's local area and immediate descendants, and because of the local temporal and spatial scales involved it is a debt whose repayment manifests as a relatively urgent concern. The agricultural capitalist is motivated to embark on some sort of rational management of the soil if only to protect his own assets, even if his management is always fitful and incomplete, and in awkward balance with the pursuit of profit.

The more fraught cases are those in which the consequences of the ecological debt rebound, not on you, or even on your descendants, but on other people living in distant spaces and times. This is the power plant whose emissions blow across a mountain range into some another nation, or the factory whose toxic dumping floats downstream into someone else's water basin, or the civilization that uses up the entire fossil fuel reserve of the planet in a single hundred-year spree. If, in the case of the soil, the agricultural capitalist cuts his own throat, we are now on more familiar ground, with the capitalist returning to his usual practice of cutting someone else's. It was this phenomenon that K. William Kapp abstracted in 1950 in *The Social Costs of Private Enterprise* as a general law of capitalism: "Capitalism must be regarded as an economy of unpaid costs, 'unpaid' in so far as a substantial portion of the actual costs of production remain unaccounted for in entrepreneurial outlays; instead they are shifted to, and ultimately borne by, third persons or by the community as a whole."[7] We find therefore that both "contradictions" of capital—both labor and ecology—are in this way predicated on the existence of structural debts, "unpaid costs," that in the case of ecology at least are becoming unavoidably and often painfully visible to us. This suggests an oppositional strategy of actualizing these unacknowledged debts, making an accounting of them in the demand that they be recognized and paid back.

The metaphorical assertion of a debt where none is admitted is therefore first and foremost a political act of anticapitalist resistance; it is an assertion that historical relations of domination and exploitation have ongoing consequences in the present, a demand that reparation or remuneration is possible and that therefore it is necessary. *Our Common Agenda,* a report published by Latin American and Caribbean intellectuals in the run-up to the 1992 Earth Summit, states the point directly: "The industrial revolution was based in large part on the exploitation of natural resources in ways which did not reflect their true costs. . . . The industrialized countries have incurred an ecological debt with the world."[8]

As Joan Martinez-Alier notes in her essay "Environmental Justice (Local and Global)," it is better to think of these sorts of "ecological debts" as incursive, or if you like *imperial,* rather than purely extractive: "In [the case of carbon emissions], Europeans act as if we owned a sizable chunk of the planet outside Europe; . . . the occupation of an environmental space larger than one's own territory gives rise to an *ecological debt* with spatial and temporal dimensions."[9] Now, to be sure, there are myriad cases of extractive ecological debt; one thinks, for instance, of the tiny island nation of Nauru in the South Pacific, whose interior was almost completely strip-mined for phosphates for use as agricultural fertilizer over the course of the twentieth century and now looks more or less like the surface of the moon, and is just as dead. This once self-sustaining island paradise, a place formerly known as "Pleasant Island," now subsists on the importation of necessities paid for through a rapidly depleting trust established during the years of the phosphorus boom, international money laundering, sales of passports to noncitizens with few questions asked, and sporadic foreign aid.[10]

So there is certainly extractive debt—but the more general form of ecological debt is not extractive but incursive. Ecological debt arises when the "unpaid costs" of capitalism in the developed nations are borne by inhabitants of the underdeveloped ones. In this sense the notion of an outsized global footprint is closely related to postcolonial studies of empire. The concept of ecological debt first arose out of Latin American political thought in the 1990s as a kind of special case of postcolonial reparations. Writing in 1994, José María Borrero Navia, one of the early popularizers of the concept, noted that ecological debt is not some abstract obligation to the biosphere as such but an obligation to "humanity, acquired by reason of often irreversible damages to the biophysical base of societies, provoked by the islands of privilege, wasteful economics and industries of barbarity, the consequences of which have been the impoverishment and exclusion of hundreds of millions of people, ethnocide, and subjugation of cultures."[11] Ecological debt is owed not to the planet but to other persons: persons who were not volitional participants in this exchange in the first place, who never signed any sort of contract but whom we must conclude are owed a moral and *legal* debt for what has been done without their consent to the places where they live.

"Our Future Is Not for Sale": Climate Debt

Another arresting example of the imperial, extraspatial debt incurred by the negative consequences cascading out of agricultural production is found in the forty-thousand-square-kilometer "dead zone" in the Black Sea brought about by fertilizer overuse in the communist bloc over three decades, starting in the 1960s. The region has begun a long and slow recovery since the fall of the Soviet Union in 1991, but this recovery is now threatened by the entry of the Danube basin into the European Union, whose Western European industrial agriculturalists are looking to buy cheap farmland and begin the cycle of fertilizer overuse and soil/water degradation all over again.[12] We might think as well of the recent Deepwater Horizon crisis in the Gulf of Mexico, where a massive spill in an offshore oil rig owned by British Petroleum reached proportions that far exceed the Exxon *Valdez* and will affect the ecology of the entire region negatively for years to come.

But the most strikingly exemplary case for this more abstract mode of "imperial" ecological debt might be the archipelago nation of Tuvalu, population twelve thousand, whose remoteness and lack of extractable natural resources have led to a largely bloodless colonial relationship with the imperial powers of Europe and North America. Tuvalu rose to prominence during the climate negotiations in Copenhagen in 2009 because it will be one of the first nations to face the devastating consequences of climate change. For a nation whose highest point is merely 4.5 meters above sea level, the effects of rising waters will be immediate and catastrophic. The existential threat to Tuvalu has lent it moral weight as the leader of the group of developing nations demanding immediate sweeping action, including a legally binding accord that would stabilize carbon at 350 ppm. These nations insist on measures that would limit the rise in global temperatures rise to 1.5 °C, demand wide-ranging financial payments from developed nations, and oppose carbon exceptions for faster-growing developing nations like India, China, and Brazil.[13] Ian Fry, Tuvalu's delegate at Copenhagen, told those gathered that for these nations the "future rests on the outcome of this meeting." When the meeting ended with none of its demands having been met, Fry concluded, "It looks like we are being offered 30 pieces of silver to betray our people and our future. . . . Our future is not for sale. I regret to inform you that Tuvalu cannot accept this document."[14]

Unfortunately, Tuvalu may not have a future at all. According to James Lewis's paper "Sea-Level Rise: Some Implications for Tuvalu," published in 1989 by the Royal Swedish Academy of Sciences, a 20 to 40 cm rise in sea level by the end of the century will leave much of Tuvalu flooded, and much or all of the population will likely need to be evacuated.[15] The early date of this paper should serve as a reminder that the climate change crisis has been widely recognized for over two decades, which have since passed without any significant action on the part of the industrialized states that produce most of the world's greenhouse gases. Moreover, if these estimates of sea level rise are found to be too conservative, naturally the situation will only be worse.

Tuvalu's relationship to global ecological crisis exemplifies "ecological debt" in its most immediate and urgent form: the relationship of a southern people facing deprivation, displacement, or outright elimination of their way of life as a consequence of the actions of the industrialized North. In what Naomi Klein has memorably called a "cruel geographical irony," the chief economist at the World Bank has estimated that "about 75 to 80 percent" of the damage caused by climate change "will be suffered by developing countries, although they only contribute about one-third of greenhouse gases"—and even that "one-third" suggests a presentist perspective that obliterates all but the most recent history of emissions.[16] The true number is closer to 20 percent of the population of the planet having emitted 75 percent of the total historical greenhouse gas emission, with the United States (5 percent global population) emitting approximately 25 percent just on its own.[17] Haiti, in contrast, emits just 1 percent of total global carbon emissions, but according to the Maplecroft Climate Change Vulnerability Index it is the world's second-most endangered nation because of climate change, behind only Somalia.[18]

In contrast to the usual political assertions of climate emergency—that we are "one planet" on a "pale blue dot," all in this together, facing a shared crisis that threatens us all *universally*—climate debt stakes its claim by insisting on particularity and difference.[19] Climate change, the argument goes, is not at all some "natural disaster"; it is not something that "just happened" like an asteroid from space; it is something the Global North has *inflicted* on everybody else, with the worst consequences having ramifications on those nations in the Global South that did not contribute to the crisis and that are worst positioned to adapt. Klein highlights the work of Bolivia's chief climate negotiator, Angelica Navarro, who has said, "Millions of people—in small islands, least-developed countries, landlocked countries as well as vulnerable communities in Brazil, India and China, and all around the world—are suffering from the effects of a problem to which they did not contribute." In Bolivia itself, the two largest cities face severe water shortages as a result of nearby glaciers melting from rising temperatures.[20]

As a policy measure, Klein writes, ecological debt (her version focuses specifically on *climate debt* because it can be so easily quantified) demands three basic categories of behavior:

1. Developed nations must recognize that they have a legal obligation to pay the costs for nations in the Global South to ameliorate the effects of climate change. In US legal parlance, this is the simple principle that the "polluter pays." That these are reparations, and not charity, additional loans, or neoliberal strategies for so-called "development" that will only worsen the problem, is key.[21] Klein quotes two activists who speak to the pressing need for a recognition of climate debt. "Climate debt is not a matter of charity," says Lidy Nacpil, a coordinator for Jubilee South. "What we need is not something we should be begging for but something

that is owed to us, because we are dealing with a crisis not of our making." An advocate for Maasai tribespeople in Kenya, Sharon Looremeta, gives a more stark appraisal: "The Maasai community does not drive 4x4s or fly off on holidays in airplanes. . . . We have not caused climate change, yet we are the ones suffering. This is an injustice and should be stopped right now."[22]

2. Developed nations must pay the cost to "leapfrog" developing nations past the dirty carbon stage of modernization toward cleaner, more sustainable technologies. The developing world cannot be expected to sacrifice its chances at industrial development because the United States and Europe have already used up the planet's entire carbon capacity for themselves. "We cannot and will not give up our rightful claim to a fair share of atmospheric space on the promise that, at some future stage, technology will be provided to us," Navarro has said.[23]

3. To the extent that carbon emissions remain necessary for development, *developed nations must bear the vast majority of carbon emissions cuts*, bringing their carbon emissions *below* even the percentage of the planetary population they represent in order to "make atmospheric space available" for the undeveloped and developing nations that have not yet used their allotment, and for whom emissions mean things like rural electrification rather than surplus bourgeois comforts.[24]

The United States' head climate negotiator, Todd Stern, has rejected any call for reparations as "wildly unrealistic" and "untethered to reality";[25] he dismissively told a news conference: "I actually completely reject the notion of a debt or reparations or anything of the like. . . . For most of the 200 years since the Industrial Revolution, people were blissfully ignorant of the fact that emissions caused a greenhouse effect. It's a relatively recent phenomenon."[26] But when Stern was senior US negotiator at the Kyoto Protocol negotiations in 1997, nearly ten years had already passed after NASA's James Hansen testified to Congress in 1988 about the imminent dangers posed by global climate change. Hansen's findings were the result of wide scientific consensus about global warming in the mid-1970s, which were based on climate models about global warming developed in the 1950s, over half a century after the concept was first proposed by Svante Arrhenius in 1896. However one chooses to narrate that history, to suggest that the North has somehow been *blindsided* by all this sudden interest in carbon and the climate is baldly disingenuous.

Suing the Present: Climate Trials

The question of precisely who the debtors and who the creditors are when it comes to climate debt is a fraught one. José María Borrerro Navia points to four categories of debtors:

1. Transnational corporations, whose power lies in creating a system of subjugation.
2. Transnational banks that play an unquestionable role in the promotion of ecological disasters in the name of development.
3. Northern governmental bureaucracies, self-affirmed as the hegemonic power, especially since the collapse of Eastern socialist bureaucracies.
4. Southern bureaucrats and elites who have engineered, directly or indirectly, ecological destruction processes in their countries.[27]

Left off the hook? Those everyday consumers in the industrialized countries fingered by Kenya's Sharon Looremeta, who "drive 4x4s or fly off on holidays in airplanes." But perhaps this is not so obscene as it might first appear. John Bellamy Foster and Brett Clark have argued that the ecologically destructive patterns of consumption on the part of everyday westerners should be thought of as a kind of cognitive "consumer trap." These consumers, they maintain, are constrained by choices that have already been made at the level of production by the transnational corporate elite. Thus any personal consumer "choice" is already determined by a system marked by deterioration and waste, a framework on which the individual consumer has essentially no leverage. He or she moreover will often lack the knowledge necessary to make a truly informed choice in the first place.[28] It was Marx himself, after all, who argued in the first chapter of the first volume of *Capital* that we can know the true workings of the system only by working at the level of production, not consumption.

And even those self-same corporate overloads are in some sense "blameless" in the sense that it is the system itself—the production treadmill of capitalism—that inevitably accelerates environmental damage and degeneration. We should not be surprised that so little has been done. What drives the "thoroughgoing deterioration of the Earth and of the nature" is the logic of capitalism itself, a mode of production that both insists (culturally) and depends (structurally) on limitless expansion and permanent growth: into new markets, into the former colonial periphery, into the peasant countryside, through oil derricks into the deepest crevices of the earth, through carbon emissions and ozone degradation into the upper atmosphere, and finally via rocket to Earth orbit—and, then, in its most cherished futurological imaginings, to orbital space stations, lunar cities, Martian settlements, asteroid belt mining colonies, sleeper ships to Alpha Centauri, and on and on. It is capitalism itself that is subject to the two-century-old Jevons paradox, the sociological law which demonstrates that improvements in energy efficiency do not correspond with reductions in consumption; innovations that consume half the fuel will simply be used twice as much.[29] "Capitalism," Foster writes in his ecological history of capitalism, *The Vulnerable Planet*, "cannot exist without constantly expanding the realm of production: Any interruption in this process will take the form of economic crisis."[30]

This is why the market solutions proposed by Lord Nicholas Stern in the *Stern Report* are rightly rejected by Vandana Shiva in *Soil, Not Oil* as mere eco-imperialism that "allows corporations to gain increasing control of the earth's resources—energy, water, air, land, and biodiversity—to continue to run the industrialized globalized economy."[31] She highlights the absurdity of a pollution reduction strategy in which "carbon credits" are given to historical polluters to financialize as profit: "Nonpolluting, nonindustrial activity does not even figure in Kyoto's CDM [Clean Development Mechanisms]. To be counted as clean, you must first be dirty."[32]

Neoliberal market solutions are especially perverse as they arise in the precise moment that multiple ecological crises inescapably demonstrate the *impossibility* of market stewardship of the environment. Market logics such as cap and trade will always reduce to the logic of Larry Summers' infamous memo to senior World Bank staff arguing that "the World Bank should be encouraging more migration of the dirty industries to the LDC [Less Developed Countries]" on the grounds that

- the lowest-wage earning nations will necessary have the lowest costs associated with the illness and death of pollution
- their mortality rate is already high; anyway such countries are "vastly under-polluted" compared to, say, Mexico City and Los Angeles, with their elevated smog levels.[33]

Summers has since claimed the memo was satire, but whatever the intended tone, the memo reflects a certain truth about the slippery operation of "efficiency" as it operates with regard to environmental economics. As Brazil's former secretary of the environment José Lutzenburger fired back: "Your reasoning is perfectly logical but totally insane. . . . Your thoughts [provide] a concrete example of the unbelievable alienation, reductionist thinking, social ruthlessness and the arrogant ignorance of many conventional 'economists' concerning the nature of the world we live in."[34]

Blissful inaction and deliberate malfeasance on the part of elites in the developed world has been so stark, in fact, that for some, including James Hansen, the operative term is not *climate debt* so much as *climate trials*. Hansen, who was arrested at a mountaintop removal coal protest against the now-infamous Massey Energy Corporation in 2009, the same firm whose Upper Big Branch coal mine collapsed in West Virginia in early 2010 after receiving thousands of dollars in fines from mine safety citations, has called for CEOs of major energy corporations to be tried for "crimes against humanity."[35] Others, like Jamais Cascio, founder of worldchanging.org, have speculated on the near-future "tobaccoification" of carbon, in reference to industry-funded denialism in the face of established scientific consensus.[36] Still others would name the Bush, Blair, and Harper administrations, for starters, as codefendants.

Science fiction writer Bruce Sterling, while generally skeptical of the potential for climate trials to put us on the road to a more rational climate policy, does not doubt their symbolic value. He memorably wrote in one of his annual "State of the World" reports that "polluting the entire sky is the biggest market failure in the history of the human race, when the Hamptons and Malibu start going under water, really rich and powerful people are gonna get mad and vengeful."[37] The recognition of the moral demand made by ecological debt provides a framework to harness the righteous anger of the rich and the poor alike, providing strategies for resistance to business as usual: forging political alliances, mass protest movements, divestment campaigns, civil disobedience, and other strategies for social mobilization. Naomi Klein highlights the way indigenous groups in Canada have attempted to leverage the nation's unpaid obligations to First Nation peoples against its WTO status and its Standard & Poor bond rating, essentially arguing that Canada keeps vast "unfunded liabilities" off its books.

The same judolike reversal of market logic might be made against transnational corporations and industrialized nations of the Global North alike. In 2008, in an astonishing act of jury nullification in the United Kingdom, six anticoal activists were cleared of criminal liability of thirty-five thousand euros of damage on the grounds that they had a "lawful excuse" to prevent the coal plant's functioning in order to prevent damage to the environment.[38] That same year, a stunt class-action lawsuit was filed by an activist in the International Criminal Court asking for "$1 billion dollars in damages on behalf of future generations of human beings on Earth—if there are any."[39]

The Future in the Present: Permaculture

Of course some number of human beings will likely survive even the worst projections of ecological catastrophe—but if we continue to let capitalism blithely take its course, those who do survive will live lives dramatically worse than the ones they might otherwise have, had we acted. Alongside the obligation to already existing humans is the obligation to the ones who *will* exist, whose inheritance we are squandering—which is an obligation to humanity as such. Without disputing the urgency of climate debt's call to defend both bio- and cultural diversity in the here and now, at the same time we must recognize, dialectically, the urgency of its call to a *shared* futurity; the recognition of ecological debt compels us to recognize a planetary commons extending in both space and time, from which global capitalism has ceaselessly appropriated more than its fair share.

In his contribution to *Red Planets: Marxism and Science Fiction,* cultural critic Carl Freedman identifies a central disjuncture in Marxist thought between the *deflationary* and *inflationary* modes of critique. "The deflationary dimension," he writes, "is represented by the attempt to destroy all illusions necessary or useful to the preservation of class society in general and of capitalism in particular"—this can be seen fairly clearly in ideology critique but also in the more specifically structural discussion of the "secret" of surplus-value in *Capital.*[40] This, Freedman suggests, has a certain figurative relationship with *noir* in prose and film.[41] While *noir* does not produce usable knowledge about the workings of capital, the genre's preoccupation with individual greed "allegorically gestures towards . . . the kind of knowledge discoverable through application of Marx's principle of the ultimately determining role of the economy."[42] It produces a kind of affective intuition that points us in the right direction, so to speak, if not getting us much of the way there.

Deflation is an economic mode, a scientific mode, and something of a cold mode—it is the mode that drives Marx's many formulae. Inflation, in contrast, is much more fragmentary and affective than deflation. It is effusive and intangible, a mode of prophecy and dreams. Marx, after all, had famously little to say about what the world would be like under communism, but the utopian impulse toward a liberatory fulfillment of history—Marx calls it history's true beginning, Engels called it "humanity's leap from the kingdom of necessity to the kingdom of freedom"—is nonetheless always the beating heart at the center of the Marxist project.[43] For Freedman, the genre most closely associated with this utopian impulse is science fiction, and he goes on to argue that, unlike *noir,* science fiction narratives can provide *better* pictures of the inflationary future than straight expository prose; because it is impossible to produce concrete knowledge of the future in the same way we can produce it of the present and the past, it is science fiction—itself a dialectic between deflationary scientific cognition and unbound inflationary estrangement—that produces our best cognitive maps of potential futures.[44]

Of course inflation and deflation function as a dialectic—we find echoes of each in the other. The cold calculus of deflation is predicated on a baseline moral recognition that the injustices that are being described *should not exist*; and the soaring heights of inflation can only surpass mere wishful thinking when they arise out of a scientific understanding of capitalist reality as it now does.

Ecocritique, like science fiction, and like the Marxist project as a whole, necessarily operates along this same dialectic of deflation and inflation. And like these other modes of criticism, ecocritique requires *both* deflation and inflation to stay vital, which is why the impulse toward the deflationary naming of various ecological catastrophes, in which terrifying scenarios draw attention to the consequences of inaction, must be matched by an inflationary, futurological impulse toward a better world for *all of us*—a transformative futurology that will always be, in some way or another, a science fiction. In that vein I want to conclude with the concept science fiction writer Kim Stanley Robinson has borrowed from Australian agriculturists Bill Mollison and David Holmgren and put to work in his novels: *permaculture,* which describes self-renewing agricultural practices that (unlike the ones Justus von Liebig both studied and developed) can be sustained indefinitely.

In an interview with the website BLDBLOG, Robinson points out that permaculture "suggests a certain kind of obvious human goal, which is that future generations will have at least as good a place to live as what we have now."[45] In that same interview he suggests permaculture as an alternative twenty-first century name for utopia. But this principle does not mean that permaculture must be defined by the penury of too-limited resources. Permaculture rejects the neo-Malthusian logic of resource scarcity and the oxymoronic paradigm of "sustainable growth" in favor of what it is essentially raw futurity, a politico-ethical imperative not only that there should *be* a future but that the people in it deserve a decent world in which to live.

And the same, of course, must be said for the people of the present: they, too, deserve a decent world in which to live. In some sense it may seem perverse to worry about the future for hypothetical persons when there are billions for whom this promise has already been broken. But we need to do both; deflation without inflation is just dead numbers, rage without hope. Only a sense that human civilization has a future can motivate us to make that future real. The science-fictional narratives of writers like Robinson are, in my view, vital in helping us to imagine an ecologically engaged politics, even a science-fictional politics. In his first novel, *The Wild Shore* (1984), he imagines an America that has been bombed back to the Stone Age, watched from the coastline by a coalition of nations eager to prevent American reunification; decades later, a character who lived through the event explains the contradictions in his own memory of America, which is incidentally our present: "America was huge, it was a giant. It swam through the seas eating up all the littler countries—drinking them up as it went along. We were eating up the world, boy, and that's why the world rose up and put an end to us. So I'm not contradicting myself. America was great like a whale—it was giant and majestic, but it stank and was a killer. Lots of fish died to make it so big. Now haven't I always taught you that?"[46] In another early book, *Pacific Edge*, Robinson advances what could be the sad maxim of human history: "Every culture is as wasteful as it can afford to be."[47] The vision of history that informs his novels foregrounds the destructive contradictions at the heart of industrial society, as he notes in an interview in *Polygraph* 22:

> I've been trying to use standard economic terms to describe the situation in ways capitalists might have to come to terms with and that might serve as entry-points to a larger discussion: that the implicit promise of capitalism was that a generation would work so hard in the working class that its children would be in the middle class, and that if extended this program would eventually lift everyone on Earth. But now resource analysis makes it clear that for the three billion living on less than two dollars a day this promise can never be fulfilled, so that capitalism is really nothing but a big Ponzi scheme, and would be illegal if run in a single state or community.
>
> Then also, the pricing we put on things, carbon especially, does not include the environmental costs of making the thing, so that we are practicing systemic predatory dumping, and the competitors we are predating on are our own children and the generations to come. So we are predatory dumpers, out-competing non-existent people, which is easy enough, but they will suffer when they come into existence, and we are cheaters.[48]

But Robinson is never as cynical as these quotes might imply: he has spent his career in pursuit of utopia, even residing in a utopian planned community in California. In his seminal Mars trilogy (1990s), his characters move through all the usual utopian forms. The Martian colonists reenact King Utopus's iconic act of closure—the digging of the trench that separates Utopia from the mainland—in their destruction of the Martian space elevator. They openly revolt against terrestrial control; when open resistance fails, they engage in hit-and-fade guerrilla tactics. They infiltrate. Some become terrorists. There is even, as it were, a traditional sudden apocalypse—not one but two Great Floods—acts of God from above and from without, which leave both Earth and Mars in position to be politically transformed. These, too, fail.

In the end there are only two sorts of revolutions that actually work in the Mars trilogy. The first is the *aeroforming* of the settlers, Robinson's analogy to *terraforming,* which sees settlers transformed by Mars in much the same way that they sought to transform it. It is the displacement in space that returns, at the end of a century obsessed with time, to provide the possibility for real human change—and it occurs because the remove to Mars forces us, but also *allows* us, to reconnect and re-embed ourselves in an ecology, to once again be part of an ecologically rational cycle. (Robinson has elsewhere called for us to imagine ourselves as terraforming Earth—noting that in fact we already are, by wrecking it.)[49]

The second utopian move is that *other* impossibility, that other thing besides the future that we no longer quite believe in: collective action in the present on behalf of the future, which is to say political agency. Robinson is a believer in coalition—in the building and nurturing of activist networks. In the end it is the tough, almost parliamentary work of reaching compromises, brokering deals, and changing minds that allows the disastrous cycle of war and revolution to be finally averted, the search for (and improbable discovery of) the missing color that might unite Red and Green. At the end of *Blue Mars* the revolutionary break is a televised speech from a group of astronaut/scientists, which underscores how utopian a thinker Kim Stanley Robinson really is. Robinson's politics is an ongoing praxis that achieves victories but is never victorious—in *Pacific Edge* (1988), Robinson defines utopia not as final, fixed fulfillment but as a process: "Struggle forever."[50] No one said it would be easy.

In *Polygraph* 22 Michael Hardt writes that during his trip to the protests in Copenhagen he noticed that there's been a significant shift on the left since the seminal Seattle protests ten years ago. Then the slogan was "We want everything for everybody"—and you still see some versions of that sign. But at Copenhagen the much more common poster was a different slogan: "There is no Planet B." The first, Hardt writes, "sounds like an absurd, reckless notion that will propel us further down the route of mutual destruction"; the other, he says, sounds like Margaret Thatcher's infamous proclamation that "there is no alternative" to neoliberal capitalism.[51] The slogan of Seattle is ambitious, inflationary, and fundamentally impossible; the slogan of the ecological activists is deflationary, anti-ambitious, and starkly realistic. I suggest that permaculture is the way to retain the inflationary spirit of the first while embracing the deflationary acknowledgment of our finitude in the second. Unlike capitalist futurity, which is self-defeatingly dependent on infinite growth on a finite planet, permaculture does not promise an impossible supersession of inevitable limits; it instead locates the promise of a better future *within* those limits. Permaculture is a mode that looks to ecological limit not as a state of emergency or as an impending disaster but as a necessary constraint, as the rules of the game we have all been playing all this time.

Hardt goes on: "Indeed the struggles against neoliberalism of the past decades have been defined by their belief in the possibility of radical, seemingly limitless alternatives. In short, the World Social Forum motto, 'Another world is possible,' might translate in the context of the climate changes movements into something like, 'This world is still possible, maybe.'"[52] Invoking the concept of ecological debt—accepting its relentless ethical demand that debts must be paid, that thefts must be made right, accepting debt and indebtedness as part of the circuits of social interconnectedness and mutual dependence that make a permaculture—helps us strike that "maybe." As the philosopher of liberation Enrique Dussel put it when he unknowingly echoed both Hardt and Robinson in his *Twenty Theses on Politics:* "The critical ecological principle of politics could be expressed as follows: We must behave in all ways such that life on planet Earth might be *a perpetual life!*"[53] In this way the rational accounting of our environmental limits and the long-delayed accounting of our ecological debts *need not* speak to withdrawal, renunciation, or defeat; it does not speak to an end to progress, of either the technological or the social sort, or of cascading disasters too far gone to remedy. In fact, in an era of climate change, ocean acidification, and Peak Everything, just to begin to name the crises, the rational consideration of ecological limits is the necessary prerequisite for any progress in our time—not in despair at what is not possible, but in hope for what still is. In this sense when we begin at last to talk about ecological debt we are speaking, in the tradition of the best of Marxism, and the most utopian of our science fictions, not of history's end but of its true beginning.

Notes

Portions of this essay first appeared in modified form in *Reviews in Cultural Theory* and *Polygraph* 22. I would like to acknowledge the contributions of my coeditors on *Polygraph* 22, Lisa Klarr and Ryan Vu, as well the other members of the *Polygraph* Editorial Collective and the Ecology and the Humanities working group at Duke. These are all people to whom I owe an abiding intellectual debt, one that I'm certain can never be repaid.

1. Fredric Jameson, *The Seeds of Time* (New York: Columbia University Press, 1994), xii.

2. K. William Kapp, *The Social Costs of Private Enterprise* (New York: Schocken Books, 1971), 231.

3. Bruno Latour, "Will Non-Humans Be Saved? An Argument in Ecotheology," *Journal of the Royal Anthropological Institute* 15, no. 3 (2009): 462.

4. Karl Marx, *Capital, Vol. 1* (New York: Penguin Classics, 1992), 638.

5. See, for instance, John Bellamy Foster *Marx's Ecology* (New York: Monthly Review, 2000).

6. See Johan Rockström et al., "A Safe Operating Space for Humanity," *Nature* 461 (September 2009): 472–75, www.nature.com/nature/journal/v461/n7263/pdf/461472a.pdf. The other two crisis thresholds are the species extinction rate and climate change. In five of the remaining seven boundaries we are either approaching or only slightly over the proposed boundary, and in the last two, total atmospheric aerosol load and chemical pollution, the relevant boundary condition has not yet been quantified.

7. Kapp, *Social Costs,* 231.

8. Quoted in Andrew Simms, *Ecological Debt: Global Warming and the Wealth of Nations* (New York: Pluto Press, 2005), 90. See Emma Torres and James C. McGowan, eds., *Our Common Agenda for the Americas* (New York: Latin American and Caribbean Commission on Development and Environment, 1994).

9. Joan Martinez-Alier, "Environmental Justice (Local and Global)," in *The Cultures of Globalization,* ed. Fredric Jameson and Masao Miyoshi (Durham, N.C.: Duke University Press, 1998), 313.

10. There's a nearly great episode of *This American Life* concerning Nauru; I say "nearly" only because there's more than a hint of neoliberal victim blaming, as if the Nauruans foolishly strip-mined their own country without anyone in the North having had anything to do with it. Jack Hitt, "The Middle of Nowhere," *This American Life* 253, hosted by Ira Glass, Chicago Public

Radio, original air date December 5, 2003, www.thisamericanlife.org/radio-archives/episode/253/
The-Middle-of-Nowhere.

11. José María Borrero Navia, *The Ecological Debt: Testimony of a Reflection*, trans. Blanca Elena
O'Byrne and Janeth Frances Cracraft (Cali, Columbia: Fundación para la Investigación y Protección
del Medio Ambiente, 1994), 13.

12. See Laurence Mee, "Reviving Dead Zones," *Scientific American* 295 (2006): 78–85.

13. This aspect of the negotiation is highlighted in Richard Black's report for BBC News, "Developing Countries Split over Climate Measures," BBC.co.uk, December 9, 2009, http://news.bbc.
co.uk/2/hi/science/nature/8403745.stm.

14. Quoted in "Future Not for Sale: Climate Deal Rejected," ABC.net.au, December 19, 2009,
www.abc.net.au/news/stories/2009/12/19/2776604.htm.

15. James Lewis, "Sea-Level Rise: Some Implications for Tuvalu," *Ambio* 18, no. 8 (1989): 458–59.

16. Naomi Klein, "Climate Rage," *Rolling Stone*, November 11, 2009, www.naomiklein.org/
articles/2009/11/climate-rage.

17. Ibid.

18. Naomi Klein, "Haiti: A Creditor, Not a Debtor," *Nation*, February 11, 2010; Maplecroft,
"Maplecroft's Climate Change Risk Atlas 2010 Highlights Vulnerable Nations and Safe Havens,"
March 9, 2009, http://maplecroft.com/about/news/climate_change_risk_list_highlights_vulnerable_nations_and_safe_havens_05.html.

19. The quoted language is meant to evoke, among other references, the final scene of Al Gore's
climate documentary *An Inconvenient Truth*, which makes precisely this appeal.

20. Klein, "Climate Rage."

21. Of course the word *reparations* conjures in the US audience the intractable political nightmare
of the debate over reparations for slavery, that is, a racialized, hot-button issue for the right wing to exploit
without any chance of anything substantive ever being passed through Congress. Klein addressed this
point in a talk at the Canadian Centre for Policy Alternatives and posted on the video-sharing site YouTube, arguing not only that this is the proper word to express the concept but, more importantly, that
it is the word Global South activists have chosen and that we should respect their choice. Naomi Klein,
"Climate Debt," YouTube, February 25, 2010, www.youtube.com/watch?v=2FtrSql3vss.

22. Quoted in Klein, "Climate Rage."

23. Ibid.

24. Indian environmentalists Anil Agarwhal and Sunita Narain have called this the difference between *luxury emissions* and *survival emissions*. See Anil Agarwal and Sunita Narain, *Global
Warming in an Unequal World* (New Delhi: Centre for Science and Environment, 1991).

25. Quoted in Klein, "Climate Rage."

26. Andrew C. Revkin and Tom Zeller Jr., "U.S. Negotiator Dismisses Reparations for Climate,"
New York Times, December 9, 2009.

27. Borrero Navia, *Ecological Debt*, 23.

28. See John Bellamy Foster and Brett Clark, "The Ecology of Consumption: A Critique of Economic Malthusianism," *Polygraph* 22 (2010): 113–32.

29. See, for instance, John Bellamy Foster, *The Ecological Revolution* (New York: Monthly
Review Press, 2009), 121–29.

30. John Bellamy Foster, *The Vulnerable Planet* (New York: Monthly Review Press, 1999), 124.

31. Vandana Shiva, *Soil, Not Oil* (Cambridge, Mass.: South End Press, 2008), 15.

32. Ibid., 24.

33. This memo has been widely posted on the Internet; see, for instance, Lawrence Summers,
"Subject: GEP," WhirledBank.com, December 12, 1991, www.whirledbank.org/ourwords/summers.
html. Vandana Shiva also discusses the memo at length in ch. 1 of *Soil, Not Oil*.

34. Summers, "Subject: GEP."

35. James Hansen, "Twenty Years Later: Tipping Points Near on Global Warming," *Guardian*, June 23, 2008.

36. Jamais Cascio, "Crimes against the Future," OpentheFuture.com, August 6, 2007, www.openthefuture.com/2007/08/crimes_against_the_future.html. See also Jamais Cascio, "Climate, Cancer, and Changing Minds," OpentheFuture.com, May 2, 2006, www.openthefuture.com/2006/05/climate_cancer_and_changing_mi.html.

37. Bruce Sterling, "State of the World 2007," January 8, 2007, The Well website, www.well.com/conf/inkwell.vue/topics/289/Bruce-Sterling-State-of-the-Worl-page03.html#post65.

38. *Lawful excuse* is a British legal term roughly analogous to *self-defense* in the United States. Michael McCarthy, "Cleared: Jury Decides That Threat of Global Warming Justifies Breaking the Law," TheIndependent.com, September 11, 2008, www.independent.co.uk/environment/climate-change/cleared-jury-decides-that-threat-of-global-warming-justifies-breaking-the-law-925561.html.

39. Mitchell Anderson, "Putting Global Warming Laggards on Trial," DeSmogBlog.com, November 22, 2008, www.desmogblog.com/putting-global-warming-laggards-trial.

40. Carl Freedman, "Marxism, Cinema and Some Dialectics of Science Fiction and Film Noir," in *Red Planets: Marxism and Science Fiction,* ed. Mark Bould and China Miéville (Middletown, Conn.: Wesleyan University Press, 2009), 72.

41. Ibid., 73–74.

42. Ibid., 74.

43. Friedrich Engels, *Anti-Dühring* (Moscow: Progress Publishers, 1947), www.marxists.org/archive/marx/works/1877/anti-duhring/ch24.htm.

44. Freedman, "Marxism," 74.

45. Geoff Manaugh, "Comparative Planetology: An Interview with Kim Stanley Robinson," BLDGBLOG, December 19, 2007, http://bldgblog.blogspot.com/2007/12/comparative-planetology-interview-with.html.

46. Kim Stanley Robinson, *The Wild Shore* (1984; repr., New York: Orb Books, 1995), 198.

47. Kim Stanley Robinson, *Pacific Edge* (1990; repr., New York: Orb Books, 1995), 3.

48. Gerry Canavan, Lisa Klarr, and Ryan Vu, "Science, Justice, Science Fiction: A Conversation with Kim Stanley Robinson," *Polygraph* 22 (2010): 207.

49. Manaugh, "Comparative Planetology."

50. Robinson, *Pacific Edge,* 95.

51. Michael Hardt, "Two Faces of Apocalypse: A Letter from Copenhagen," *Polygraph* 22 (2010): 271.

52. Ibid.

53. Enrique Dussel, *Twenty Theses on Politics* (Durham, N.C.: Duke University Press, 2008), 86–87; see also 114–15. Of course, Dussel quickly admits, the relentless march of entropy means life on earth can never *really* be perpetual—but, he quickly adds, that doesn't mean we shouldn't do our best.

Index

Contributors

Morris Berman is a cultural historian and author of a trilogy on the decline of the American empire: *The Twilight of American Culture; Dark Ages America;* and *Why America Failed.* He has taught at a number of universities in Europe and North America, most recently at the Tecnológico de Monterrey in Mexico City.

Gerry Canavan is Assistant Professor of Twentieth- and Twenty-First-Century Literature at Marquette University. He has coedited special issues of the journals *American Literature* and *Polygraph* and has published articles in *Lit: Literature, Interpretation, Theory; Science Fiction Film and Television;* and *Extrapolation.*

Eleanor Courtemanche is Associate Professor of English at the University of Illinois at Urbana-Champaign. She is the author of *The "Invisible Hand" and British Fiction, 1818–1860: Adam Smith, Political Economy, and the Genre of Realism.*

Kennan Ferguson is Associate Professor of Political Science at the University of Wisconsin–Milwaukee and the author of *All in the Family: On Community and Incommensurability* and *William James: Politics in the Pluriverse.*

Stephen L. Gardner is Associate Professor of Philosophy at the University of Tulsa and author of *Myths of Freedom: Equality, Modern Thought, and Philosophical Radicalism.*

Michael Allen Gillespie is Professor of Political Science and Philosophy at Duke University. He is the author and editor of many books and articles, including *The Theological Origins of Modernity* and *Homo Politicus, Homo Economicus* (coeditor).

Donald D. Hester is Professor of Economics, Emeritus, at the University of Wisconsin–Madison. He is the author of *The Evolution of Monetary Policy and Banking in the US.*

Elaine Lewinnek is Associate Professor of American Studies at California State University, Fullerton, and author of *The Working Man's Reward: Chicago's Diverse Early Suburbs and the Roots of American Sprawl.*

Joel Magnuson is an Instructor of Economics at Portland Community College. He is the author of *Mindful Economics: How the US Economy Works, Why It Matters, and How It Could Be Different.*

Peter Y. Paik is Associate Professor of Comparative Literature at the University of Wisconsin–Milwaukee. He is the author of *From Utopia to Apocalypse: Science Fiction and the Politics of Catastrophe* and coeditor of *Aftermaths: Exile, Migration, and Diaspora Reconsidered.*

Mary Poovey is the Samuel Rudin University Professor of the Humanities and Professor of English at New York University. Her books include *Genres of the Credit Economy: Mediating Value in Eighteenth- and Nineteenth-Century Britain* and *A History of the Modern Fact: Problems of Knowledge in the Sciences of Wealth and Society.*

Genese Marie Sodikoff is Assistant Professor of Anthropology at Rutgers University, Newark. She is the author of *Forest and Labor in Madagascar: From Colonial Concession to Global Biosphere* and editor of *The Anthropology of Extinction: Essays on Culture and Species Death.*

Michael Tratner is a Professor of English at Bryn Mawr College. He is the author of *Crowd Scenes: Movies and Mass Politics; Deficits and Desires: Economics and Sexuality in Twentieth-Century Literature;* and *Modernism and Mass Politics: Joyce, Woolf, Eliot, Yeats.*

Julianne Lutz Warren teaches in the areas of environmental humanities and sciences at New York University. She is the author of *Aldo Leopold's Odyssey: Rediscovering the Author of "A Sand County Almanac."*

Merry Wiesner-Hanks is Distinguished Professor of History at the University of Wisconsin–Milwaukee. Her books include *The Renaissance and Reformation: A History in Documents; The Marvelous Hairy Girls: The Gonzales Sisters and Their Worlds;* and *Religious Transformations in the Early Modern World: A Brief Study with Documents.*

Richard D. Wolff is Professor of Economics, Emeritus, at the University of Massachusetts, Amherst. His books include *Democracy at Work: A Cure for Capitalism, Contending Economic Theories: Neoclassical, Keynesian and Marxian* (coauthored with S. Resnick), and *Capitalism Hits the Fan: The Global Economic Meltdown and What to Do about It.* His work is available at rdwolff.com and democracyatwork.info.